GW00984635

Customer-Centered Supply Chain Management

A Link-by-Link Guide

Fred A. Kuglin

AMACOM

American Management Association

New York · Atlanta · Boston · Chicago · Kansas City · San Francisco · Washington, D.C.
Brussels · Mexico City · Tokyo · Toronto

This book is available at a special
discount when ordered in bulk quantities.
For information, contact Special Sales Department,
AMACOM, a division of American Management Association,
1601 Broadway, New York, NY 10019.

*This publication is designed to provide accurate and authoritative informa-
tion in regard to the subject matter covered. It is sold with the understanding
that the publisher is not engaged in rendering legal, accounting, or other
professional service. If legal advice or other expert assistance is required, the
services of a competent professional person should be sought.*

Library of Congress Cataloging-in-Publication Data

Kuglin, Fred A.
    *Customer-centered supply chain management : a link-by-link guide /
Fred A. Kuglin.*
        p.   cm.
    Includes index.
    ISBN 0-8144-0408-1
    *1. Business logistics—Cost effectiveness.   2. Delivery of goods—
Management.   I. Title.*
    HD38.5.K848   1998
    658.5—dc21   *98-16552*
                                                                      CIP

Printing number

10 9 8 7 6 5 4 3

Contents

For my wife, Karin, and my children, Heidi and Karl. May they rise to the challenge of continuously learning in our ever-changing world, while taking the time to enjoy life and add back to the less fortunate.

Acknowledgements

This book was an effort that combined a passion for completion with the support from many family members, friends, and professional associates. I first want to thank my beautiful wife, Karin, who provided me with unwavering support, patience, and critical advice from start to finish to make this book a reality. Thanks also to my children, Heidi and Karl, for their patience and understanding during the many evenings and weekends that I worked on the book. Special thanks go to my parents, Fred and Lillian, who provided me with the early guidance to never give up on a personal goal, despite the many setbacks and naysayers that surface on the path of life. In addition, I want to thank Tom Gunn and Dana Scannell, who were constant sources of support and whose help made this book a reality. Also, I want to thank Dr. John Coyle, Mike Glynn, Ann Robledo, Gabriella Semerena, and Jeanne Moeller, who at various times supported me in this effort.

I specifically want to thank my high school English teacher, who said I would never be a published author. Without his help, I would never have had the initiative or the determination to make my dream a reality.

Lastly, I want to thank the many clients I have served over the past several years. The quality of the learning experiences I have gained with my clients has only been eclipsed by the long-standing value of our relationships.

Customer-Centered Supply Chain Management

Introduction

Customer-Centered Supply Chain Management

Leadership Through Transformation

Recently, I had the pleasure of traveling to Tokyo to visit the executives of some leading Japanese companies. One executive in particular spent considerable time discussing with me the way Japanese and Americans do business, particularly in the areas of managing change, transformation, and customer-centered supply chain management.

He was amazed at the amount of time and effort we Americans invest in copying and duplicating Japanese practices; yet, he commented, we frequently miss the essence of these practices. He referred to these efforts as "productizing philosophies." As an example, he pointed to just-in-time (JIT), a supply chain method of reducing or eliminating waste in the manufacturing process. When the just-in-time philosophy was developed and popularized by Toyota, Japan was a poor country that could not afford waste in manufacturing. Also, land prices were so high in Japan that most companies could not afford an elaborate warehousing network. According to my Japanese executive associate, those were the reasons just-in-time was created.

As many readers know, American companies adopted just-in-time as a means of duplicating the Japanese success. Some by-products that many of those companies realized from their attempts to copy JIT were higher transportation costs, higher supplier costs due to uneven supplier production schedules, and higher supplier inventories throughout their supply chain. In addition, their efforts produced dissatisfied executives. The potential effects of critical factors such as customer demand, assembly schedules, supplier lead times, transportation lengths of haul, and land prices in the United States had not been considered when just-in-time manufacturing programs were put in place. Instead of customizing the Japanese supply chain philosophy to fit the needs of the enterprise, many American companies simply copied the practices of the Japanese.

Toward the end of our conversation, the Japanese executive mentioned that land prices have been declining in many parts of Japan for the past few years. Many Japanese companies are now considering using warehouses to decrease their transportation costs. With some amusement, he asked me, "What new program will you Americans come out with when we Japanese start using warehouses again?" The point was well taken.

Looking for Silver Bullets

Americans haven't limited themselves to copying from the Japanese. There are many customer-centered value chain management "programs" on the market that have an underlying philosophy similar to just-in-time. Efficient Consumer Response (ECR), quick response (QR), continuous replenishment (CR), and flow-through warehousing (frequently called cross-docking) are similar customer-focused programs that are designed to make enterprises more efficient in particular functions in their order-to-cash value chain cycles. If properly implemented, these programs can produce just the results for which they were intended.

Each one of these programs seems to be positioned by its advocates as the "silver bullet" that will enhance overall, long-term business performance merely by plugging the program into a company's operations. Time after time, executives are disappointed with results after adopting programs such as these because their expectation level was too high. (In my opinion, many executives also set themselves and their organizations up for failure by looking for quick fixes to complex problems. Reengineering to cut costs without focusing on growth is just one example of this.)

The confusion over how to proceed is not confined to a select few senior managers. Seminar after seminar bombards executives with programs, philosophies, and processes that promise great results. Quality, enterprise resource planning, reengineering, activity-based management, enterprisewide technology applications, and others permeate the marketplace with their methodologies and gurus who proclaim that they have the answer to managing change successfully.

Many of these approaches have merit, but they cannot stand alone and function as silver bullets.

All too often, silver-bullet approaches have too narrow a scope or they focus on the wrong things. Programs that concentrate on efficiencies of individual supply chain components miss what is most important about supply chain management: the customer and a true commitment to quality. Quality programs, spawned by the coveted Baldrige Award and the ISO 9000 series, can have a major impact on an enterprise. However, many executives have embraced quality as a quick fix and not as a philosophy on how to do business. They have therefore had limited success with quality because their business focus was too narrow.

The answer is not to copy the best practices of industry leaders but to reengineer the order-to-cash process. The ability to plan, implement, and manage this transformation process is what will differentiate future winners from losers. Companies like Frito-Lay recognized this early and were able to regain their industry leadership with a process, from concept to implementation, to reengineer and manage the customer value chain over time in a changing environment. Bridging the gap between concept and implementation is a difficult task. Organizations that can do it successfully will reap the benefits of differentiating themselves from their competitors. Those that cannot will at best be followers within their industry; at worst, they will fail to survive in the long run.

Customer-Centered Supply Chain Management Defined

The term *supply chain management* has been around for approximately fifteen to twenty years. Its definition varies from one enterprise to another. Because of the different business functions that retailers, carriers, and manufacturers perform and the types of companies with which they deal, the supply chain and extended enterprise for each of these three industries look very different. For this book, the focus will be on supply chain management within a manufacturing extended enterprise.

My definition of *supply chain management* for a manufacturer is as follows:

> The manufacturer and its suppliers, vendors, and customers—that is, all links in the extended enterprise—working together to provide a common product and service to the marketplace that the customer is willing to pay for. This multicompany group, functioning as one extended enterprise, makes optimum

use of shared resources (people, processes, technology, and per-formance measurements) to achieve operating synergy. The result is a product and service that are high-quality, low-cost, and delivered quickly to the marketplace.

To define *customer-centered supply chain management,* I would expand on the *supply chain management* definition as follows:

> The manufacturer and its suppliers, vendors, and customers—that is, all links in the extended enterprise—working together to provide a common product and service to the marketplace that the customer *desires and* is willing to pay for *throughout the life cycle of the product and service.* This multicompany group, functioning as one extended enterprise, makes optimum use of shared resources (people, processes, technology, and performance measurements) to achieve operating synergy. The result is a product or service that is high-quality, low-cost, delivered quickly to the marketplace, *and achieves customer satisfaction.*

Despite improvement programs, restructurings, layoffs, and other streamlining efforts, many companies are as far from effective customer-centered supply chain management as they have ever been, and they still retain their mass-production mentality. In mass production, the company is built around the plant. The internal transactions that make up the order-to-cash cycle—order entry, purchasing, transportation, and distribution—all revolve around the manufacturing function. The manufacturer tries to drive the lowest cost from suppliers and service providers.

People Issues

Powerful market forces are demanding that manufacturers transform their way of satisfying customer demand through the production and delivery of goods. The processes many manufacturing enterprises use today, from customer order through delivery of the goods to actual cash, are under severe stress, with globalism being perhaps the most powerful of the forces stressing the order-to-cash processes.

The success or failure of an enterprise hinges on the ability of its senior managers to plan, implement, and manage the necessary transformation process. External changes in an enterprise's environment and marketplace drive internal changes within the enterprise. The same external factors also drive competitors to reformulate their strategies, thereby further changing the external marketplace and environment. Adapting continually to this vicious cycle of change will, over time, put the enterprise in a competitive position within its industry—provided its people measure up to the challenge of doing so.

The changing dynamics of the global environment and the shift of power from the manufacturer to the retailer (as in the case of Wal-Mart) demand that manufacturers rethink the way they work with other companies in their customer value chain. Adversarial relationships with suppliers and a command-and-control approach may have worked in the past, but they now act as barriers to the mutually beneficial strategies and partnerships that manufacturers must use in order to survive under the new and changing rules.

Little has been done to knock down these barriers because companies either don't know the barriers are hindering them, don't know how to go about removing them, or greatly underestimate the importance of people issues in bringing about change.

In my opinion, universities have contributed to the problem by doing little or nothing to prepare students for people issues in business. When I visit universities to review their business curriculum, I often find that many of our top universities monopolize a business student's course load with function-driven classes. Very few emphasize in their courses the "soft," or people, skills needed to influence, rather than control, the behavior of others. It is these soft skills that are used to influence suppliers, vendors, customers, and people within the company to work together as a single, extended enterprise to produce a product and deliver it to the customer.

Does customer-centered supply chain management sound theoretical? To a company steeped in mass-production culture, it probably does, but to best-in-class companies like Wal-Mart and Frito-Lay, it is *modus operandi*. The ability to measure up to the achievements of today's Wal-Marts and Frito-Lays will be the price of admission to tomorrow's global marketplace. Companies that rigidly adhere to a functional, single-enterprise approach to the marketplace will quickly fall behind their competitors.

The Customer-Centered Supply Chain Management Change Process

This book provides executives with a step-by-step methodology to develop a complete plan, starting with a business strategy, to design and implement a customer-centered supply chain management change process in their enterprise. When implemented properly, this step-by-step methodology will enable the enterprise to achieve best-in-class performance in its customer value chain in terms of cost-effectiveness, quality, cycle time, information, and customer satisfaction. This best-in-class performance will enable growth with a low-cost base.

This step-by-step methodology, called the customer-centered supply chain management change process, is introduced in Chapter 1 (see Exhibit 1-1) and serves as the foundation for the book. Each chapter has two sections: The first describes the philosophy of a particular stage of the customer-centered supply chain management change process; the second is the step-by-step process methodology that supports the philosophy.

The outline of the book is as follows:

Chapter	Chapter Title	Process Methodology
1	Customer-Centered Value Chain Management: Leading Transformation Within the Global Business of Manufacturing	Getting Started
2	Business Strategy	Foundation
3	The Quality Commitment	Quality
4	The Transformation Journey Begins: Supply Chain Management Design	Transformation Design
5	Inter-Enterprise Innovation: How Is Your Company Positioned?	Innovation
6	Understanding the Current (As-Is) State of the Supply Chain	As-Is
7	Converting Theory Into Reality: Building the Bridge to Transform the Supply Chain	Bridge
8	Results Matter! Measuring Performance After Implementation	Performance Results
9	Supply Chain Alternatives	Core Competencies— Supply Chain Alternatives
10	The Executive Perspective: Pulling It All Together	—

A Simple Lesson Learned

Several years ago, I was the area logistics manager for a large food company located in the Midwest. Our group was going through a change process, and the truck driver member of our change process team offered me some advice that I have not forgotten to this day.

He told me that he only had a high school education, yet he totally endorsed change. However, he said it is important not to forget the fundamentals of our business.

He went on to say that, regardless of the output of the change process, we would still manufacture products, load trailers, dispatch drivers, and deliver products to customers. The "how" might be different, but the fundamentals would remain the same. He also advised me to focus on integrating our strategic process meetings with our tactical process meetings to make sure that when we discussed strategy the majority of our workforce could relate to the strategy discussions from their tactical views of their job responsibilities.

And finally, he said that the people who perform the fundamental tasks of the supply chain—the delivery sales representatives, the truck drivers, the warehouse employees, and the plant floor workers—all have a certain pride in their work and want to improve the operations of the supply chain. He suggested that they would be an excellent source of ideas on how to change the operations of the supply chain if they were just asked for their input in a sincere manner.

Conclusion

As I developed the customer-centered supply chain management change process, I incorporated those words of wisdom from my truck driver friend. He may have been just a truck driver in his own eyes, but I would have him on any of my business change teams today. As they map out a change process for growth that begins with a business strategy, companies must never lose sight of implementation and their business fundamentals.

Like the truck driver on our team, many executives also recognize the need for change, yet when faced with the day-to-day demands of running their companies, they find it hard to initiate the change process. These executives often ask, "How do I get started?" Chapter 1 provides the answer.

Chapter 1

Customer-Centered Value Chain Management

Leading Transformation Within the Global Business of Manufacturing

It is nine o'clock on a Saturday morning in May of 2002. The time has arrived for Steve Robinson to part with $50,000 for a new car. For months, he has been thinking about retiring his six-year-old Chevy Blazer, decidedly obsolete by the standards of the day. The last straw that spurred him to action was when one of his teenage children said several days ago that she was ashamed to be seen riding in such an old vehicle.

After heated discussions, the Robinsons have agreed on a sporty new Ford Explorer as their vehicle of choice. Over recent years, the Explorer has evolved from its original utilitarian design, and some of the latest models have all the features of a top-of-the-line luxury vehicle.

Before leaving home to order the Explorer, Steve dials to channel 469 on his Web television, which he still thinks of from time to time as just a television with cable. He notifies his local bank that he plans to purchase a car within the next seventy-two hours, reserves $50,000 for payment when he makes the purchase electronically, and receives approval for the funds transfer. The entire transaction takes only fourteen keystrokes. Steve still uses the keyboard attached to the television monitor—a fact that does not escape his son, who constantly admonishes him to be "up-to-date" and use either the remote or the voice recognition and response module to work with the monitor.

An hour later, Steve arrives at Sam's Club to make the final decision. He pauses briefly at a large overhead sign that proclaims "Welcome to Sam's Virtual Reality Car Showroom" and then proceeds to the sign-in station. After he has entered his universal identification number and bank credit line password, the showroom's system instantly identifies him and grants him access, recording the bank approval for $50,000.

The showroom has four sets of seats where shoppers can experience, through the wonders of virtual reality technology, the look and feel of different car makes and models in a variety of driving environments. As he settles into one of the seats, Steve specifies to the system that he wants to try out a black, four-door 4×4 Explorer with all the options, including an in-car fax hooked into the onboard trip computer. Next, the system prompts him to request a test drive to challenge the sport utility vehicle and his ability to handle it under adverse weather and road conditions. Steve decides to take a virtual reality drive on an October day in New Hampshire, first under sunny conditions, then in the rain. Both the smooth, pleasant drive and the beautiful fall colors exceed his expectations. He is sold.

At the upper right-hand corner of the keyboard is a large red button labeled BUY. Pushing the button, Steve says good-bye to his $50,000 and triggers the process that will cause his new car to roll off the assembly line five days from today and be delivered to his house two days after that. Seven days seems an eternity, but he is glad to be making the purchase.

Leaving the showroom, Steve muses about the big red button. Why not voice recognition technology? he wonders, recalling his son's comment that everyone has been using it for quite a while. Concluding that the button is a gimmick to heighten the thrill of making the purchase, Steve turns his thoughts back to the Explorer and heads for home.

Virtual reality car showrooms? In a Sam's Club? Voice recognition in an interactive purchasing process? Secured electronic attachment of funds through a cable channel? A universal personal identification number complete with on-line personal information accessible anywhere with the use of a password? All this sounds futuristic. . . . Or does it?

The reality is that the technology to do all these things is here today. Applications and processes have been and are being developed at this moment to make these technologies viable for the consumer marketplace.

Silicon Graphics offers a 3-D system that uses audiovisual virtual reality technology for designing and testing automobiles, eliminating the need to build a physical prototype. The same technology was successfully used to help rebuild whole city blocks in Los Angeles after the riots. It was also used to design a model of the Atlanta Olympic complex to show to members of the International Olympic Committee before any physical buildings were constructed.

Is Your Company's Supply Chain Positioned for the Future?

Although technology alone cannot transform an enterprise's supply chain, technology does have profound implications for the immediate future of supply chain management, separating the winners from the losers. Experts agree on two things: First, the winners will be those who use technology and core competencies effectively to satisfy the ever-changing demands of customers; second, there will be more losers than winners.

Globalization and technology are impacting almost all industries (most likely including yours) and creating the need for significant change within manufacturing enterprises. How is your company positioned to take advantage of change and leverage your core competencies to achieve total customer satisfaction? Will your company be a winner or a loser?

Many companies, and even Wall Street, focus on using technology as a change agent. Granted, technology can provide the stimulus for change and can even help transform certain industry supply chain segments, as Amazon.com is doing for electronic book purchases. But technology is only one aspect of the overall supply chain transformation process. If that process is to succeed, it must be strategy-based and process-driven.

The purpose of this book is to help supply chain executives undertake a strategy-based and process-driven change management effort that will ensure the long-term success of their enterprise.

It is a simple fact that change is not optional. Five years from now, if your company uses the same processes to produce the same products as it does today, chances are that your company will have lost market share, revenues, and profits. Even worse, your competitors will have filled the marketplace void and improved their image as market leaders.

The Customer-Centered Supply Chain Management Change Process

To assist the executive in migrating his or her enterprise to world-class performance, I have designed the customer-centered supply chain management change process, illustrated in Exhibit 1-1. This process

Exhibit 1-1. The customer-centered supply chain management change process.

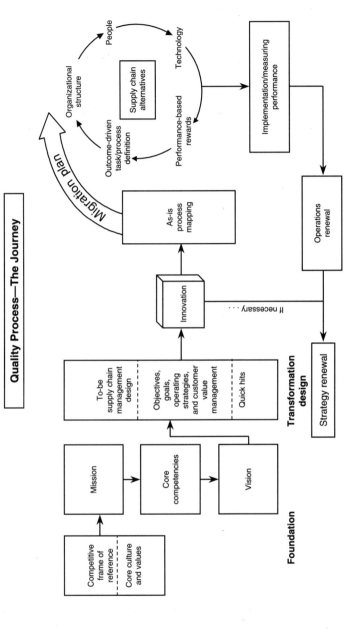

walks the executive through a transformation effort that starts with the business strategy of the corporation and ends with the implementation of a transformed supply chain. The chapters and corresponding process methodologies in this book are all based on the customer-centered supply chain management change process. The following subsections provide an overview of the process.

Business Strategy

Many aspects of the "virtual" corporation are materializing. In a virtual corporation, many entities join forces throughout the supply chain to produce a common product or service. When the product reaches the end of its life cycle, the virtual corporation disbands to form other alliances to produce other products or services.

The virtual corporation operates in a worldwide scenario of international markets and competitors, shorter product life cycles, and consumers with best-in-class expectations. The traditional stakeholder cast of employees, stockholders, unions, and communities will be joined by new stakeholders—telecommunications providers, information technology partners, logistics vendors, and financial institutions.

In the coming era of virtual corporations, a company's survival will depend increasingly on its ability to identify and focus on its core competencies. The key will be not only how to blend your company's core competencies with the core competencies of other companies to produce a product or service but how to do it quickly at low cost and with high quality. Thus, there are three key questions to ask now:

1. What are your company's core competencies?
2. Does your organization partner with other companies quickly and successfully today, working together to address such issues as organizational behavior, information technology/electronic commerce, performance-based rewards, and customer satisfaction?
3. How quickly does your company adapt to and take advantage of change?

Speed and adaptability are critical to the future of your company's supply chain. Partners in the automotive assembly industry must learn how to produce an automobile with such a short life cycle that they can manufacture only 50,000 automobiles and still make a profit. This will be a quantum leap from today's industry break-even production levels, which range from 250,000 to 400,000 automobiles. In the food industry, supply chain partners must be able to work together to produce a profitable product with a life cycle of less than one year. In the near future, traditional approaches to partnering and capital investments in product portfolios will no longer work.

How does your company plan for the future? If you can answer yes to all of the following questions, your company has passed the planning acid test and is ready for the future:

- ☐ Does your company have a strategic plan covering the next three to five years?
- ☐ Are the senior managers aligned with the plan?
- ☐ Is the plan well communicated throughout the organization?
- ☐ Is it updated at least once every six months?
- ☐ Is the strategic plan linked to the annual operating plan?
- ☐ Does the annual operating plan include supply chain design and performance measurements?
- ☐ Are your supply chain partners included in the overall planning process?
- ☐ Do your employees know how they are performing day in and day out?
- ☐ Do they know how their job duties fit within the design and operation of the total supply chain?
- ☐ Do they know the role their job plays in the strategic plan?
- ☐ Does your company have in place the communications network needed to implement a major change in the strategic plan in a matter of days?

If you answered no to one or more of these acid-test questions, your company may have difficulty competing in the future. Changes happen so fast that only those companies that have a balanced business strategy linking their annual operating plans, supply chains, and employees will be able to adapt quickly to the changes and take advantage of them. The foundation process methodology is designed to help you establish a balanced business strategy for your enterprise.

The Quality Commitment

By the year 2000, the marketplace will expect manufacturers to achieve levels of quality that are rarely attained today. It is entirely possible that successful manufacturing executives will be measuring the quality of their products in terms of defects per *billion* units produced!

The quality process will have to be tightly woven into the very fabric of the supply chain. In fact, the extended enterprise will be so challenged to be the low-cost provider to the marketplace and achieve total customer satisfaction that there will be little tolerance for waste and sources of customer dissatisfaction. At the best companies of the future, quality will be so much a part of every process and of every employee's daily job performance that the word *quality* will cease to be part of their vocabulary.

Assembling an automobile and delivering it to a customer in seven calendar days will require a well-synchronized supply chain process with virtually no defects in parts and subsystems. Every supply chain participant will be required to focus on the end customer's requirements and expectations. The performance of the supply chain as a whole will be only as good as its slowest-moving, least-effective task, activity, function, or company. Poor performers must and will be replaced quickly to upgrade the performance of the overall supply chain.

How does your company incorporate quality into its supply chain process? Answering the following questions will give you a picture of how your company is positioned to meet the quality demands of the next several years:

- ☐ Does your company have a quality project, program, or process?
- ☐ Is your quality effort aimed at satisfying customers?
- ☐ Are the company's customer satisfaction measurements customer-provided?
- ☐ Is your rewards structure tied to these customer satisfaction measurements?
- ☐ Do your supply chain partners use the same customer-provided satisfaction measurements?
- ☐ If you asked your employees, would they know what these customer satisfaction measurements are?
- ☐ Do your employees know how the supply chain is performing, on a daily basis, vis-à-vis these customer satisfaction measurements?

If you answered no to one or more of these questions, the odds are that your company is not prepared to achieve the quality levels that the marketplace will demand in the next several years. Because the performance of the supply chain is limited by its weakest link, the poorest performers risk being quickly phased out to improve the overall chain. To avoid being phased out, executives must incorporate a commitment to quality into every activity within their organization.

It is the essence of quality that should be captured within a transformation process.

The Transformation Journey Begins: Supply Chain Management Design

The virtual corporation will be successful only if every functional organization and company understands both the overall supply chain order-to-cash process and its own distinct role within that process. In the future, these roles will be clearly defined in terms of the final product to be produced. Production of the final product, coordination of the flow of materials, and communications facilitating all processes will be dramatically different. By studying today's best-in-class companies, which are already starting to operate like this, we can get a preview of how the supply chain will function when virtual corporations become the norm.

In the automotive industry, the best assembly plants will produce a significant percentage of their automobiles in response to demand rather than for inventory. An assembly plant will receive the "build" signal from a virtual reality car showroom, such as the Sam's Club mentioned at the start of the chapter, which will provide a complete bill of materials for the automobile. Upon receiving the same build signal, suppliers will manage the flow of parts and subsystems to the assembly plant to ensure that the assembly is completed within the targeted five-day schedule (e.g., five days as described earlier in the chapter).

The build signals to the assembly plants and suppliers will be audiovisual. Audio technology will be used to communicate the signals to a culturally diverse workforce. Visual information will eliminate the piles of paperwork that are now generated during the automotive assembly process.

The complete design specifications for each stage of the automotive assembly will be available to all involved employees. The life cycles of automobiles in the future will be so short that once an automobile is in production, its replacement will already be finishing the design phase. Today's proprietary secrecy surrounding the design will give way to the sharing of information.

The design of the order-to-cash supply chain will focus entirely on the final product and the consumer. The guiding force will be customer value management. Each potential member of the supply chain will be screened for quality, cost, and responsiveness to the customer value management process design. Its culture and information technology will also have to "fit" with the rest of the chain. All members of the chain will be putting their own companies at risk when a new company becomes a partner. For best-in-class extended enterprises, the screening process will be demanding.

If you could start with a clean sheet of paper and an unlimited budget, how would you design your company's future supply chain? If a competitor started its supply chain from scratch, could your company meet and exceed this competitive challenge? How is electronic commerce reshaping your industry from a clean-sheet perspective? Do you know who your best customers are and how to keep them as lifelong customers? The day may come when your company will compete with an archrival or a new company for the same partnership slot in an extended enterprise supply chain. Will your company win? Your company's future may depend on it!

Inter-Enterprise Innovation: How Is Your Company Positioned?

Chapter 5 examines innovation, which is how companies like Motorola, Microsoft, and Intel continue to reinvent themselves, and globalism, which can be an opportunity for growth above U.S. rates. Transformation teams must look at the following three levels of innovation:

1. *Value refinement:* a process to find better ways to satisfy the values and needs of the supply chain customer. The key to value refinement is to increase the efficiency of the current supply chain business model.

2. *Value creation:* a process to break the industry mold or current business model. As I explain in Chapter 5, the unmet values of existing customers must be reviewed and strategies developed to leverage competencies or infrastructures to satisfy those unmet values. Value creation efforts usually establish new linkages between supply chain partners.

3. *Migrating value:* a process involving the creation of ways to take over value-added activities within the supply chain. Migrating value out of other supply chains and into the enterprise's adds value to the enterprise while leveraging its core competencies.

Not only are there tremendous opportunities for growth in the global economy, but the failure to pursue a global strategy carries a number of risks. Contrary to common belief, a global economy has been present for years. Companies like Coca-Cola and General Motors have been building an impressive network of subsidiaries, alliances, and joint ventures around the world for several decades. It is no surprise that the greatest percentage of their company profits are now being generated outside the United States.

However, historians will view the last eleven years of the twentieth century as a time of rapid transformation and convergence of the world's economies. During this time frame, the former Soviet Union collapsed; several countries like Brazil, Argentina, China, and India started to emerge economically by combining political, social, and economic stability; and advances in technology allowed emerging countries to "leapfrog" developed countries in selected industries without the sunk, stair-step investment costs.

The emergence of trading blocks with open borders has influenced the shape of the global economy and will continue to do so. Trading alliances like NAFTA, the European Union, ASEAN, and MERCOSUR are creating powerful incentives for companies to alter their behavior and do business under the terms of the alliance agreements. Companies that ignore the rules of these alliances will find that their products and services will be high-cost and thus noncompetitive in the alliances' member countries.

How does your company incorporate innovation and globalism into its business strategy? Answering the following questions will help you define how your company is positioned to do business globally after the year 2000:

- [ ] Does your company actively pursue value refinement, value creation, and migrating value efforts?
- [ ] Does your company realize at least half of its revenues from international operations?
- [ ] Is your customer relationship strategy aimed at satisfying customers in multiple countries?
- [ ] Are the company's customer satisfaction measurements tailored to be country-specific?
- [ ] Does your company run its international operations in a decentralized manner?
- [ ] Do you have supply chain partners that are global?
- [ ] Do the employees of your international operations know what the corporate business strategy is and how it interrelates with the business strategy for their country?

If the answer to any of these questions is no, then your company must revisit what it means to be global. For some industries (like bakery/bread), it does not make sense to be global, although even in such industries, some companies are expanding into nearby countries. (For example, Bimbo, in Mexico, is expanding into other Latin American countries, driven primarily by the severe recession in its home market. Despite the fact that the bakery/bread industry is low-value, involves local production, is driven by local consumption, and is not conducive to globalism, Bimbo is searching for ways to survive the lingering Mexican economic troubles.) Most industries, however, are globalizing.

Companies must also learn to tailor products to local preferences. For example, Tupperware entered into a joint venture with Disney to produce plastic lunch boxes in Brazil that showed a picture of Mickey Mouse with a soccer ball. The response was so overwhelming that the annual production was exceeded by demand in just two months, resulting in the development of a black market for these lunch boxes.

Understanding the Current (As-Is) State of the Supply Chain

"Where is your enterprise today?" Some executives will privately answer this question in terms of where their enterprise is *not*. The trouble is that these executives are too far removed from day-to-day operations. They also have functional backgrounds like finance or marketing and lack a working knowledge of the operations of their extended enterprise.

In addition, many enterprises still struggle with having employees work entirely within a vertical or functional area. These employees frequently work in ignorance of how their output affects other supply chain participants. Despite what has been written about horizontal integration of supply chains, the majority of enterprises still appear to operate in vertical or functional work groups.

The process mapping of the current (as-is) state of the supply chain by the involved work groups accomplishes many goals. The transformation team must have an understanding of the as-is state of the supply chain to measure against the future state and assess the "gap" that needs to be addressed. The individual work groups can use the as-is mapping to understand the linkages in the supply chain. These linkages—which involve the movement of goods, information, and financial transactions—determine how the output of each vertical or functional work group affects the other work groups in the supply chain.

The linkages are measured in terms of cost, quality, and time. By combining the definition of these linkages with their measurement, the transformation team can start to map how the supply chain is performing in its current state.

However, the key is to perform this exercise *after* the development of the design or future (to-be) state. When I lead these exercises, the transformation teams often immediately start to redraw the as-is maps to directionally reflect the design work. In addition, these teams frequently embrace the concept of eliminating non–value-added activities before the formal exercise of redrawing the as-is map as a to-be map.

The hidden value of this effort is that it creates a visual representation of the supply chain to which the participants can refer when discussing interfunctional activities. As a result, it can be the focal point of continuous improvement thinking in a collaborative manner. When I was the area manager for a large snack food manufacturer in the Midwest, we placed our detailed as-is map in our "war room." Whenever we had interfunctional meetings, this map was instrumental in separating fact from fiction regarding how the supply chain operated. Until we had the map, there were many arguments over the as-is state and the supply chain linkages. Thus, the focus was on bridging the gap to what was being proposed and not on clarifying what was happening at the present time.

Does your company have a supply chain as-is process map? Is it prominently displayed so that employees in all functions can use it? Is it continually modified as improvements are made? Does this map define the supply chain linkages? If the answer to any one of these questions is no, then you have opportunities to make improvements that can positively affect the performance of the enterprise's supply chain.

Converting Theory Into Reality: Building the Bridge to Transform the Customer Supply Chain

If performed properly, the process of building the bridge from the current (as-is) state to the future (to-be) state is an ongoing one. The to-be state should be continually redefined while the as-is state is continually improved. However, the bridge isn't built overnight. It takes a carefully orchestrated migration plan to make sure the bridge you construct will withstand the demands that will be placed upon it.

The migration plan involves the following five key sections, which are discussed in detail in Chapter 7:

1. Outcome-driven task and process definition
2. Organizational structure
3. People/responsibility charting
4. Technology
5. Performance-based rewards

When the as-is process map is modified to reflect the future (to-be) state, the map needs to be defined to the task level to be operationalized. The use of responsibility charting is critical, both to define the outcome-driven tasks and process activities and to assign roles and responsibilities for each task. The summary of the responsibility charts determines the job duties and responsibilities of each employee. This summary provides the base for developing the organizational structure around supply chain processes (rather than functional or vertical activities).

The technology of the redesigned supply chain should support the outcome-driven tasks and process activities. The performance-based rewards should be customer satisfaction–based and support a teamwork environment.

Where is your company today? Do you have integrated information throughout the supply chain feeding decision support systems for your employees? How useful are your company's executive information systems? Do you have the ability to produce accurate, daily profit-and-loss statements? Do you even have one set of numbers today?

Again, this bridge doesn't just materialize. To assess the readiness of your organization to build the bridge, ask yourself the following questions:

- ☐ Does your enterprise have a formal process for employees to collaboratively define its responsibility charts?
- ☐ Do these responsibility charts support pushing decision making down to the lowest levels in the organization?
- ☐ Are the tasks and activities developed by the employees who are directly involved?
- ☐ Are employees free to eliminate non–value-added activities without political pressure from senior executives to keep those activities?
- ☐ Is the organizational structure process-oriented and/or horizontal in nature?
- ☐ Do your people have the skills needed to function in the new supply chain environment?
- ☐ Does the enterprise have the human resources expertise that will be required in order to promote, retrain, demote, and outplace existing employees as it transitions to the new supply chain environment?
- ☐ Does the enterprise have the right technology to support the redesigned supply chain?
- ☐ Is the rewards structure aligned with the redesigned supply chain and the resultant customer-based team goals?

Companies like Wal-Mart and NUMMI are continually enhancing their bridges to redefined future states. It is this continuing adaptation to the marketplace that differentiates winners from losers.

Results Matter! Measuring Performance After Implementation

As mentioned earlier in the chapter, performance measurements must change as the supply chain changes. Each member of the chain must be measured by the ultimate customer's requirements and expectations. As the customer changes, so must performance measurements.

Food-processing companies face this challenge every day. Each time an item goes over a point-of-sale scanner, a customer casts a vote for that particular product. Quality, price, product appearance, brand name, and company image all play important parts in a customer's buying decision.

With shorter product life cycles in the future, it is imperative for research and development departments of food companies to understand the dynamics and trends of consumer demand. Today, the research and development cycle from concept to store shelf is thirty to sixty days for new products and two to four weeks for line extensions. In order to gain a competitive advantage in emerging trends, the cycle will have to be compressed to a third of what it is today. To do this, companies will expand their research and development staffs to include supplier, retailer, and actual customer representatives working full-time to develop new products. The payoff will be a higher success rate for new products (historically, the failure rate has been 80 percent) and savings resulting from the shorter cycle.

Best-in-class food manufacturers will also be able to measure their performance hour by hour across all distribution channels. Today, only the largest retail outlets compile point-of-sale data, which are usually provided through an overnight "batch" system. Hour-to-hour measurement will enable companies to produce an accurate daily, and perhaps hourly, profit-and-loss statement.

How does your company measure performance today? Does it use activity-based costing to allocate costs effectively? How well will your company be able to measure its performance in the year 2000? Are your performance measurements calibrated by your customers? The measurement system must be right to enable the enterprise to measure progress. Nothing is more unsettling than for an executive to have measurements that indicate positive results only to have the "real" numbers and the competitors indicate otherwise.

Supply Chain Alternatives

There will be no room for average performers in the next decade. Companies will have to be low-cost, high-quality providers of products and services. They will be forced to recognize, develop, and focus on core competencies and give serious consideration to outsourcing the other competencies.

For example, food-processing companies have been putting greater emphasis on manufacturing, sales, and marketing of branded products while farming out the manufacturing of private-label and entry-level products, and this trend can be expected to continue. Today, some companies are pursuing this strategy to a limited extent. In the next several years, the industry will be divided into two tiers: (1) entry-level and private-label products and (2) branded products. The first tier of products will perhaps be produced largely by contracted companies with low overhead and regional production capabilities. The second tier, which will include only those products that have true brand equity, will be produced by the major food processors.

This production-outsourcing strategy will accelerate the outsourcing of logistics. Shared distribution channels will emerge, enabling these channels to coordinate the delivery of noncompeting products from multiple companies direct to retail stores. For example, yogurt, hamburgers, tacos, and pizza may be delivered from multiple manufacturers to multiple retailers on the same truck without the services of a wholesaler or distributor.

The customer measures the performance of the total supply chain. If your company is to continue performing any supply chain activity that is not a core competency, it should have a compelling reason for doing so. (Frito-Lay's store-door delivery system is a good example of a non–core competency activity that is critical to keep. It not only provides frequent access to customers but also serves as a barrier of entry for competitors.)

Outsourcing has two phases: The first is the decision to outsource, which usually involves both assessing the value of outsourcing to the company and clearing the emotional hurdle of outsourcing. The second involves selecting the right third party as your outsourcing partner. Chapter 9 presents easy-to-follow methodologies that will enable you to progress through both of these phases.

Before proceeding to the getting-started process methodology, let's finish the story of how the components of the automotive supply chain have interacted to deliver Steve Robinson's new Ford Explorer:

The day has finally arrived for the Explorer to be delivered, right on schedule, seven days after Steve ordered it. A large vehicle resembling a truck, with a satellite dish and antennas, pulls into the Robinsons' driveway.

Before delivering the utility vehicle, the attendant prepped it as it was being transported from the railroad's receiving yard to the buyer's house. One final detail remains before the vehicle is unloaded: taxes. The attendant invites Steve into the truck to pay the taxes electronically from the onboard computer. After the taxes are paid, the vehicle's title is printed.

Next, the attendant hooks the Explorer up to a diagnostic monitor and starts it. He then unhooks the vehicle and backs it out of the truck while an electronic imaging machine "scans" the Explorer's interior and exterior.

At long last, the Explorer is parked in the Robinsons' driveway. Prep work on the vehicle is finished, taxes have been paid, and Steve now holds the title. Before departing, the attendant hands Steve a CD containing the engine diagnostic results and imaging screens of the interior and exterior for Steve's records. A duplicate of these records will be kept permanently on file at Ford's worldwide headquarters in Dearborn under Steve's global personal identification number.

As the truck pulls away, the proud new owner marvels about the changes that have taken place in the past five or six years. His son's voice breaks the silence: "Dad, can I borrow the Explorer?" Steve then realizes that there are some things that will never change.

Process Methodology
Getting Started

Many executives share a vision for their enterprise that involves dramatic change. Their vision, albeit specific to their own industry, is comparable to the vision I have just described for the automobile industry in terms of the degree of change involved. As I mentioned in the Introduction, these executives often ask me the same question: "How do I get started?"

The first step in my customer-centered supply chain management change process is the getting-started process methodology. The steps of this methodology, which are illustrated in the accompanying process flowchart and described in detail in this portion of the chapter, are designed to help executives begin the transformation effort in an organized and comprehensive way. Following this process methodology properly will enable you to begin your change effort with the right frameworks, executive sponsors, and performance expectations to help ensure success.

To get started, the executive sponsor must develop for the enterprise an awareness and understanding of the significance of the change process. Because the customer supply chain is how the enterprise provides goods and services to its customers, changing the supply chain involves transforming the heart and soul of the enterprise.

Executives must recognize that it takes time to transform a supply chain while the supply chain is concurrently performing its day-to-day activities and tasks. When handled properly, a transformation effort can take from six to twenty-four months to complete, and executives must be committed to supporting the effort throughout this long but necessary time frame.

A.1: Recognize and Establish the Need for Supply Chain Management Transformation

If an enterprise is to start a transformation effort involving its supply chain, there must be an overriding need to do so. For example, the

THE SUPPLY CHAIN MANAGEMENT CHANGE PROCESS
Process Methodology
Getting Started

A.1

Recognize and establish
the need for supply chain
management transformation.

A.1.a

Identify key
executive sponsors.

A.1.b

Identify and select
process champions.

A.1.c

Define the scope of the
transformation effort.

A.1.d

Select and customize the
transformation
framework.

A.1.e

Develop a high-level
baseline of
expected results.

A.1.f

Formulate the business
case and present it to key
executive sponsors.

A.1.g

Assess executive
commitment to transforming
the supply chain.

Low

High

A.1.h.1

Stop the process;
exit.

A.1.h.2
Communicate the process
to employees and enter
supply chain partner

Proceed to the next stage.

order-to-cash cycle time, order-fill percentage, or costs may be producing customer dissatisfaction and/or be noncompetitive with key competitors. Perhaps your company is the industry leader, and you want to place even more distance between it and your competitors. Whatever the reason, it must be clearly defined.

It is important in this step to tie the recognition of the events driving the need for transformation with the establishment of the need itself. For example, your enterprise is the industry leader in a specific line of building materials. One of your marketplace differentiators is your order-to-cash cycle time of seven days. In the past few months, your market share has dipped a little, while reports from the field tell of competitors' matching your cycle time of seven days.

As the enterprise executive, you recognize the value of your cycle time core competency and its relationship to your industry-leading market share. You also recognize the threat competitors present if they can consistently match or beat your cycle time. Thus, you establish the need to transform your enterprise's order-to-cash cycle time in order to preserve your leadership position within the industry.

This is a critical step. To start the process, identify (recognize) the driving forces behind the perceived need to transform your supply chain. Then, establish the need to transform, linking the need to the driving forces. Use the preceding scenario as an example.

A.1.a: Identify Key Executive Sponsors

In every company, there exists a select group of executives who are the key decision makers. Most of the time, but not always, these executives are the business unit leaders of critical business or internal functions. They have the autonomy to make significant decisions and the signature authority to approve the resources to support those decisions.

The key executives who are directly involved in supply chain activities should be identified and selected as transformation sponsors. There should be no more than three or four sponsors, with one executive functioning as the transformation team's overall executive sponsor.

A.1.b: Identify and Select Process Champions

Once the senior executive recognizes and establishes the need for transforming the customer supply chain and selects the key executive sponsors, the process champions must be chosen. The key executive sponsors should take the lead in this selection.

Process champions should be picked based on their past performance, their ability to influence people, and their enthusiasm for embracing and leading change. Process champions should not be selected based on their political connections within the company. Many transformation efforts are doomed to failure the minute a political "appointee" becomes a process champion. Employees often equate "transformation" with "losing jobs." An individual who is selected as a process champion is usually assured of continuing employment after the transformation effort. Choosing a nonperforming political appointee as a process champion sends a strong signal to employees that whom you know matters more than what you have accomplished. Avoid this at all costs! Select process champions who can coordinate and lead the transformation effort with the respect and support of the employees.

A.1.c: Define the Scope of the Transformation Effort

Successful transformation efforts must be focused. The need to change the supply chain must therefore be translated into a scope of the change effort. The key sponsors and process champions must decide which supply chain components are to be included in the transformation effort and which will be excluded. Resources are limited, so to maximize their utilization, they must be deployed only to the activities that are "within scope." The scope of the transformation effort should be very tightly defined. For example, the executive may select the procurement and inbound transportation of parts and subsystems from suppliers to an automobile assembly plant as the scope of the change effort. The driving forces may be inventory control and cost reduction. Thus, the delivery of finished automobiles would be considered "out of scope."

The executive sponsor and the process champions should identify the scope of the transformation effort, with the process champions and the transformation team defining what activities will be considered "within scope." The scope of the change effort should be defined in a published document, ensuring that the key sponsors and process champions are in full agreement regarding the scope.

A.1.d: Select and Customize the Transformation Framework

Although there are numerous transformation methodologies on the market, it is important to recognize that methodologies are only road maps. These road maps are all based on a similar, high-level framework and must be converted from this high-level framework to a customized methodology that fits the enterprise's individual needs. Executives must avoid selecting an "off-the-shelf" methodology and implementing it without customization. It is this approach used by some consultants that creates the executive perception of process models' being "only theoretical." Of even greater importance is to avoid selecting a management consulting company that adheres rigidly to its methodologies. Just as it is the success of the journey that counts and not the road map, so it is the outcome of the change effort that counts and not the transformation methodology per se.

Most of the transformation methodologies on the market are based on a high-level framework similar to the one shown in Exhibit 1-2. Any transformation process should include such basics as activities, anticipated timelines, milestones, and deliverables. Emphasis should be placed on the "implementability" of change and the involvement of key employees. You can use the framework presented here as a starting point and adapt it to the needs of your organization.

However, the process need not be perfect or exact. Throughout the change effort, significant learnings will be realized that will contribute to an ongoing revision of the transformation methodology. So the important thing is to establish the transformation framework with the concurrence of key executives and get the process under way.

A.1.e: Develop a High-Level Baseline of Expected Results

The deliverables of the transformation effort must be quantifiable and measurable. They must also be focused on the driving forces behind the need for change. For example, if cycle time needs to be reduced, then an expected result could be to cut the order-to-cash cycle time from seven to four days. If costs are to be reduced, then an expected result could be to cut the order-to-cash cost per unit by 10 percent. If customer satisfaction is to be increased, then an expected result could be perfect order-fill rates.

The executive establishing the high-level baseline of the transformation effort's expected results must keep the number of targeted results to one or two at most and keep the measurement process simple.

Thus, for this step, the senior executive, the executive sponsor, and the process champions must collectively decide on one or two performance categories that will be used to measure the results of the transformation effort and establish the goals within each performance category.

Exhibit 1-2. Business process transformation methodology—
basic framework.

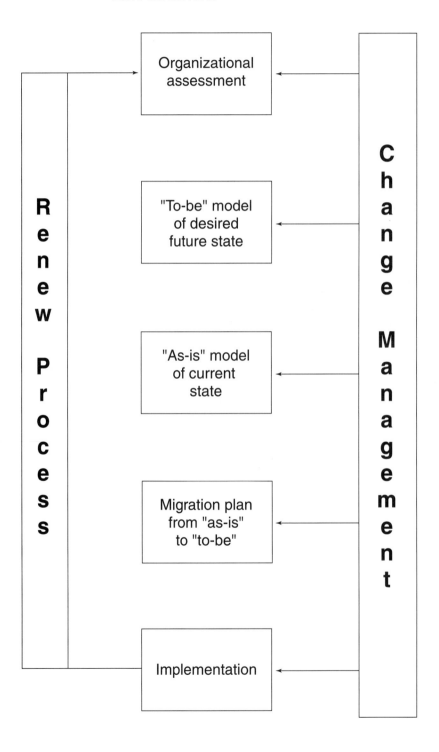

A.1.f: Formulate the Business Case and Present It to Key Executive Sponsors

The process champions must match the expected results of the transformation effort with the costs associated with the effort. The costs need to be defined in two ways: the anticipated direct costs associated with undertaking the change effort and the anticipated indirect costs associated with not undertaking the effort.

The cost/benefit business case must also focus on the business value of the effort. Higher customer satisfaction measurements must be associated with an increase in sales or market share (if the market is expanding) or the prevention of a loss in sales or market share (if the market is contracting); lower costs should produce higher profits or higher market share; and so on.

In addition, it helps to perform a sensitivity analysis on costs and benefits to focus on the probability of the results' being achieved. Any measure, ranging from payback to present value, can be used if your assumptions are documented.

Thus, an executive sponsor might position the order-to-cash transformation of the supply chain to reduce cycle time from seven to four days. The costs would be the cost of the project—say, $375,000. The benefit would be the three-day reduction in cycle time or a 2 percentage point increase in market share. Each market share point represents $500,000 in annual revenue and $100,000 in profit. Whatever the measurements, speak the language of the senior executive! It is critical to prepare the presentation using language and terms that senior executives are used to.

A.1.g: Assess Executive Commitment to Transforming the Supply Chain

At this point, it is time for the senior executive, the executive sponsor, and the process champions to decide collectively either to proceed with the transformation effort or to stop the process. The executive sponsor must assess whether there is sufficient commitment within the executive ranks to support the transformation process through its implementation.

A.1.h.1: Stop the Process; Exit

If there are any doubts about the executive commitment, *stop the process and exit!* There is no reason to subject the enterprise to a change effort if the executive team does not totally concur in terms of its support and commitment.

A.1.h.2: Communicate the Process to Employees and Enterprise Supply Chain Partners

If the executive commitment is high, then the executive team must proceed with communicating the process to the enterprise's employees. *Honesty is critical.* If cost is the primary driver, *then say so!* People are the key to the success of any transformation effort. Honesty and integrity will help people support the organization after the change is made. It is important for the executive sponsor to present the process to the employees and to connect the process with executive integrity. You have one chance to start the process properly and connect with your employees. *Do it right!*

Please don't forget your supply chain partners. They have a significant stake in the outcome of the customer-centered supply chain management change process. They should either participate in the transformation effort or at least be informed of the effort from the start. True partnerships are also built on trust and integrity. Don't let your partners find out about a transformation effort through the grapevine. Be in control of the way the process is communicated, and you will be in control of your partnership relationship.

One way to accomplish this is to make a simultaneous announcement to employees and your supply chain partners. If you have large, diverse employee groups and supply chain partners, you could use a video teleconference. If you have a small, concentrated group, you could hold a meeting and invite your supply chain partners to participate. Whatever you decide, please treat your partners as you would want to be treated if they were transforming their supply chains.

Conclusion

This chapter has focused on how the executive can get the supply chain management change process under way. After successfully completing the getting-started process methodology, it is time to advance to the next stage of the process.

Chapter 2 discusses the impact of change and the important role that business planning plays in taking advantage of change. Chapter 2's process methodology outlines the steps by which the executive can either establish or reinforce the enterprise's competitive frame of reference, core culture and values, mission, vision, and core competencies (at a high level), all of which are critical to establish the foundation for the customer-centered supply chain management change process.

Chapter 2

Business Strategy

As I illustrated in Chapter 1 with the virtual reality car showroom, there are forces of change affecting manufacturing that are accelerating the need for enterprises to adapt quickly to change. These forces, led by electronic commerce and globalism, are combining to create an environment that rapidly separates winners from losers. Winners will be the companies that create flexibility in their value chains so they can adapt quickly to change and grow. Losers will be the companies that fail to do so.

In the past several years, I have had the pleasure of working with several senior executives around the globe. The senior executives of the successful companies all had one thing in common: They were able to develop a business vision for their enterprise and then effectively mobilize their employees and resources in the direction needed to achieve that vision. In essence, these senior executives were able to formulate and implement strategic plans consistently.

The less successful companies also had one thing in common: Their senior executives seemed to lack a strong vision, which contributed to a lack of unity in purpose among their executive staff. The result was a preoccupation with short-term results and a distinct inability to respond quickly to changing consumer demands in the marketplace.

Because the business vision plays such a critical role in establishing a foundation for enterprises to create opportunities out of constant change and thereby achieve long-term success, this stage of the customer-centered supply chain management change process is called the foundation (Exhibit 2-1). In this chapter, I've included both a business vision framework and a process that executives can use to establish a vision for their enterprise.

Exhibit 2-1. The customer-centered supply chain management change process.

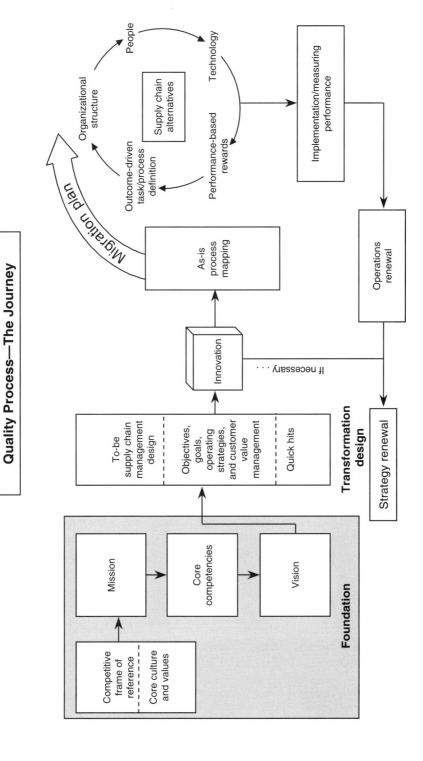

Major Change Forces and Their Effects on Manufacturing

This section provides a quick overview of globalism, the impact of change on the *Fortune* top 50 for the past quarter century, and how the two major forces of change in manufacturing—electronic commerce (discussed briefly in Chapter 1 in connection with the changes it is creating in the automotive assembly value chain) and globalism—are impacting the high-tech manufacturing industry.

Globalism

The movement toward globalism in the world's manufacturing environment can be described by analyzing the driving forces behind globalism and the changes that these forces have brought about.

One such driving force is the global investment flow. The total of foreign direct investment owned by U.S. companies increased from $146 billion in 1977 to $327 billion in 1988. More than 40 percent of the total investment was in manufacturing. By 1988, the total of foreign direct investment owned by foreign countries in the United States was $328.8 billion, or roughly equal to the foreign direct investment owned by U.S. companies in that year. Approximately 37 percent of the foreign direct investment in the United States was in manufacturing.[1]

By 1995, the U.S. direct investment abroad had increased to $711.6 billion (36.2 percent in manufacturing), while the total foreign direct investment in the United States had risen to $560.1 billion (37.5 percent in manufacturing).[2] The strength of the U.S. economy and the U.S. leadership in the application of technology helped fuel the investments on both sides. The impact of these numbers can be realized by focusing on one figure: In 1973, the amount of foreign direct investment in the United States was only $22 billion. The United States has evolved from the world's *dominant* economy to the world's *leading* economy.

1. Committee for the Study of the Causes and Consequences of the Internationalization of U.S. Manufacturing, Manufacturing Studies Board, Commission on Engineering and Technical Systems, National Research Council, "The Internationalization of U.S. Manufacturing: Causes and Consequences" (Washington, D.C.: National Academy Press, 1990), p. 59.
2. Bureau of Economic Analysis, U.S. Department of Commerce, Economics and Statistics Administration, "Survey of Current Business," Vol. 73, No. 12 (December 1996), pp. D-62, D-64.

Exhibit 2-2. Domestic versus international/global customer supply chain management activities.

Domestic Customer Supply Chain Management Activities	*International/Global Customer Supply Chain Management Activities*
Purchasing/procurement	Purchasing/procurement
Inbound transportation	Inbound transportation
Warehousing	Warehousing
Outbound transportation	Outbound transportation
Order processing	Order processing
Accounts/freight receivables	Accounts/freight receivables
	Customs brokerage
	Customs duty drawbacks
	Global inventory tracking
	Ocean shipping
	• Consolidation
	• Crating/packing
	• Deconsolidation
	Trade financing
	Foreign currency management
	Insurance (land, sea, air)
	Bonded warehousing and distribution
	Multilingual customer service
	Export/import administration

Another driving force behind globalism is the growth of technology sources around the world. An indicator of technology sources is the mix between U.S. and foreign applicants for U.S. patents. In 1970, 27 percent of U.S. patents were awarded to foreign applicants. By 1988, this figure had risen to 48 percent.[3]

The growth in foreign investment is combining with the growth of technology sources around the world to change the manufacturing infrastructure globally. Manufacturing plants are being located closer to their markets and sources of technology and farther from sources of raw materials and labor. This movement places enormous pressure on an enterprise's value chain. Raw materials and work-in-process goods must be transported across longer supply lines and across national borders to accommodate this infrastructure change. In addition, financial transactions and telecommunications across national borders vastly increase the complexity of supply chain management as compared to traditional, domestic supply chain management activities. (See Exhibit 2-2.)

3. "Internationalization of U.S. Manufacturing," p. 59.

The Impact of Change as Reflected in *Fortune's* Top 50 Industrial Corporations

The need for flexibility to adapt quickly to change is being accelerated by globalism. Unfortunately for many companies, it is already too late. Let's take a look at a twenty-year span of the *Fortune* top 50. I will focus on the impact of change on our country's largest industrial corporations and, in particular, the high-tech industry. The rise and fall of many of the *Fortune* top 50 companies can be attributed to senior executives' success or failure in establishing a business vision, perceiving change in their industries, and adapting to that change.

The year was 1971. Richard Nixon was president of the United States; gasoline was thirty-eight cents per gallon; and mass production ruled the business of manufacturing. Transportation was largely regulated; the United States dominated the world economy; and I was just graduating from high school.

The *Fortune* top 50 industrial corporations in 1971 included companies like IBM, Rapid-American, United Aircraft, Singer, Litton Industries, Firestone Tire & Rubber, Greyhound, Swift, and Ling-Temco-Vought. (See Exhibit 2-3.)

By 1996, Bill Clinton had been reelected president; gasoline prices had risen to $1.15 per gallon; and mass production had begun to be replaced by lean production. (Lean production has been defined as "[t]he use of teams of multi-skilled workers at all levels of the organization and the use of highly flexible, increasingly automated machines to produce volumes of products in enormous variety with significantly less resources than mass production. [Its] goals . . . are continuing declining costs, zero defects, zero inventories, and endless product variety.")[4] Transportation had largely been deregulated, and the United States had become just another major player in the world economy.

Between 1971 and 1993, more than 40 percent of the names in the *Fortune* top 50 list had changed. (There was even greater change by 1996. However, *Fortune* had by then changed its list to include the largest U.S. corporations rather than the largest industrial corporations.) Mergers, acquisitions, market changes, and bankruptcies contributed to this large turnover. Many corporations maintained their rankings, while others rose into the top 50.

In 1971, IBM dominated the high-tech industry. Twenty-five years later, IBM was still the world's largest high-tech company, but it had endured some tough years. The compression of technology caused IBM to struggle for a vision, a business direction, and a way

4. James P. Womack, Daniel T. Jones, and Daniel Roos, *The Machine That Changed the World* (New York: Simon & Schuster, 1990), pp. 13–14.

Exhibit 2-3. The Fortune 50 largest U.S. industrial corporations.

	1993			1971	
Rank	Company	Sales ($ Millions)	Rank	Company	Sales ($ Millions)
1	General Motors	133,621.9	1	General Motors	28,263.9
2	Ford Motor Co.	108,521.0	2	Standard Oil (N.J.)	18,315.2
3	Exxon	97,825.0	3	Ford Motor Co.	16,433.0
4	IBM	62,716.0	4	General Electric	9,425.3
5	General Electric	60,823.0	5	IBM	8,723.6
6	Mobil	56,576.0	6	Mobil Oil	8,243.0
7	Philip Morris	50,621.0	7	Chrysler	7,999.3
8	Chrysler	43,600.0	8	Texaco	7,529.0
9	Texaco	34,359.0	9	International Tel. & Tel.	7,345.7
10	E. I. DuPont	32,621.0	10	Western Electric	6,045.2
11	Chevron	32,123.0	11	Gulf Oil	5,940.0
12	Procter & Gamble	30,433.0	12	Standard Oil of California	5,143.2
13	Amoco	25,336.0	13	U.S. Steel	4,928.2
14	Boeing	25,285.0	14	Westinghouse Electric	4,630.5
15	PepsiCo	25,020.7	15	Standard Oil (Ind.)	4,054.3
16	ConAgra	21,519.1	16	Shell Oil	3,892.4
17	Shell Oil	20,853.0	17	E. I. DuPont de Nemours	3,848.2
18	United Technologies	20,736.0	18	RCA	3,711.8
19	Hewlett-Packard	20,317.0	19	Goodyear Tire & Rubber	3,601.5
20	Eastman Kodak	20,059.0	20	Ling-Temco-Vought	3,358.7
21	Dow Chemical	18,060.0	21	Procter & Gamble	3,178.1
22	Atlantic Richfield	17,189.0	22	Atlantic Richfield	3,134.8
23	Motorola	16,963.0	23	Continental Oil	3,051.0
24	USX	16,844.0	24	Boeing	3,039.8
25	RJR Nabisco	15,104.0	25	Union Carbide	3,037.5
26	Xerox	14,981.0	26	International Harvester	3,016.3
27	Sara Lee	14,580.0	27	Swift	2,996.2
28	McDonnell Douglas	14,487.2	28	Eastman Kodak	2,975.9
29	Digital Equipment Corp.	14,371.4	29	Bethlehem Steel	2,963.6
30	Johnson & Johnson	14,138.0	30	Kraftco	2,959.6
31	Minnesota Mining & Mfg.	14,020.0	31	Lockheed Aircraft	2,852.3
32	Coca-Cola	13,957.0	32	Tenneco	2,840.6
33	International Paper	13,685.0	33	Greyhound	2,616.1
34	Tenneco	13,255.0	34	Firestone Tire & Rubber	2,483.6
35	Lockheed	13,071.0	35	Litton Industries	2,466.1
36	Georgia-Pacific	12,330.0	36	Occidental Petroleum	2,400.0
37	Phillips Petroleum	12,309.0	37	Phillips Petroleum	2,363.2
38	Allied Signal	11,827.0	38	General Foods	2,281.9
39	IBP	11,671.4	39	North American Rockwell	2,210.7
40	Goodyear Tire	11,643.4	40	Caterpillar Tractor	2,175.2
41	Caterpillar	11,615.0	41	Singer	2,099.4
42	Westinghouse Elec.	11,564.0	42	Monsanto	2,087.1
43	Anheuser-Busch	11,505.2	43	Continental Can	2,081.5
44	Bristol-Myers Squibb	11,413.0	44	Borden	2,069.6
45	Rockwell Int'l	10,840.0	45	McDonnell Douglas	2,069.0
46	Merck	10,498.2	46	Dow Chemical	2,052.7
47	Coastal	10,136.1	47	W. R. Grace	2,048.9
48	Archer Daniels Midland	9,811.4	48	United Aircraft	2,028.7
49	Ashland Oil	9,553.9	49	Rapid-American	1,990.6
50	Weyerhaeuser	9,544.8	50	Union Oil of California	1,981.4

Sources: *Fortune* (May 1972), p. 190; *Fortune* (April 1992) p. 220. Used with permission.

to manage change. In 1992, the company posted a net loss of $5 billion (including a $7.2 billion pretax charge), and its stock had declined more than 70 percent from its 1987 high, wiping out more than $70 billion in market value for its shareholders.[5] By early 1997, IBM's stock had fully recovered to the level of its pretrouble days.

IBM is certainly not alone in its struggle to adapt to change. Digital Equipment Corporation (DEC) was subjected to the same compression of technology as IBM but has been unable to recover as IBM did. Both IBM and DEC are in an industry that has been and continues to be in a period of accelerated change. Industry experts believe that there will be more change in the next five years than there was in the previous twenty years. In the following subsection, we'll consider why there is so much change in the high-tech industry and how that change affects DEC and others.

The High-Tech Manufacturing Industry

High-tech manufacturing is one of the most dynamic industries in the world. Twenty-plus years ago, in the era of IBM and the mainframe, the microprocessor was invented, bringing about massive change in the high-tech industry.

A microprocessor is a computer on a silicon wafer, or "chip," a set of transistors that process data. Every eighteen to thirty months, researchers have achieved a fourfold increase in the number of transistors placed on a chip, giving rise to enormous computing power in small microprocessors.[6] This explosion in computing power transformed the industry, first from mainframes to minicomputers and later to PC-based workstations and networked computers. This change has divided the industry into a number of segments with rapidly emerging leaders.

The growth of desktop computing and network computing power, along with the birth of the Internet, is bringing electronic commerce to many parts of the extended enterprise. Employees at all levels can now adapt electronic commerce to their specific needs.

IBM has historically been a vertically integrated company. For many years, IBM controlled the hardware and software marketplace with its proprietary architecture, and its mainframe business was highly profitable.

In the early 1980s, IBM turned to outside suppliers for components in order to bring its personal computer to market faster. Because the contracts IBM signed with Intel and Microsoft allowed them to market to IBM's competitors, Compaq and other competitors were

5. Michael W. Miller, "IBM Shares Fall Further as Analysts and Computer Experts Urge More Cuts," *Wall Street Journal*, December 17, 1992, p. A3.
6. John Markoff, "IBM Problems Traced to Size," *Dallas Morning News*, Business Section, December 16, 1992, p. 1D.

soon producing IBM-compatible personal computers. Within a few years, Intel's microprocessors and Microsoft's disk operating system (DOS) became a de facto standard in most personal computers except Apple's. The IBM-clone market became an industry segment unto itself.

With the aforementioned explosive growth in microprocessor technology, the integration of software into business operations, and the standardization of software products across multiple hardware manufacturers, the high-tech industry has become extremely price-competitive. PCs have become commodities, driving volume through the supply chain and forcing manufacturers to lower their costs and prices.

The outlook is for even greater change. Satellite-based telecommunications, integrated with individual users through a series of networks, promises integrated connectivity for virtually unlimited products and services. Industry experts believe that satellite-based telecommunications will impact the value chains of automotive companies and have an even more profound impact on the value chains of computer manufacturers.

The rush is on for high-tech companies to demonstrate competency and vie for market share in one of three major groups: satellite-based telecommunications, high-tech hardware manufacturing, and software and service providers that support the networks. To offer one-stop shopping to users, companies must participate in the other groups through alliances, joint ventures, or mergers. The need to have a business vision has never been greater, but merely having a vision is not enough. As I mentioned earlier in the chapter, in order to be successful, a senior executive must mobilize the enterprise's employees and resources in the direction necessary to achieve the vision.

Intel has exhibited an intent to dominate the microprocessor industry segment and to expand its presence in the industry segments close to its microprocessor segment. In 1997, Intel aggressively moved into the networking business. When Intel announced it was cutting prices for its network adapter cards (the circuit boards that connect a desktop computer to a network cable), the market value of 3Com's stock dropped more than $2 billion. This was not the first time Intel had expanded its presence beyond the microprocessor industry segment. In 1993, it invaded the turf of many of its primary customers by expanding its production of motherboards. Its competitors were powerless to stop Intel.[7]

What's to come? Intel's chief executive officer recently told *Forbes*, "A few years from now every computer will be multimedia ready and network-management ready. Computers without those things

7. Nikhil Hutheesing, "Excuse Me If I Invade Your Business," *Forbes*, March 10, 1997, pp. 158–162.

will be as meaningless as computers without memory."[8] Intel's CEO seems to have a very clear vision indeed of where his industry and his company are headed.

The Vision Framework

For the executive transforming a supply chain in a high-tech industry, flexibility and adaptability to an ever-changing product mix and product life cycle are essentials. Any change effort that is focused on the supply chain and *not* connected to a strong business vision will be a waste of time. Given the fast pace of change within the industry, such an effort could even cause a significant drop in marketplace presence despite the best intentions of all involved.

In this section, we'll examine a framework that will help the executive develop a strong business vision, using EDS and DEC as concrete examples of the relationship between the business vision and corporate success. Then, in the following section, we'll see how to develop a linkage between this vision and the enterprise's employees and resources that will be used to make that vision a reality.

The EDS Manufacturing Business Vision

EDS is a world leader in the use of information technology, especially in data center outsourcing. To assist senior executives in their efforts to develop a vision for their enterprise, EDS developed the EDS Manufacturing Business Vision (Exhibit 2-4) with the help of Tom Gunn, who is now the process engineering chief information officer with General Motors. The EDS Manufacturing Business Vision is a framework, or template, to enable senior executives to pull together their efforts in a multitude of common areas, which are called core concepts.

The core concepts of the EDS Manufacturing Business Vision are:

- Global Approach to Business
- Core Culture and Values
- Balanced Business Strategy
- Leadership
- Responsive Enterprise
- Competitive Advantage Enablers
- Value-Added Pipeline[9]

8. Ibid., p. 162.
9. Thomas G. Gunn, "21st Century Manufacturing: Creating Winning Business Performance," 1991, p. 28.

Exhibit 2-4. EDS manufacturing business vision.

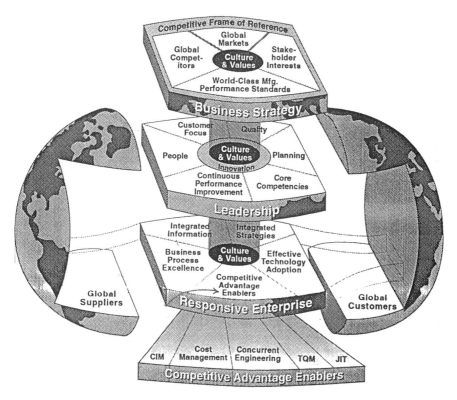

Source: Thomas G. Gunn, "21st Century Manufacturing: Creative Winning Business Performance" (New York: HarperCollins 1991), p. 29. Used with permission.

Two of the core concepts employed in the EDS Manufacturing Business Vision—the core culture and values and the balanced business strategy—provide such a useful framework for developing your own vision that I have incorporated them into my customer-centered supply chain management change process. Let's briefly consider these two key core concepts and their relevance to the development of a vision for the enterprise.

Core Culture and Values

For any organization to create lasting change, top management must define a core culture that incorporates the principles by which the organization operates. As employees accept and share these principles, they become the foundation for the corporate values.

To promote corporate values, manufacturing and logistics executives must define desired attributes for the enterprise's employees and screen its new employees accordingly. Downsizing puts a greater burden on each employee to be more productive and to make a greater contribution to the success of the enterprise. An employee's success, and the success of other employees with whom he or she interacts, often hinges on the employee's alignment with the corporate culture and value base. It is difficult to achieve world-class performance in supply chain management if employees do not perceive that top management is strongly committed to them.

Balanced Business Strategy

A global manufacturer's business strategy must maintain a balance among the forces of its world marketplace. These forces include global competition, stakeholders, and world-class performance standards. A successful and balanced business strategy is the basis for a product portfolio strategy to penetrate new and underdeveloped markets aggressively and maintain existing, developed markets. Each market requires a unique approach to the supply chain and its activities.

The aim of a world-class manufacturer is to produce world-class results. World-class performers must continually search for ways to improve if they are to retain their world-class standing. For example, Motorola expects to improve its defect rate to the point where defects are reported in number per *billion* parts![10]

It is hard for senior executives to understand the need to recreate their vision when their companies are world-class performers and highly profitable. However, in my opinion, it is essential for senior executives to do just that. The time to change is when you are on top. A company can pay a huge price if it becomes complacent, especially when it is on top.

Digital Equipment Corporation: The Price of Resting on One's Laurels

For DEC's fiscal year 1996 (which ended on June 30, 1996), total operating revenues were $14.563 billion, virtually unchanged from 1993 and only slightly higher than in 1991. DEC incurred an operating loss of $44 million and a net loss of $112 million. Since 1990, DEC has

10. G. Christian Hill and Ken Yamada, "Staying Power: Motorola Illustrates How an Aging Giant Can Remain Vibrant," *Wall Street Journal*, December 9, 1992, p. 14.

incurred net losses in every year but one (1995). DEC's total losses since 1990 have been approximately $5.8 billion![11] The peak year for DEC was 1988. Net income was $1.306 billion on total operating revenues of $11.475 billion, or 11.4 percent. Its revenues had increased 22 percent over the prior year, and optimism was pervasive about the continuing success of its minicomputer product line. DEC had a return on equity of 18.9 percent and a return on assets of 14.1 percent. Its stock traded in the $99–$199 range, providing true value for its shareholders.[12] By the first quarter of 1997, DEC's stock was trading at around $28.[13]

The consensus of opinion in the investment community is that DEC failed to anticipate the marketplace movement from minicomputers to desktop computers and that it was slow to move from hardware to services. In fact, "service and other revenues" in 1996 were $6.2 billion, or virtually unchanged from $6.235 billion in 1992.[14] In addition, there is an opinion in the marketplace that DEC's executives failed to develop a vision for the company that identified its core competencies and then leveraged them. The failure to renew its vision at the peak of its profitability in 1988 placed DEC at the mercy of the fast-changing high-tech industry. DEC has paid a high price for complacency. In early 1998, Compaq announced its acquisition of DEC.

In the past three to five years, DEC has been an active supporter of supply chain management. Many of its executives have been involved with key logistics associations and have provided a certain amount of marketplace thought leadership on the subject. However, DEC's financial performance since 1988 bears out the key premise of this book: To transform a supply chain, executives must start at the strategy level. The vision for the company, constructed in an iterative fashion by identifying and leveraging core competencies, must first be established in order to provide the right foundation for the transformation effort.

The balanced business strategy core concept combines the global marketplace, competitors, stakeholder interests, and world-class performance standards to define an enterprise's competitive frame of reference. Once the competitive frame of reference has been defined, the senior executive can use it as a platform from which to initiate the

11. "Digital Equipment Corporation—1996 Annual Report to Shareholders," eleven-year financial summary, from: http://www.digital.com/info/finance/annual96/11year.html.
12. Ibid.
13. *Dallas Morning News,* Business Section, stock tables, NYSE, "Digital," March 21, 1997, p. 5D.
14. "Digital Equipment Corporation—1996 Annual Report to Shareholders."

vision, or strategic-planning, process. Thus, the vision framework feeds the vision process, forging the first link in the creation of a process that will enable the enterprise to take advantage of change. For the executive, the next step is to establish the vision process.

The Vision Process: Strategic Business Planning

Now that the executive and the transformation team have established the enterprise's core culture and values and defined the competitive frame of reference, they need a process to pull this information together and actually create a vision for the enterprise. Numerous books have been written on strategic business planning and strategic management. In my experience, successful business planning revolves around three key principles: keeping the process simple, developing a vision with which the senior executive team can align itself, and connecting the vision to the annual operating plans of the enterprise's operating divisions.

I have pulled together a simple vision/business-planning process to help the senior executive get started. One critical *caveat* is that you get out of any process what you are willing to put into it. The purpose of this process is to develop a vision statement for the enterprise that can be used as a basis for designing and implementing an effective supply chain. My intent is to keep things simple.

The Mission Statement

An enterprise's competitive frame of reference includes the following elements:

- Global competitors
- Global marketplace
- World-class performance standards
- Stakeholder interests
- The enterprise's core culture and values

These areas feed an exercise that is overworked and often misunderstood—namely, the development of a mission statement.

A good mission statement should be no more than twenty-five to thirty words long and span no more than two sentences. (I have seen mission statements as long as two pages!) A mission statement should answer the question "Why does your enterprise exist?" It should include the product, market, and geographic mix of the enterprise's product portfolio. It should also mention the interests of key stakeholders and the enterprise's competitive advantage enablers in the marketplace.

As an example, let's construct a mission statement for DEC. (Please note that this is in no way intended to offend DEC or infringe on its operations.)

Sample Mission Statement for DEC

DEC will maximize shareholder value by delivering computer *services* and *related products* to its global customers. DEC will achieve global marketplace eminence by listening to its customers and translating their needs into winning products and services that measurably improve their business performance.

Although simple, this mission statement addresses the product and market (computer services and related products), the geographic area (global), key stakeholders' interests (shareholder value), and the company's competitive advantage enabler (listening to customers; translating customer needs into winning services and products that measurably improve the customers' business performance).

To restore itself to marketplace competitiveness, DEC has to develop a clear vision of what it must do to become a world-class leader in today's dynamic global marketplace. The company must anticipate marketplace changes and be flexible enough to meet changing customer demands in a timely, cost-effective way with superior-quality services and products.

A good exercise is to compare your company's mission statement (if one exists) to the sample statement for DEC. If your company has no mission statement, create one with your management team. If it has a mission statement but it is not concise or realistic, redo it. The key is to have a mission statement that succinctly expresses why your business exists.

Core Competencies

To be leaders, global manufacturers must identify their core competencies and use them to build a marketplace presence and image. Core competencies can be based on an individual employee's contribution or the collective knowledge of a group of employees. Value chain partners that bring complementary core competencies will contribute to the success of the total effort.

Identifying the core competencies is key to the development of a vision for the enterprise. Honda's core competency is building engines. Home Depot's core competency is the do-it-yourself self-help philosophy of its employees. A core competency must be something that your company does so well that it provides a competitive advantage in the marketplace and perhaps serves as a barrier of entry against competitors. In addition, it must not be easily duplicated. (Note: Being the low-cost producer or provider *can* be a core competency if the cost differential is large enough to have a significant impact on the marketplace price of the product. Wal-Mart is a good example of a company in which *low cost* [Everyday Low Prices] is a core competency.)

Apple Computer, formed in the mid-1970s, focused on the personal computer industry segment. Ease of use, its core competency, enabled Apple to lead the industry in personal computer sales in only a few years. For a while, Apple enjoyed record sales and earnings, primarily driven by the premium prices that were charged for this ease-of-use capability.

Microsoft's Windows operating system, which greatly improved the ease of use of IBM-compatible PCs, eroded Apple's competitive advantage. Now, Microsoft's Windows 95 and Office 97 are the standard for the marketplace. As a result, Apple has been cutting prices and restructuring to preserve market share. During 1996, its market share plummeted to 5.2 percent, down from 7.9 percent a year earlier. Apple's earnings declined from $530.4 million in 1992 to a net loss of $816 million for fiscal year 1996 (which ended September 30, 1996).[15] This example shows that if competitors can easily duplicate a company's core competencies, its market share and earnings are at risk. A company must consistently enhance its existing core competencies or develop new ones to strengthen its marketplace leadership.

When you have defined your enterprise's competitive frame of reference, identified its core culture and values, developed a mission statement, and identified the core competencies, you are ready to develop your vision statement.

The Vision Statement

The vision statement expands on the mission statement and involves the next lower level of detail. This is critical in order to establish a linkage between the company's mission and its strengths, weaknesses, and leadership as well as the opportunities and threats facing it. Let's take a look at the vision statement of EDS as an example:

15. Peter Burrows, "Apple: What Is Steve Jobs Up To?" *Business Week*, March 17, 1997, pp. 116–117.

Sample Vision Statement: EDS

The Company will be globally recognized as the premier provider of Information Technology Services on the basis of our contribution to the success of our customers.

We will be a market-driven company, operating with strong business units focused on specific market segments and market leadership. In response to market demand, we will sustain aggressive growth, expand our markets, and be a truly global corporation.

We recognize that our success is driven by conscientiously serving the interests of customers, employees, and stockholders. We are foremost committed to understanding our customers' needs and helping them succeed in their marketplace. In doing so, we will be a preferred employer worldwide, offering unmatched employee opportunity, and we will provide significant stockholder return.

Our commitment to our customers will be legendary.[16]

The product is information technology services. The geographic scope is global. The *vision* is to be globally recognized as the premier provider in the industry.

The market is subsegmented into specific markets with strong business units focused on these markets. The *vision* is to be a market-driven company in response to market demand.

The competitive advantage enabler is the recognition that the company's success is driven by serving the interests of customers, employees, and stockholders. The *vision* is customer success, being a preferred employer worldwide, and significant stockholder return.

A core competency is identified in the last point: Legendary commitment to its customers provides the company with a distinct marketplace competitive advantage and serves as a barrier against the entry of other firms.

Once the vision statement is completed, the next steps include defining how the company will do business (quality) and designing the enterprise to achieve its vision. Aggressively redefining your company's vision can yield numerous benefits. Not renewing the company's vision, and subsequently its operations, can be disastrous.

For supply chain management, the key lesson is to be flexible and competent. Adapting quickly and effectively to a changing business climate is a must for supply chain partners. Failure to do so will result in the supply chain's inhibiting the enterprise's efforts to realize its business vision. Customer dissatisfaction will ensue, along with declining financial performance.

---

16. EDS vision statement. Used with permission.

Process Methodology Foundation

Change is pervasive in global manufacturing and rampant in the high-tech industry, which is evolving into a global, tightly connected network of telecommunications and hardware manufacturing, with services and software connecting the two. To achieve and sustain world-class performance, an enterprise needs visionary leadership to anticipate change and determine how to respond appropriately. In order to take advantage of change, an enterprise must have a supply chain that quickly and effectively adapts to evolving business conditions.

As I mentioned earlier in this chapter, the success of any supply chain transformation effort depends on the senior executive's ability to establish a vision for the enterprise, then mobilize the employees and resources in the direction needed to achieve the vision. But the dilemma for executives is how to develop a vision of the future while still managing the enterprise for short-term profitability. This section presents the methodology for a step-by-step process (illustrated in the accompanying process flowchart) that executives can use to define the enterprise's business vision in the context of its current business realities. The deliverables from successfully completing this process will be a competitive frame of reference, the core culture and values, a mission statement, a vision statement, and an identification of the enterprise's core competencies at a high level. These deliverables combine to establish the foundation for the supply chain management change process.

B.1: Define the Competitive Frame of Reference

The enterprise's competitive frame of reference includes global competitors, global markets, stakeholder interests, and world-class perfor-

THE SUPPLY CHAIN MANAGEMENT CHANGE PROCESS
Process Methodology
Foundation

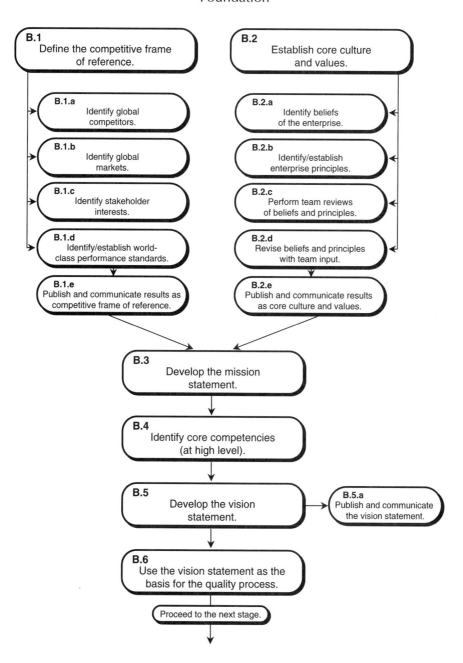

mance standards. It also includes the enterprise's core culture and values, but these latter factors are so critical to the enterprise that I have covered them in a separate series of process definition steps.

B.1.a: Identify Global Competitors

The executive team knows (or should know) who the competitors are better than anyone inside or outside the enterprise. However, it is critical for the executive team to identify the global competitors in a way that positions them competitively vis-à-vis the enterprise.

The executive team should identify and categorize the enterprise's global competitors based on size, strength of product portfolios (market shares in product categories), perceived core competencies, and marketplace tendencies. The executive team should then rank the competitors in three levels:

Level 1 competitors
Level 2 competitors
Level 3 competitors

Level 1 competitors pose the largest threat to the enterprise. These competitors must be monitored closely, with action plans defined to respond to their marketplace actions.

Level 2 competitors pose a moderate threat to the enterprise. These competitors usually threaten specific products and/or specific geographic regions. Although they do not pose as large a threat as level 1 competitors, they can seriously impact the performance of a product or region if ignored.

Level 3 competitors usually pose a low-level threat to the enterprise. Executives frequently refer to these competitors as "irritants." Often, they are small local or regional competitors that offer one or two "niche" products or services. They may be very good at what they do but lack the location or critical mass to have a major impact on the enterprise's overall performance. These competitors must be identified, because they may be acquisition candidates for the enterprise or the competition. In addition, these companies are the type with which a large company like Wal-Mart may contract. When this happens, these companies explode out of level 3 and instantly become level 2 competitors.

B.1.b: Identify Global Markets

The executive team should next identify the global markets for the enterprise's product portfolio. Although I have placed this step after the identification of global competitors, it could be performed before, or the two steps could be performed simultaneously. The key point is that when the two steps are completed, their results must be combined in order to assess the competitive environment of the enterprise.

The global market should be assessed based on the following criteria:

- Size of market
- Growth trends
- Political stability
- Currency stability
- Competitor/enterprise market position

The size of the market is important. For example, Argentina is a relatively stable country politically and is enjoying a strong economic growth rate. Its total population is roughly 34 million people. The majority of the population is literate and has had a relatively high per capita income level for Latin America. Brazil has only a moderate level of political stability, yet it has had a stronger economic growth rate than Argentina. Although Brazil has had a lower literacy rate and lower per capita income than Argentina, it has 167 million people, or almost five times the population of Argentina. If only 40 percent of the population of Brazil can afford the products of your enterprise's supply chain, it still amounts to twice the potential of Argentina if 100 percent of the Argentine population could afford your products.

The executive team must assess every country and region using these criteria to determine the market position of each competitor enterprise in each country and region. For the transformation process, a matrix of global markets, with a ranking of market potential (high, medium, and low), risk (high, medium, and low), and competitive position (dominant, competitive, and weak) should be developed (Exhibit 2-5). However, the sales and marketing executives should develop an in-depth market plan that details the sales and marketing strategies within each market.

B.1.c: Identify Stakeholder Interests

Once the global competitors and global markets are identified and assessed, the interests of the enterprise's stakeholders must be identified. Stakeholders include shareholders, employees, unions, communities, the environment, and supply chain partners.

The executive team must realize that mapping the stakeholders' interests will be like mapping a series of concentric circles. There will

Exhibit 2-5. Global market matrix.

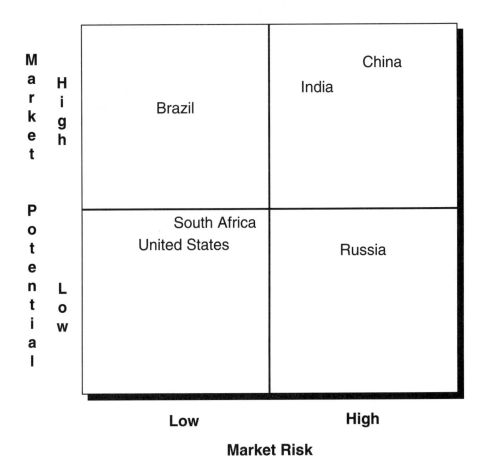

be overlapping areas that indicate the presence of common interests and not-overlapping areas that indicate an absence of common interests. As long as there is some overlap with the mainstream of the enterprise, it will be possible to establish a viable connection between stakeholders and the enterprise's vision. The executive team should focus on those stakeholders whose interests do not overlap at all with the interests of the mainstream of the enterprise's stakeholders. These stakeholders are potential sources of resistance to any transformation effort, and if they are strong enough, they could derail the change process. Thus, stakeholders should be rated on three criteria: their ability to absorb change, their teamwork philosophy or alignment with the enterprise, and the site of their impact on the enterprise. A highly unionized manufacturing organization provides the setting for a good example of the need to align powerful stakeholders to the change process. When the Saturn division of General Motors was created, the United Auto Workers (UAW) was welcomed as an equal partner in the overall change process. Today, the UAW continues to support the Saturn environment and the team concept that makes Saturn unique among American carmakers. An early 1998 union vote continued this support, despite a slowdown in sales of Saturn.

The reverse scenario is equally compelling. When General Motors was deciding whether to close either the Ypsilanti, Michigan, or Arlington, Texas, plant due to overcapacity, the UAW took two distinct positions. With the Ypsilanti plant, the UAW was combative and resistant to most work-rule changes. As a result, despite a significant cost advantage at the start of the negotiation process, the Ypsilanti plant was closed. The Arlington plant remained open, largely due to the work-rule changes and cooperative partnership with the UAW.

The learning here is that in order to minimize the threat of derailing the change process, an effort needs to be made to influence the UAW in such a way as to move its interests into the concentric circles of management.

B.1.d: Identify/Establish World-Class Performance Standards

The best-in-class companies frequently have world-class performance standards. These companies set the marketplace expectations in the areas of pricing (cost), quality of the product and service, cycle time, and relevant information that is useful in the purchasing decision.

The executive team must identify these best-in-class performance standards as they apply to the enterprise. In doing so, the team will want to consider the performance standards of some of the competitors whose strength was measured in step B.1.a. After the best-in-class or world-class performance standards are established, the team must rank the enterprise's performance standards against the best-in-class standards.

The gap between the enterprise and best-in-class companies is the space that must be closed if it is negative or the space that must be preserved and expanded if it is positive. However, the executive team must realize that this gap is dynamic. Best-in-class companies improve continually. *The enterprise has to improve at the same rate as the best-in-class performer just to stay even!* Or the enterprise has to improve at the same rate as its closest competitor if it is to maintain the market leadership position it enjoys today.

The executive team should perform a benchmarking effort to identify these performance standards. Customers, academia, suppliers, and trade associations are excellent sources of information. These standards should be high-level (such as the number of days required for the order-to-cash cycle). Later in the process, there will be steps that get into lower-level performance indexes.

B.1.e: Publish and Communicate Results as a Competitive Frame of Reference

When steps B.1.a through B.1.d have been completed, the information that has been developed, taken as a whole, defines the enterprise's competitive frame of reference. The executive team should pull all this information together into a document and selectively distribute it to key members of the management team. The results should be communicated to employees as well.

This step is potentially dangerous. Although employees and other stakeholders have a right to be informed about the direction of the company, the information in the competitive frame of reference document has significant value to competitors. The communications to employees must therefore be thorough enough to create an awareness and understanding of the enterprise's competitive position but not so detailed that information leaks to competitors could compromise the enterprise's operations. Executives must use good judgment when determining the balance in this trade-off.

B.2: Establish Core Culture and Values

As mentioned in the first portion of the chapter, for lasting change to be created, the executive team must define and establish the core culture of the enterprise. This core culture must incorporate the principles by which the organization operates. As employees accept and internalize these principles, they become values of the enterprise.

B.2.a: Identify Beliefs of the Enterprise

A belief of an enterprise is a state of mind in which stakeholders place trust and confidence in the enterprise. Wal-Mart employees, called associates, believe that if they work hard and support the Wal-Mart philosophy, they will be granted job security. The many charitable and civic associations in Saint Louis believe that Anheuser-Busch is an excellent corporate sponsor of the Saint Louis community. These beliefs are developed and cultivated over time by companies, usually through consistent and voluntary actions that add value to stakeholder groups.

The executive team must identify and document the current beliefs about the enterprise. Stakeholders, including supply chain partners, should be surveyed to determine what beliefs actually exist.

B.2.b: Identify/Establish Enterprise Principles

The executive team must differentiate principles from beliefs. Principles are the rules or code of conduct that companies require their employees, and sometimes their stakeholders, to follow. These principles can range from conflict-of-interest rules to dress codes to provisions regarding drug and alcohol abuse. Frequently, these principles set the guidelines for professional behavior that contribute to the corporate image and integrity.

For example, Wal-Mart has a principle that no employee can accept any gift, including lunches from vendors. Conversely, vendors are prohibited from even offering gifts to employees. In either case, the employees are subject to termination and the vendors are subject to contract cancellation if an offer is made and not reported by the other party. Another example is the rule that many companies now have that a driving while intoxicated (DWI) conviction is grounds for immediate termination.

The principles of the enterprise must be identified and documented. Start with the code of conduct and proceed throughout the enterprise to determine what principles exist.

B.2.c: Perform Team Reviews of Beliefs and Principles

The process champions should take the identified beliefs and principles of the enterprise to as many employees as possible for validation. This process step usually begins with diverging thoughts on the beliefs and principles but frequently ends up with converging opinions. The executive team should then collect the results from the many team reviews for the next process step.

B.2.d: Revise Beliefs and Principles With Team Input

The diverging and converging opinions identified in step B.2.c should be considered as input to revise the enterprise's existing beliefs and principles. The executive team should exercise care so as not to compromise the enterprise's current beliefs and principles in order to satisfy the radical opinions of a minority or dissident group. However, valuable input will enhance the continual improvement process, ensure employee ownership of the beliefs and principles because of their involvement in the process, and contribute to the publication of a credible document.

B.2.e: Publish and Communicate Results as Core Culture and Values

When beliefs and principles are internalized, they become intrinsically desirable or valued by the employees who internalize them. Step B.2.d, if facilitated properly, allows for this internalization to take place through the employees' active participation in the process itself.

By using the preceding steps to identify and revise the enterprise's core culture and values, the executive team will ensure that the core culture and values that are ultimately published and communicated to employees will have credibility. It is this state of trust, confidence, and support that executives need in order to build their vision and mobilize employees behind it.

Completing the Foundation Process

At this point in the process, the executive should be prepared to lead the development of the mission statement, the identification of the enterprise's core competencies (at a high level), and the development of the vision statement. (You may wish to refer to the discussion of the development process for each of these steps in the first portion of the chapter.)

As you go through this process, it should be easy to see how executives can get themselves into a bind from a business-planning standpoint. I have known highly results-oriented executives who did not want to take the time to develop the enterprise's competitive frame of reference and core culture and values adequately and dove right into the development of their mission statement. Without exception, developing the mission statement became a painful process for the participants.

Furthermore, each mission statement developed in this fashion became a collection of thoughts associated with all the steps involved in the development of the competitive frame of reference and the core culture and values. Did you ever see a mission statement that was 50–150 words, one huge run-on sentence that started strategically and ended tactically? One mission statement I know of got so involved that it even detailed a 10 percent reduction in the rate of errors per order-entry clerk! And this was from a *Fortune* 500 company!

Once the mission statement and vision statement are developed and the core competencies identified, it is important to publish the vision statement and communicate it to the employees and supply chain partners (step B.5.a). It is also important to identify the vision statement as the basis for the quality process that is to be performed following the development of the foundation (step B.6).

Conclusion

As you can see, the foundation process is critical to establish purpose, clarity of vision, and stakeholder commitment to the transformation of the supply chain. It must be performed in a thorough manner. Shortcuts in the foundation process will only increase the enterprise's risk of failing to achieve the desired results from the transformation process.

The executive has now started the supply chain management change process and established a foundation for change within the enterprise. The next step is to develop the process for how the enterprise will conduct business in the future. This process is simply called quality.

Chapter 3
The Quality Commitment

"What is your definition of quality?" the purchasing executive of a large mass-merchandising company asked the contract negotiations team of a major consumer electronics company. The time was the spring of 1997, and the event was the opening day of its annual contract negotiations meeting.

The members of the contract negotiations team were excited to hear the question. In their exhaustive preparation for the meeting, they had dedicated about a dozen of the more than 330 overheads they had prepared to quality. The company's vice president of sales took the lead and, in eloquent fashion, presented his company's quality story. Overhead after overhead was filled with product defect measurement statistics, information on quality circles on the factory floor, and endless quality slogans. At the end of the presentation, it was obvious that the whole negotiating team was feeling very good about its quality presentation and the opening of the contract negotiations. In a different setting, I am sure high fives would have been exchanged among the team members. As it was, the team members only gave each other thumbs-up gestures of approval.

After a few moments of silence, the large mass merchandiser's purchasing executive stood up, walked to the overhead projector, placed a blank overhead on the projector, and wrote the following: "Quality in a product or service is not what the supplier puts in. It is what the customer gets out and is willing to pay for."[1]

After he had finished writing, the purchasing executive observed to the consumer electronics company team that the word *customer* or *consumer* was nowhere to be seen on any of their slides. He suggested that the contract negotiations restart the following week, after the

---

1. Peter Drucker, *Innovation and Entrepreneurship: Practice and Principles* (New York: HarperBusiness, 1993), p. 228.

team had had time to reorient its quality focus around the ultimate customer. He also told the team members that their ultimate customer was not his company but the final consumer. You could hear a pin drop in the room as the meeting came to an abrupt end.

After the meeting, I overheard a hallway conversation among the members of the consumer electronics company negotiating team. One individual commented that he thought the quality movement was dead. I suggested to him that although "the bloom" was gone from TQM (total quality management), the fundamental concepts supporting quality have never been stronger or more pervasive in the marketplace.

Many readers will recognize the quotation written by the purchasing executive as being from Peter Drucker's *Innovation and Entrepreneurship.* Regardless of whether you are a Drucker fan, his comment about quality is very insightful. Just ask the consumer electronics company negotiating team! In addition to contract positioning, the purchasing executive sent a profound message to his supplier—a message that was reinforced by the one-week delay in the opening of negotiations and the electronics company's embarrassment at having its inwardly oriented quality focus pointed out during negotiations with its largest customer. The message was that quality is a commitment focused on the final customer, not a project internal to your own company.

The Vision/Quality Connection

After the manufacturing and logistics executives complete the foundation process methodology and establish a vision for their enterprise, it is important for the executives to determine how their enterprise will do business. The philosophy of how an enterprise will conduct its business is critical to the overall success of the customer-centered supply chain management change process. It will serve as a basis for how other companies will approach partnering with the enterprise. The greater the focus on the buying values of the ultimate customer in the supply chain, and the more thorough the definition and greater the understanding of such a philosophy, the greater the chance that supply chain partners will interact successfully. Assessing, defining, and incorporating the customer-based philosophy of how an enterprise conducts business is called the quality process.

The quality process is the next phase beyond the vision (or foundation) process for executives to follow in their journey to customer-centered supply chain management change (see Exhibit 3-1). It is a natural extension of the competitive frame of reference, core competencies, mission, and vision steps of the foundation process. It is also *the* critical link between business strategy and business process transformation. The quality process methodology in the second part of this chapter has been designed to provide the executive with the process steps to forge this critical link.

One industry where quality and customer-centered supply chain management are prevalent is electronics. Let's take a look at the electronics industry, its size, major companies within the industry segments, and how one company (Motorola) has become synonymous with the word *quality.*

Overview of the Electronic Equipment Industry

The global electronic equipment industry is composed of several diverse segments, including electrical equipment, semiconductors, defense electronics, electronics instrumentation, and even household appliances. The many product groups range from electronic toys to stereo systems and from medical-testing electronics to defense electronics. These products are used in most other industry groups, including agriculture, medical, defense, aerospace, high-tech, food, retail, and even chemicals.

The electronic equipment industry is large. The Integrated Circuit Engineering Corporation (ICE), a Scottsdale, Arizona, market research company, estimates that global sales of electronic equipment will rise from $690 billion in 1994 to $1.1 trillion by 1999. This growth rate far exceeds the gross domestic product growth rates of the United States and other developed countries.[2]

In addition, the electronic equipment manufacturing growth rate drives the growth rate of electronic equipment distributors. The North American electronics distribution industry has grown from approximately $16 billion in 1994 to a projected $25 billion in 1997.[3]

The electronics industry provides parts and supplies to other industry assemblers as well as finished products to retailers. For example, Motorola manufactures silicon wafers for the high-tech industry and assembles its own two-way, wireless radios. I will use a supply

2. "Standard & Poor's Industry Surveys: Electronics," August 3, 1995, pp. E15–E16.
3. Ibid., p. E16.

Exhibit 3-1. The customer-centered supply chain management change process.

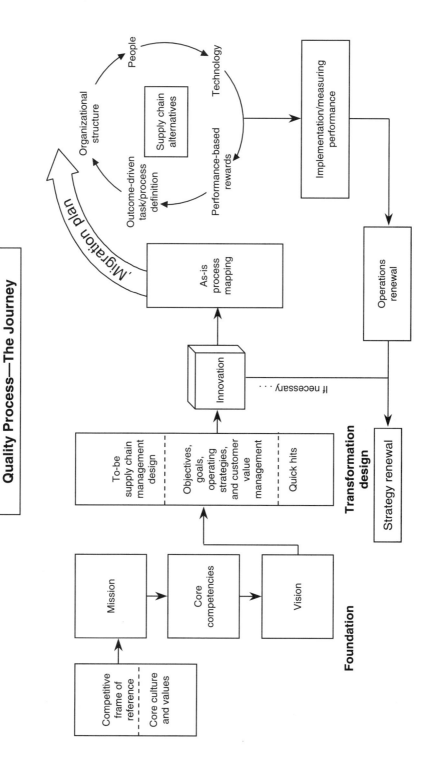

Quality Process—The Journey

People

Technology

Organizational
structure

Supply chain
alternatives

Performance-based
rewards

Outcome-driven
task/process
definition

Implementation/measuring
performance

Migration plan

As-is
process
mapping

Operations
renewal

Innovation

If necessary . . .

To-be
supply chain
management
design

Objectives,
goals,
operating
strategies,
and customer
value
management

Quick hits

Strategy renewal

**Transformation
design**

Mission

Core
competencies

Vision

Competitive
frame of
reference

Core culture
and values

Foundation

chain approach to categorize companies in certain industries, even though the lines between industries are often blurred.

The demand for quality has been and continues to be strong among customers who purchase electronics products. These customers have now come to expect quality from the service supporting these products as well. (Have you ever been at a special family gathering and had a camera or video-cam malfunction? As consumers, we *expect* these products to work perfectly all the time.)

Electronics companies must focus on quality as it relates to the products and services that customers demand. High quality has become the norm, or the price of staying competitive in the electronics business. The key is that quality is now being *defined by the customers*, not by the suppliers, manufacturers, distributors, or transportation companies. It takes a structured process to ensure that the supply chain meets those customer-defined needs with respect to quality.

Motorola: Combining Vision and Quality

Motorola has historically demonstrated the enviable skill of anticipating and taking advantage of change. Its founder, Paul Galvin, foresaw that technology would make his "battery eliminator" obsolete, so he quickly invested in car radios. Motorola progressed to two-way radios and televisions and even invented the walkie-talkie along the way.[4]

In 1949, Paul Galvin and his son Robert invested in integrated circuits and semiconductors. By 1974, Robert Galvin anticipated the Japanese surge into consumer electronics. He sold Quasar, his consumer electronics company, to Matsushita Electrical Industrial Company of Japan. Robert Galvin then invested in the microchip and wireless device industries. Now, Motorola is the global market leader in cellular phones and infrastructure, pagers and messaging, two-way radios, and microchips used to control devices other than computers.

Christopher Galvin, who became Motorola's CEO in 1997, is the son of Robert and the grandson of Paul. He has continued to reinforce Motorola's dominance in the infrastructure end of its businesses and to push into new technologies like the semiconductor-packed "smart" credit cards. In fact, Motorola's dominance in the infrastructure area has helped buffer its earnings from the competitive pressures in the cellular, paging, and modem markets.[5]

---

4. G. Christian Hill and Ken Yamada, "Staying Power: Motorola Illustrates How an Aging Giant Can Remain Vibrant," *Wall Street Journal*, December 9, 1992, pp. 1, 14.
5. "Motorola," *Value Line Investment Survey*, January 24, 1997, p. 1062.

The keys to Motorola's success are focused in a few critical areas. The company has an intelligence department that assesses technology developments, marketplace conditions, competitor activities, and potential new products. In essence, its balanced business strategy is continually evolving and improving. However, a major reason for Motorola's success is its commitment to quality.

Motorola's Commitment to Quality

In 1987, Motorola adopted a corporate mission that included a five-year goal of "Six Sigma Quality." This goal means no more than 3.4 defects per million parts. By the end of 1991, Motorola had achieved 40 defects per million, versus 6,000 defects per million at the end of 1986. This dramatic reduction in defects has resulted in cost savings of $900 million in 1992 and $3.1 billion since the start of the program.[6]

How was Motorola able to achieve such a tremendous reduction in defects? It started by defining its goals not in terms of defect measurements but in terms of business. The company focused on increased market share, with "Six Sigma Quality" and reduced cycle items supporting its market share goal.

Motorola's operating strategies included limiting its supplier base, negotiating long-term partnership agreements with its remaining suppliers, and implementing a total cost measuring system (TCMS) that included quarterly reviews with its suppliers. The total cost measuring system involves mutual goal setting, measuring achievement toward those goals, and taking action to improve performance based on results. In other words, Motorola was committed to quality and expected its suppliers to be committed with it as partners in the process.

Motorola also focused on customer satisfaction. The company has organized around "total customer satisfaction" teams, which have the authority to make production changes and establish work rule procedures that impact defect rates or cycle times. Bonuses are tied to defect rates and cycle times and are paid to team members just as they are to their superiors. Even seven years ago, in 1991, Motorola spent $70 million training and developing its employees. In addition, Motorola estimates that these teams produce an estimated four new or improved products *each day!* As a result, Motorola was one of the first winners of the Malcolm Baldrige National Quality Award (see Exhibit 3-2).

Motorola is not the only company in the electronics industry to

6. Hill and Yamada, "Staying Power," p. 14.

Exhibit 3-2. The Baldrige Award.

- August 20, 1987, President Ronald Reagan signed the Malcolm Baldrige Quality Improvement Act.
- The four goals of the Malcolm Baldrige Quality Award are:
  1. Helping to stimulate American companies to improve quality and productivity for the pride of recognition while obtaining a competitive edge through increased profits;
  2. Recognizing the achievements of those companies that improve the quality of their goods and services and providing an example to others;
  3. Establishing guidelines and criteria that can be used by businesses, industrial, governmental, and other organizations in evaluating their own quality improvement efforts; and
  4. Providing specific guidance for other American organizations that wish to learn how to manage for high quality by making available detailed information on how winning organizations were able to change their cultures and achieve eminence.

Source: Christopher W.L. Hart and Christopher E. Bogan, *The Baldrige: What It Is, How It's Won, How to Use It to Improve Quality in Your Company* (New York: McGraw-Hill, 1992), p. 13.

---

be recognized for quality achievements. Westinghouse Electric Corporation's Commercial Nuclear Fuel Division was a 1988 winner of the Baldrige Award. This division was able to reduce defects per thousand from 50 to .05 and reduce manufacturing cycle time by 40 percent, and was determined to be the best in its industry as defined by customer satisfaction.[7]

In addition, General Electric (GE) Fanuc Automation North America, Inc., received ISO 9001 certification (Exhibits 3-3 and 3-4). Because many of GE's largest European customers required ISO 9001 certification as a condition of doing business with them, GE pursued and received this certification, thereby reinforcing its commitment to its customers.

Armstrong World Industries, Inc., BPO, which manufactures and markets acoustical ceiling systems for residential and commercial markets, received the 1995 Baldrige Award. Using 250 improvement teams operating throughout its seven manufacturing facilities and its headquarters, Armstrong has improved output per manufacturing employee by 39 percent and sales per manufacturing employee by 40 percent since 1991. These results were attributed to employee involvement, recognition, gainsharing, eliminating non–value-added activities, and active sharing of best practices among all facilities.[8]

---

7. Christopher W. L. Hart and Christopher E. Bogan, *The Baldrige: What It Is, How It's Won, How to Use It to Improve Quality in Your Company* (New York: McGraw-Hill, 1992), p. 26.
8. Frank Cap, "From the Rust Belt to the Baldrige Award," *Journal for Quality and Participation*, Vol. 19, No. 7 (December 1996), pp. 46–51.

Exhibit 3-3. ISO 9000 series (International Standards Organization).

- Founded in 1946 to develop manufacturing, trade, and communications quality standards, formulated under an EC (European Community) directive.
- Over 111 countries have adopted ISO 9000 standards.
- American National Standards Institute is the U.S. member body to the ISO.
- Offer a standardized way of evaluating and certifying a company's quality management and quality assurance system.
- Certification benefits
  - Worldwide recognition through the use of universally accepted quality standards
  - Access to international markets restricted by government mandates for ISO 9000 Certification.
  - Use of certification label in sales/marketing activities.
  - Listing in the International "Certified Supplier" directory.
  - Improved productivity and reduced costs.
  - Elimination of duplicate, costly, time-consuming audits by prospective customers.

ISO 9001

Ascertains a company's ability to design, develop, produce, install, and service a product. Company must identify, plan, and carry out—under controlled conditions—production and installation processes that directly affect quality.

ISO 9002

Determines a supplier's ability to produce a good product, as well as to inspect and test it correctly.

ISO 9003

Establishes a basis for supplier assessment when the only interest is to ensure that the manufacturer is capable of inspecting and testing properly.

ISO 9004

General guideline that provides direction for installing and maintaining a comprehensive quality system.

The Quality/Supply Chain Connection

The Motorola, Westinghouse, General Electric FANUC Automation North America, Inc., and Armstrong World Industries, Inc., BPO examples clearly show top management commitment and support for the companies' quality processes. This support reinforced the companies' ability to manage in the face of change and take advantage of change. Although top management supported the quality commit-

Exhibit 3-4. ISO 9001 requirements.

The basic requirements of ISO 9001 are contained in 20 clauses. The following are the clauses contained in *ANSI/ASQC Q9001—1994, Quality Systems-Model for Quality Assurance in Design, Development, Production, Installation and Servicing.*

1	Scope
2	Normative reference
3	Definitions
4	Quality-system requirements
4.1	Management responsibility
4.2	Quality system
4.3	Contract review
4.4	Design control
4.5	Document and data control
4.6	Purchasing
4.7	Control of customer-supplied product
4.8	Product identification and traceability
4.9	Process control
4.10	Inspection and testing
4.11	Control of inspection, measuring, and test equipment
4.12	Inspection and test status
4.13	Control of nonconforming product
4.14	Corrective and preventive action
4.15	Handling, storage, packaging, preservation, and delivery
4.16	Control of quality records
4.17	Internal quality audits
4.18	Training
4.19	Servicing
4.20	Statistical techniques

Source: Tom Tobor with Ira Feldman, *ISO 14000: A Guide to the New Environmental Management Standards* (Chicago: Irwin, 1996), pp. 27–31.

ment in all these companies, what made their quality awards possible was the support and leadership of all employees in the quality process.

I believe that manufacturing and logistics executives have a prime opportunity to lead the overall quality effort within their organizations. Because of the very nature of their functional responsibilities, these executives interface with virtually all the enterprise's internal functional groups. In addition, logistics often has interactions that are most valuable to the enterprise—interactions with customers. From order entry through customer service to the final delivery of ordered goods, manufacturing and logistics professionals have frequent and substantive contact with the supply chain's customers. It is this customer connection that opens the door for the manufacturing and logistics executives to focus their efforts horizontally beyond their functional boundaries and become the quality leaders within their enterprise.

The Journey to World-Class Quality in Supply Chain Management

To assist supply chain executives in leading the quality process within their enterprises, I have developed the "Journey to World-Class Quality in Supply Chain Management" (Exhibit 3-5). It blends the common themes of the quality gurus' philosophies with logistics operations, support activities, and results measurements to produce a quality benchmark matrix for executives.

Logistics Operations

Compressed Order-to-Delivery Cycle Times

In many industries, the supply chain that has the fastest and most consistent order-to-delivery cycle time has a distinct competitive advantage. Globalism is creating longer transportation routes, which, in turn, create the need to reduce order lead times. Furthermore, product life cycles are shrinking. This is dictating the need to shorten order-to-delivery cycle times to avoid obsolescence costs. A few companies are responding dramatically. For its circuit breaker boxes, General Electric (GE) has cut the lead time from order to delivery from three weeks to three days![9]

In today's competitive marketplace, quality in process must include best-in-class cycle times. Tomorrow's world-class companies may compress their cycle times by an order of magnitude of five or ten just to stay world-class.

The goal for manufacturing and logistics executives is to understand the customers' needs and be the best in the industry in responding to those needs. From the ultimate customers' perspective, it is the supply chain's performance that counts. It is not enough for your enterprise to be best-in-class in cycle time if your supply chain part-

9. John G. Parker, "Global Manufacturers See Logistics as Critical Skill," *Transport Topics* (November 30, 1992), p. 20.

Exhibit 3-5. Journey to world-class quality in supply chain management.

	Average	Competitive	World-Class
Logistics Operations			
• Compressed order-to-delivery cycle times	Below top 3	Top 3 in industry	Number 1 in industry
• Lowest landed cost	Limited measurement capability	Low landed cost—internal focus	Lowest landed cost—customer involvement
• Quality of customer deliveries	Less than 97.5%	97.5% to 99.5%	Greater than 99.5%
Support Activities			
• Organizational structure	Functional efficiency	Use of cross-functional teams	Horizontal integration internally as well as with customers and suppliers
• Application of information technology	Automating manual functional efficiency processes	Vertical, functional efficiencies	Supply chain processes; balanced business and supply chain strategies
• Employee involvement	Autocratic organizational behavior	Use of teams—problem solving	Self-directed, empowered employees—trust, integrity
Results			
• Measurement of customer satisfaction	Customer complaints	Customer feedback questionnaires	Customer performance reviews
The Quality Process			
• Supply chain planning	Functional activity	Horizontally reengineered supply chain processes	Ongoing horizontally reengineered supply chain processes and alignment to vision and customer needs
• Supply chain control	Functional, cost-based	Multifunctional, profit-and-loss–based	Horizontal, profit and loss by product or like businesses logistics; performance = percentage of optimal/zero waste
• Supply chain improvement	Functional, internally based	Root-cause analysis, corrective action implemented	Root-cause analysis, corrective action, and reengineered processes to ensure compliance with customer needs

ners are not. Customers only see one final product and service, regardless of how many enterprises partnered to produce and deliver that final product and service. The entire supply chain must be number one in cycle time for its partners to be viewed as world-class.

Lowest Landed Cost

Globalism and a worldwide excess of industrial capacity are contributing to extreme price pressures for industrial and consumer products. "If you can't sell a top-quality product at the world's lowest price, you're going to be out of the game," General Electric Chairman Jack Welch told *Fortune*.[10]

Supply chain costs as a percentage of total product costs depend on the value of the product, length of supply lines, length of the product life cycle, and manufacturing cost sensitivities. Logistics costs, for example, can be as high as 30 to 40 percent of the value of the product in industries such as petroleum, chemicals, food manufacturing, and general retailing. On the other hand, logistics costs can total no more than 5 to 10 percent of the value of a product in industries like apparel, furniture, and tobacco.[11] The bottom line is that logistics must be an integral part of an organization's effort to be a low-cost provider.

During the 1980s, deregulation of transportation lowered many rates across multiple modes of transport. It was relatively easy for logistics executives to produce lower cost numbers without much effort or focus on total logistics. This one-time windfall, which benefited many supply chains in many industries, is often called "the deregulation dividend."

World-class companies, however, were focusing on total supply chain costs. Furthermore, the 1980s are over, and the year 2000 is almost here. It is critical for executives to look beyond the vertical/functional costs such as transportation and focus on all supply chain costs, including the cost of inventory.

The optimal approach is to involve customers and supply chain providers in the decision process. The movement of goods, facilitated by the movement of information, involves the networking of multiple supply chain activities. The involved supply chain partners must therefore work together to optimize the whole process and minimize the landed cost to the ultimate customers. When all is said and done,

10. Stratford Sherman, "How to Prosper in the Value Decade," *Fortune*, November 30, 1992, p. 91.
11. James E. Morehouse, "Improving Productivity in Logistics," *Handling & Shipping Management*, Presidential Issue (1984–85), p. 12.

it is the final price of the product, driven by its final landed cost, that customers consider in their purchasing decisions.

Quality of Customer Deliveries

One way to think about the quality of customer deliveries is in terms of the "seven R's of customer satisfaction," which consist of the traditional six R's plus a critical seventh R:

1. The right product
2. Delivered to the right place
3. At the right time
4. In the right condition and packaging
5. In the right quantity
6. At the right cost

and

7. To the right customer

At the heart of the seven R's of customer satisfaction is the delivery of what was ordered when the order was needed by the customer. The standard measurements for the quality of customer deliveries are order-fill rates and on-time deliveries. The entire supply chain must be measured on its performance in these categories.

Order-fill rates must be pegged at least at 99.5 percent to be considered world-class. Admittedly, it is not easy to juggle global supply lines, thousands of line items, and hundreds to thousands of suppliers and still produce the lowest landed cost and the shortest order-to-cash cycle time, with a 99.5 percent order-fill rate and 99.5 percent on-time delivery. However, L. L. Bean's example of a 99.9 percent order-fill rate proves that it is possible to achieve these levels consistently. In doing so, L. L. Bean and other world-class companies represent their supply chain partners when their effectiveness is viewed from the customer's perspective.

The quality concept of "zero defects" must apply with customer deliveries because a 99.5 percent order-fill rate and on-time delivery record still translate into one failure per two hundred deliveries. Although this is a magnitude less than the manufacturing defect measurement of world-class quality, which is currently expressed in terms of defective parts per *million* and will someday be expressed in terms of defective parts per *billion,* the operational complexities of customer deliveries, in my opinion, far exceed the complexities of a standardized manufacturing process, so the comparison is not apples to apples. However, the fact looms large that *even with a 99.5 percent order-fill rate and on-time delivery record, there is still one unhappy customer out of every two hundred customers served.* Supply chain executives must therefore focus on "perfect" customer deliveries as a basis of world-class performance in customer-centered supply chain management.

Example: Whirlpool In 1991, Whirlpool Corporation established its "Quality Express" effort to meet the changing needs of its customers. When Whirlpool surveyed its dealers (Whirlpool's customers), it discovered that the dealers were expecting three things: faster order-to-delivery cycle times, consistent deliveries, and emergency delivery capability when needed. When Whirlpool benchmarked its competitors, it realized that improved customer deliveries were not optional. In addition, Whirlpool recognized that two of its three consolidated divisions or business units (Whirlpool and KitchenAid) demanded customized delivery capabilities to meet their marketplace needs.

In an effort to improve customer deliveries, Whirlpool created the environment to establish the ERX Logistics joint venture (Quality Express). This joint venture included Elston Richards, a warehousing company, and Missouri-Nebraska Express (MNX), a trucking company. This joint venture provided the management, systems, and human resources to utilize Whirlpool's infrastructure in an integrated fashion. ERX Logistics replaced all common carriers and dedicated its service to providing the highest-quality customer deliveries for the two divisions or business units.

The results are solid. On-time delivery rates rose to 99.8 percent. Before ERX Logistics, this measure could not be obtained. "We couldn't even measure on-time rates before Quality Express. We guesstimated that it was in the [80 percent range], but I don't know if it was that high," Jim Grant, Whirlpool's manager of regional distribution, told *Financial World.*[12]

Looking back from 1997, the contract between ERX and Whirlpool to manage the Quality Express network has created a flexible relationship that enabled the supply chain to adapt to changing needs without having to reopen contract negotiations for every change. This has allowed Quality Express to adapt to the consolidation of Whirlpool's customer base. In its six years, Quality Express has been enhanced to meet the emerging channel needs. Kenco Logistics Services (KLS) now operates the Quality Express network in the Southeast, while ERX continues to operate the network in the rest of the United States.

"Quality Express truly is an enabler of Whirlpool's supply chain. One of the reasons that Whirlpool has been successful with Quality

12. Ronald Fink, "Group Therapy," *Financial World*, September 28, 1993, p. 61.

Express is that it has allowed Whirlpool to quickly adapt to changing sales strategies. This includes the concurrent focus on builders, individual consumers, local retailers, and large national accounts," observed Tom Wright, general manager of Whirlpool logistics.[13]

As a result, Whirlpool has been able to create a competitive advantage vis-à-vis its competitors by providing distinct logistics services to the ever-changing and emerging distribution channels.

Support Activities

Organizational Structure

As mentioned earlier in this section (in the "Compressed Order-to-Delivery Cycle Times" subsection), customer supply chain management involves multiple functions and external supply chain partners behaving organizationally as one enterprise to produce and deliver a common product or service. For the executive, this means that purchasing, procurement, transportation, warehousing, order processing, and inventory management not only must link together but must link horizontally with other enterprise functions (engineering, manufacturing) and with customers and suppliers. The focus must be on how the activities of one function impact and influence the activities of other functions and other companies.

The use of cross-functional teams is a good first step in the quality transition. (Armstrong World Industries, Inc., BPO has 250 improvement teams among its 2,500 employees!) However, it is critical for team members to transcend their functional identity and assume a team identity. It takes a special culture to accomplish this, in addition to a properly aligned rewards structure and performance measurement system.

In order to achieve world-class quality, executives must focus on the customers. It is obvious that horizontal integration brings a company closer to those customers and that customer-centered supply chain management is critical to executives' success in meeting customer needs.

Application of Information Technology

The movement of information across an extended enterprise supply chain is a key enabler for the supply chain to behave organizationally

---

13. Conversation with Tom Wright, April 1997.

as one entity. This should be at the top of the list for logistics executives as they pursue the path to world-class quality in logistics.

Functional efficiencies and the horizontal effectiveness of product manufacture and delivery depend heavily on accurate, timely information. (Even the quality process relies on the application of information technology. Armstrong World Industries, Inc., BPO's employees use computer networks and conference calls to share best practices between the company's improvement teams.)

The investment in information technology and the development of the architecture baseline must support the enterprise's balanced business strategy and the resulting logistics strategy. Often, difficulties in functional activities like warehousing drive the move to solve short-term problems. Applications of technology are used to remedy the difficulties, only to miss the really critical underlying issues.

A major merchandiser of electronic goods implemented a random-access storage (RAS) computer model within its Florida warehouses as a means to access unused space. The company perceived its problem as being a lack of space due to increasing line items and a standard warehouse layout. Within eighteen months after RAS was implemented, however, the same problems returned.

The real issue was that the company's purchasing department operated as an independent, vertical function. Its sole measurement criterion was cost. Furthermore, the purchasing department refused to enter into annual contracts that dictated volumes and cost. It preferred to play the "spot" market, using its size to drive costs down on one-time purchases. The purchasing department's decisions produced an inventory turnover rate of only two to three times a year. Its closest competitor had an inventory turnover rate of six to eight times a year.

Before investing in information technology, the Florida merchandiser should have focused on the competitive aspect of the application of information technology and looked at the entire supply chain process. This competitive aspect would have included a product-line review and rationalization based on performance, which might have enabled the merchandiser to determine that its real need was to have fewer warehouses with a higher rate of inventory turnover rather than to improve the utilization of space in its existing warehouses. It could then have solved its warehouse problems and several others with better-placed investments.

Employee Involvement

One of the themes common to the philosophies of the major quality gurus is employee involvement. The transition from the autocratic, directive managerial style so successful during the mass-production days of the 1950s, 1960s, 1970s, and early 1980s to a style that focuses on employee involvement will not be easy for many executives. However, it is a transition that must be made because our workforce is changing.

The explosion of technology, the decline of our educational system, and the disproportionate growth of women, minorities, and immigrants in our workforce have contributed to training, remedial and on-the-job education, and language complexities of significant proportions. In addition, cultural differences and two-income family demands (such as child care and time off) enter into the equation in a big way. These trends are expected to increase significantly throughout the next decade.

With the low unemployment rate in the United States, many executives believe that there is a shortage of skilled, productive workers. With companies having fewer yet more productive employees operating in expanded job roles, retention of employees becomes a critical success factor. Managers must adapt their management styles to create an atmosphere of trust and integrity. The late W. Edwards Deming, one of the world's most respected quality advocates, professed that managers must drive out fear so that everyone may work effectively for the company. Empowered and self-directed employees will tend to be happy, contented, and productive employees.

The executives of supply chain enterprises must lead their organization in employee involvement. Employees often have significant responsibilities that involve inherent trust. For example, order-entry personnel frequently operate in the capacity of customer service representatives. Private-fleet truck drivers often leave their homes for days without returning. The enterprise's executives implicitly trust that these drivers will make all deliveries on time while obeying all federal, state, and local laws; be drug- and alcohol-free; and be courteous to everyone. Warehouse personnel are often self-directed, working without on-site supervision. Purchasing agents work with suppliers, often developing strong personal and professional relationships that can transcend enterprise relationships.

Each of these examples shows supply chain employees operating in either an empowered or a self-directed role and relying on influence to accomplish their tasks. Whether they realize it or not, manufacturing and logistics executives have an initial base of employee involvement to expand and showcase for the rest of their organization.

Many executives, successful for years with command-and-control managerial styles, will have difficulty adapting to the emerging complexities and demands of employee involvement. Manufacturing and logistics executives can provide leadership through coaching and helping their counterparts adapt to employee involvement.

Results

Measurement of Customer Satisfaction

Customer satisfaction must be the primary focus of all quality processes as well as the primary measurement of the entire supply chain. Furthermore, the measurement of customer satisfaction must be externally, not internally, based.

Logistics and manufacturing executives have frequently used customer complaints as a basis for measuring customer satisfaction—that is, they measure customer *dis*satisfaction. Although this is a small step in the right direction, it doesn't even come close to measuring customer satisfaction or dissatisfaction accurately. A recent study determined that less than 5 percent of unhappy customers of large ticket durable goods or services ever have their complaints reach the manufacturer.[14] What's even more astounding is that each unhappy customer is estimated to tell ten other people about his or her complaint!

If they are to progress on the path to world-class quality in customer-centered supply chain management, executives must go beyond measuring customer complaints. The first major step is relatively easy: *Ask the customer!*

The customer feedback questionnaire is a good way to start measuring customer satisfaction. Such a questionnaire can be transaction-based and relatively simple. National Car Rental asks every customer returning a rental car, "Was your rental satisfactory?" The question also appears on every rental return form (Exhibit 3-6) and is incorporated into National's Emerald Aisle Rapid Return System. The answer, a simple yes or no, is incorporated into National's database to measure customer satisfaction. In addition, if the answer is no, the counter employee is trained to address the problem or concern immediately. On the back of their business cards, employees also carry "National's Quality Commitment" (Exhibit 3-7).

Customer satisfaction can also be measured through the use of monthly or quarterly questionnaires. Xerox sends out 40,000 questionnaires per month, receiving approximately 10,000 responses.[15] Although this effort can be expensive and time-consuming, Xerox be-

---

14. Technical Assistance Research Programs (TARP) Institute, "Consumer Complaint Handling in America: An Update Study, Part II" (Washington, D.C.: U.S. Office of Consumer Affairs, March 31, 1986), p. ES-2.
15. Barry Farber and Joyce Wycoff, "Customer Service: Evolution and Revolution," *Sales & Marketing Management* (May 1991), p. 48.

Exhibit 3-6. National Car Rental's rental return form.

For faster car return,
please record odometer and fuel gauge readings.

Odometer

Did you purchase fuel during this rental?

☐ *Yes*   ☐ *No*

If yes, please indicate the current fuel tank level below.

E   *¹/₈*   *¹/₄*   *³/₈*   *¹/₂*   *⁵/₈*   *³/₄*   *⁷/₈*   *F*
☐   ☐   ☐   ☐   ☐   ☐   ☐   ☐   ☐

Fuel Gauge

Date   *Time*

National's Customer Satisfaction Commitment

> *Was Your Rental Satisfactory?*
>
> ☐ *Yes*   ☐ *No*
>
> *National is committed to providing the highest level of customer satisfaction in the industry. Your comments are important. If we have not met your expectations, one of our location personnel would be pleased to assist you, or we will contact you by phone.*

NEED ASSISTANCE?

- *Call the National Car Rental phone number shown on the Paper-Less Express rental document.*

- *If there is no response, or if you are not in the same city where you rented your car, call toll-free 1-800-367-6767 in the continental U.S. for 24-hour emergency road service.*

Exhibit 3-7. National's Quality Commitment, shown on back of business card.

National's Quality Commitment

All of us at National Car Rental pledge to:
- Provide defect free products and services to our customers and each other.
- Fully understand the requirements of our jobs and the systems that support us.
- Fulfill these requirements on time every time.

---

lieves that the benefits far outweigh the costs. It is not surprising that Xerox is recognized as a leader in customer satisfaction.[16]

The best customer satisfaction measurement technique includes customer participation in performance reviews. Whether these reviews are performed one-on-one or with horizontal teams, the intent is the same. Customer satisfaction should be a part of everyone's performance appraisal, merit raises, and incentive/bonus plans.

The best feedback from these performance reviews is how to improve one's operations. Whether it's order-fill rates, on-time deliveries, damaged goods, or customer service issues, the customers' input will allow for corrective action and improvement in customer satisfaction. The goal must be to give the customers what they want every time and thereby achieve a 100 percent customer satisfaction rate.

Although measuring customer satisfaction is critical to the success of any company, it is mandatory for the supply chain executive due to the very nature of customer supply chain management as a customer-contact, customer-driven series of activities.

The Quality Process

I have selected Joseph M. Juran's trilogy (see Exhibit 3-8) as a framework for the supply chain quality process. (Joseph M. Juran is another quality guru who is recognized as one of the top leaders in his field.) This process has three aspects: supply chain planning, supply chain control, and supply chain improvement.

---

16. Otis Port and Geoffrey Smith, "Beg, Borrow, and Benchmark," *Business Week* (November 30, 1992), p. 74.

Exhibit 3-8. The Juran trilogy.

1. *Quality planning:* the activity of developing the products and processes required to meet customers' needs
2. *Quality control:* the activities that prevent operating results from worsening once the quality plan is implemented by the operating forces
3. *Quality improvement:* the organized creation of beneficial change; improvement of chronic performance to an unprecedented level

Quality is product performance that results in customer satisfaction and the freedom from product deficiencies, which avoids customer dissatisfaction.

Source: Adapted from Joseph M. Juran, *Juran on Planning for Quality* (New York: Free Press, 1988), pp. 4–5, 11–12, 332.

Supply Chain Planning

Using Juran's definition of quality, supply chain quality can be defined as the product and service performance that results in customer satisfaction and the freedom from product and service deficiencies, which prevents customer dissatisfaction. Thus, the first step is for supply chain executives to obtain customer participation in defining customer needs.

The customer expectations and needs that are identified must be translated into measurable standards. For example, three high-level standards, as shown in the logistics operations portion of the "Journey to World-Class Quality in Supply Chain Management" matrix (Exhibit 3-5), are order-to-delivery cycle times, landed cost, and quality of customer deliveries (order-fill rates and on-time deliveries). These three standards are only a recommendation for customer-specific measurement. Each customer has its own needs, and executives must be flexible in defining needs on a customer-by-customer basis.

Once customer needs are identified, executives must assess the enterprise and supply chain's ability to meet those needs. If the enterprise and supply chain can meet customer needs with existing processes, then executives should proceed to address the issue of supply chain control.

If the enterprise or the supply chain is *not* capable of meeting customer needs as defined by the jointly developed standards (for example, 99 percent order-fill rate), however, then the supply chain processes require transformation. When supply chain processes are transformed, it is critical that the changes be aligned with the customers' needs and expectations.

This is the first step in the supply chain quality process. World-class supply chain performance begins with listening to customer needs and expectations, then designing the processes that will enable the enterprise to meet and exceed those needs and expectations.

Supply Chain Control

Measuring supply chain performance in terms of customer standards begins the true journey to world-class quality in customer-centered supply chain management. Conformance to customer expectations is the anticipated end result for the whole process.

Initial measurements after implementation of the quality process will show the variance between actual performance and expected performance. If this variance is significant, the enterprise may need to revisit the supply chain planning phase and reexamine the transformed supply chain processes that support the customer standards. If the supply chain processes were changed significantly, it may take a few tries to coordinate people and technology smoothly within the new processes.

Philip Crosby is another leading quality expert and an advocate of zero defects. A concurrent measurement system that incorporates this philosophy is to measure actual performance as a percentage of optimal performance. Although it can be difficult for employees to comprehend this measurement at first, it does reveal the true waste in a process and the amount of performance improvement that can be attained.

It is important to note that it must be possible to relate cost measurements to the enterprise's profit-and-loss statements. Companies have been known to develop separate cost performance systems for customers and processes that do not tie in to any internal accounting statements. These separate systems defeat the very essence of what a quality process is intended for and should be avoided.

The reviews of performance to standards should feed the customer performance reviews. These reviews should be established around a product or like groupings of products and should include the horizontal or cross-functional teams responsible for customer satisfaction. To achieve maximum focus and results, it is recommended that merit raises and bonuses—of both team members and senior executives—be tied to these reviews.

Supply Chain Improvement

The measurement of supply chain performance versus customer standards will produce the variance, or amount of improvement required to meet the customers' needs. As mentioned earlier in the chapter, significant variances may reveal the need to transform the supply chain processes employed to meet the customers' needs.

A root-cause analysis should surface where breakdowns in service have occurred and where corrective action is needed to improve performance. This process is ongoing. The more comfortable people become with the measurement and performance processes, the easier the root-cause analysis will become. Continual performance improvement is at the heart of this ongoing supply chain improvement step.

As the measured performance level comes closer and closer to consistently meeting and exceeding customer requirements, the need for standards decreases. Deming's philosophy is to eliminate standards and improve, continually and forever, the system of production and service. Once the quality process is implemented and producing world-class results, I believe Deming's philosophy is right-on.

All too often in my visits with company senior managers, I find evidence that they ignore the vision and quality process steps. They have a tendency to charge ahead into the business design and transformation phases. Pressure for short-term results, familiarity with tactical day-to-day operational activities, and an inability to pull a vision together strategically are just three of the reasons I have identified that drive this type of behavior.

However, short-term moves produce short-term results, if any. The lack of a plan that includes the foundation and quality processes increases the chances that the enterprise's venture into customer-centered supply chain management change will be less than successful. It also contributes to an attitude of reacting to change rather than managing and leading change.

Is the quality movement dead, as our friend from the consumer electronics company said? In fact, the quality movement has never been more vigorous. The quality process is the definition of how a company will do business. It is the critical link between business strategy and business process transformation. Robert C. Forrest, senior vice president and general manager of Corning TPD, a 1995 Baldrige National Quality Award winner, had this to say about the role of quality in his company: "Let me warn you, you won't hear our people mention the word *quality* very often. If you want to look at our quality plans, they will take you through our business plans. If you ask them what their quality objectives are, they will show you their business objectives. And if you ask me for our quality organization chart, I'll give you the name of everyone in TPD."[17]

The following quality process methodology is designed to help

17. Cap, "From the Rust Belt to the Baldrige Award," p. 51.

the executive connect the foundation process (discussed in Chapter 2) with the transformation design process (discussed in Chapter 4)—that is, build the critical link between business strategy and change. The quality process methodology includes logistics operations, enterprise support activities, needed results measurements, quality process activities, and an analysis of the gap between the enterprise and its best-in-class competitors. The "Journey to World-Class Quality in Supply Chain Management" (Exhibit 3-5) is the framework for this quality process methodology.

Process Methodology Quality

As I mentioned earlier in this chapter, the quality process methodology (illustrated in the accompanying process flowchart) is a natural extension of the foundation process methodology. In simple terms, the foundation establishes the mission and vision, or the business strategy for the enterprise. The quality process establishes how the enterprise will do business and is designed to link the foundation, or business strategy, with the transformation of the supply chain.

If you tend to perceive the quality process primarily in terms of the additional work you think will be involved, keep two things in mind: First, if the change process is executed properly, there is a complementary overlap between the quality process and transformation rather than a duplication of effort. Also, I would remind you of the "silver-bullet syndrome," discussed in the introduction, and reemphasize that true quality is a process, not a project.

I have designed the quality process to include an assessment of the current state of the supply chain against industry norms or standards, specifically focused on customer satisfaction. As you will see in the supply chain design and implementation phases of the customer-centered supply chain management change process, the work performed in the quality process methodology will provide input for the overall transformation process.

In this regard, it is important to note that the quality process methodology contains a number of steps that involve what might be termed documentation and packaging. The executive team should not dismiss these steps as mere formalities. Consistency in documentation and packaging at this stage of the transformation process will pay off during later stages of the process, when the availability of well-organized information will enable the executive team to spend less time on format and appearance and more time on content and substance.

THE SUPPLY CHAIN MANAGEMENT CHANGE PROCESS
Process Methodology
Quality

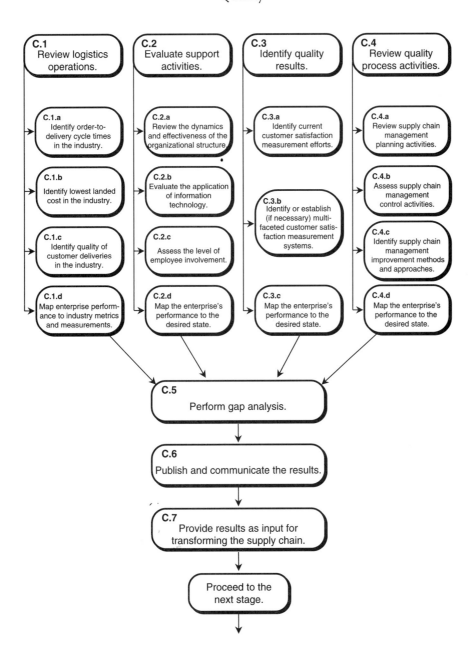

C.1 Review logistics operations.

C.2 Evaluate support activities.

C.3 Identify quality results.

C.4 Review quality process activities.

C.1.a Identify order-to-delivery cycle times in the industry.

C.2.a Review the dynamics and effectiveness of the organizational structure.

C.3.a Identify current customer satisfaction measurement efforts.

C.4.a Review supply chain management planning activities.

C.1.b Identify lowest landed cost in the industry.

C.2.b Evaluate the application of information technology.

C.3.b Identify or establish (if necessary) multi-faceted customer satisfaction measurement systems.

C.4.b Assess supply chain management control activities.

C.1.c Identify quality of customer deliveries in the industry.

C.2.c Assess the level of employee involvement.

C.4.c Identify supply chain management improvement methods and approaches.

C.1.d Map enterprise performance to industry metrics and measurements.

C.2.d Map the enterprise's performance to the desired state.

C.3.c Map the enterprise's performance to the desired state.

C.4.d Map the enterprise's performance to the desired state.

C.5 Perform gap analysis.

C.6 Publish and communicate the results.

C.7 Provide results as input for transforming the supply chain.

Proceed to the next stage.

C.1: Review Logistics Operations

C.1.a: Identify Order-to-Delivery Cycle Times in the Industry

Using the list of global competitors identified in foundation process methodology step B.1.a (Chapter 2), the executive team must determine the competitors' order-to-delivery cycle times for key product groups. Once these times have been determined, they need to be ranked with the best-in-class times that have been identified.

Information on order-to-delivery cycle times is usually not readily available, but it can be obtained with a little effort. Academic research projects are one source to tap. The executive team may even want to fund a research project through top supply chain or logistics universities such as Penn State. In fact, this university has even set up the Penn State Center for Logistics Research to accommodate these types of benchmarking efforts. Customers are another source. Key, high-volume customers may willingly give you the information. I have even known some companies to have employees order competitors' products on a routine basis to assess supply chain cycle times.

The executive team needs to rank the competitors in three groups: the industry leader, the top three including the industry leader, and the rest of the industry. Later in the process, there will be a step in which you will rank your enterprise vis-à-vis its competitors. At this point, however, it is valuable to document learnings gained by identifying the competitors' rankings.

C.1.b: Identify Lowest Landed Cost in the Industry

The same list of competitors used in step C.1.a for cycle time benchmarking should be used for determining the lowest landed cost. University research groups, annual reports, 10Ks, investment research reports, and other public-domain information should provide enough data to enable the executive team to perform a landed cost analysis.

A helpful hint is to break up the supply chain into individual components. Key supply chain costs include purchase prices of raw materials, parts and/or subsystems, inbound transportation, manufacturing/processing, warehousing, outbound transportation, sales and marketing, general and administrative, and customer distribution. Some costs (such as transportation) may be readily available. For those that are not (such as manufacturing/processing), a simulation costing model may help you develop an estimate.

Costs are continually changing, so don't feel you have to be exact. There should be enough separation between competitors to place them naturally into three groups: industry leaders, average competitors, and industry laggards. Remember, it is the competitive positioning that is important, not the exactness of the numbers!

It is even more critical to assess and rank the measurement capability of each competitor. World-class performers in the industry will have the lowest landed costs, the measurement system to track those costs, and the involvement of their customers in keeping costs low. The competitive companies will have a strong measurement system but will be internally focused in measuring the costs. The average performers will have limited measurement capability.

C.1.c: Identify Quality of Customer Deliveries in the Industry

The two important performance indexes for measuring the quality of customer deliveries are order-fill rates and on-time deliveries. With the help of selected customer supply chain management experts, I have identified a performance level of 99.5 percent in each of these categories as the threshold for best-in-class performance. A performance level of 97.5 percent to 99.5 percent in each category would be considered competitive, while a performance level of less than 97.5 percent would be considered average.

The key to these performance indexes is that the measurements must be performed by the customers and not manipulated by the enterprise. In addition, the information has to be clean. The enterprise must not change customer orders to match inventory levels. The goal is to measure customer satisfaction. Although customer deliveries must match customer orders, these figures *cannot* be made to agree by tampering with the data on customer orders.

C.1.d: Map Enterprise Performance to Industry Metrics and Measurements

After performing steps C.1.a, C.1.b, and C.1.c, the executive team must map the enterprise's performance to the industry metrics, which will provide a competitive positioning ranking as it pertains to these critical customer satisfaction measurements. The team should document these rankings but not publish them until the rest of the quality process methodology steps are completed.

If the previous three steps have been done properly, this step should be relatively easy. Since most executives will want to know immediately where their enterprise or function ranks with respect to competitors, this step is often blended into the previous three, regardless of whether the process calls for the blending. However, there is value in keeping this step separate from the previous three, since this step is *internally focused,* whereas the previous three are *externally focused.*

C.2: Evaluate Support Activities

C.2.a: Review the Dynamics and Effectiveness of the Organizational Structure

Reviewing the dynamics and effectiveness of the organizational structure is very straightforward. Annual reports, stockholder meetings, investor reports, and even the competitors' public relations departments are prime sources of information. As stated earlier in this portion of the chapter, customers can also provide a wealth of knowledge in this area.

World-class performers in customer-centered supply chain management have horizontal integration both internally with their organizational structure and externally with their suppliers and customers. Enterprises that are competitive have a functional organizational structure and rely on the use of cross-functional teams to increase their supply chain's effectiveness. Average performers are easy to identify: They still rely on functional efficiency to drive their enterprise's performance.

The executive team must look under the rug, so to speak, when assessing their enterprise's ranking in this area. I know of a few companies that boast of geographical business unit organizational structures but operate in the same functional manner as they have for years. The key is the supply chain focus on the customer and not a focus exclusively on functional efficiency. Thus, the executive team must identify where the enterprise ranks in terms of organizational effectiveness. This information should be documented and held for step C.5.

C.2.b: Evaluate the Application of Information Technology

The evaluation of the application of information technology is performed at a high level and is also straightforward. The "customers" for the application of information technology are primarily internal users. The executive team should interview the actual users of information technology and place each user group into one of three categories: very satisfied/competitive advantage, satisfied/gets the job done, and not satisfied/competitive disadvantage.

The very satisfied/competitive advantage category often includes the application support for supply chain processes and strategies. The satisfied/gets the job done category includes application support for vertical, functional activities. The not satisfied/competitive disadvantage category frequently involves the investment in systems applications that just automate manual functions.

The results should be compiled, with an overall rating given to the information systems group.

C.2.c: Assess the Level of Employee Involvement

Assessing the level of employee involvement in the organization causes more anxiety and stress among the executive ranks than other steps. Employee involvement is a result of a number of factors. Perhaps the greatest driving force behind the level of employee involvement is the leadership style of the executive team.

The world-class performers in customer-centered supply chain management, like Wal-Mart, have self-directed and empowered employees who operate in an environment of trust and integrity. The competitive companies use cross-functional teams to solve operational problems. The average performers are frequently the companies that have not changed with the times and still exhibit the autocratic style of organizational behavior that was successful in the 1950s through the 1970s.

The executive team may consider hiring a human resources consultant to assess the true level of employee involvement. I personally know of a *Fortune* 100 company whose president announced in its annual report a major corporate initiative to improve employee empowerment. Although the behavior of the executive team did change, its style became more, not less, autocratic. The president was upset to discover that employee involvement had then become worse, not better. A closer look at the situation revealed that the direct reports to the president had indeed become more empowered, but since no one had worked with them to change *their* behavior, they had become empowered to be more autocratic! The employees who must become empowered are the ones who "touch" and interface with the customers and supply chain partners on a day-to-day basis, not the executives.

When the executive team has categorized the enterprise in terms of its level of employee involvement, this information should be documented for use in step C.5.

C.2.d: Map the Enterprise's Performance to the Desired State

The support activities examined in steps C.2.a through C.2.c should be mapped to the world-class performance levels identified in each step and the individual gaps pinpointed. This information should be summarized in a user-friendly format and held for use in step C.5.

C.3: Identify Quality Results

C.3.a: Identify Current Customer Satisfaction Measurement Efforts

The next step is for the executive team to identify the current customer satisfaction measurement efforts and categorize them as to their effectiveness. World-class supply chain performers have their customers participate in group and sometimes individual performance reviews. Several world-class companies also take these customer reviews into account in determining merit raises and bonuses for supply chain employees. Competitive companies use customer feedback questionnaires to assess customer satisfaction—a technique that is useful if the questionnaires are employed consistently and if the percentage of returns is high. Average companies still use customer complaints as a measure of customer dissatisfaction.

The use of these measurement efforts is actually cumulative. World-class performers still use customer complaints and customer feedback questionnaires in addition to involving customers in performance reviews. Competitive companies use customer complaints as well as customer feedback questionnaires. When the executive team ranks the enterprise, it must look for all three measurement efforts and not simply stop when one is found.

C.3.b: Identify or Establish (If Necessary) Multifaceted Customer Satisfaction Measurement Systems

Identifying or establishing multifaceted customer satisfaction measurement systems is one of the few action steps in the quality process methodology that precedes the actual transformation process. When the executive team assesses the enterprise's customer satisfaction measurement efforts and finds gaps between those efforts and world-class performance, immediate action must be taken. Customer satisfaction is what supply chain transformation is all about.

The executive team leading the customer-centered supply chain management change process must be able to assess the baseline of customer satisfaction accurately *before* the supply chain is transformed! If the baseline of customer satisfaction is not known, how can the executive team possibly assess the degree of improvement in customer satisfaction produced by the transformation effort?

The action plan is simple. If the enterprise is already using customer complaints and customer feedback questionnaires to measure customer satisfaction, then the executive team should lead the design and implementation of a system for involving customers in performance reviews. If the enterprise is average and just uses customer complaints, then the executive team should lead the design and implementation of customer feedback questionnaires as well as a system for involving customers in performance reviews.

C.3.c: Map the Enterprise's Performance to the Desired State

Once again, mapping the enterprise's performance to the desired state involves documenting the information gathered in the previous steps, including information on the operational actions taken in step C.3.b, and holding that information for use in step C.5.

C.4: Review Quality Process Activities

C.4.a: Review Supply Chain Management Planning Activities

The supply chain management planning activities should focus on the continual improvement of customer satisfaction. Quality, as defined earlier in the chapter, consists of listening to customers, assessing their needs, and then developing products and processes that meet those needs.

As you can see, if taken literally, this step could subsume the whole supply chain redesign process methodology. For the purposes of the quality process methodology, however, the executive team should concentrate on assessing how supply chain planning is performed.

World-class companies conduct their supply chain planning around horizontally transformed supply chain processes and align their planning activities to the enterprise's vision and the customers' needs. Furthermore, world-class companies perform these planning activities continually to ensure continuity of purpose. Competitive companies will have advanced their planning activities to focus on the transformation of supply chain processes. However, they may or may not be able to perform these activities on an ongoing basis, and they may not align these activities to both the customers' needs and the enterprise's vision. Average companies perform supply chain management planning activities functionally.

The executive team should document the enterprise's current level of performance with regard to supply chain planning activities and hold the information for use in step C.5.

C.4.b: Assess Supply Chain Management Control Activities

Measuring the performance of the supply chain versus customer standards is critical to achieve conformance to those standards. However, implementing change within the enterprise can be disruptive to its day-to-day operations. Juran's definition of quality control is: "the activities that prevent results from worsening once the quality plan is implemented by the operating forces" (Exhibit 3-8). If we recognize the overlap between the quality process and transformation as a whole and then substitute the word *transformation* for *quality plan*, we will have the essence of this step in this process methodology.

World-class companies measure cost performance on a horizontal, profit-and-loss basis. These profit-and-loss statements are often organized according to products and like businesses. In some cases, conformance to customer standards is measured in terms of "percentage to theoretical optimal" (for example, 100 percent order fill) or zero waste. Competitive companies have multifunctional profit-and-loss statements with functional cost centers. Although this is a good start, competitive companies still need profit-and-loss statements that are organized by products or like businesses in order to drive their product portfolio and asset investment decisions. Average companies still have functional, cost-based systems. The roll-up mechanisms of these systems will be virtually useless for measuring operating results after the supply chain is transformed.

The executive team must determine in which group the enterprise falls and then document that information for use in step C.5.

C.4.c: Identify Supply Chain Management Improvement Methods and Approaches

This step in the quality process involves comparing performance versus customer standards, doing a root-cause analysis on the areas in which significant shortfalls are observed, and identifying improvement methods and approaches to close the performance gaps. The executive team should focus on identifying the gaps and determining why they exist, and then recommend corrective actions for the transformation teams to implement.

In ranking the enterprise, the executive team should use the following guidelines to distinguish between world-class, competitive, and average performance. World-class performers do a root-cause analysis of performance shortfalls versus customer standards, recommend corrective action, and then implement that corrective action by transforming their processes. Competitive companies perform a root-cause analysis and implement corrective action, but they do not necessarily transform their processes to do so. The shortcoming of this approach is that, unless processes are transformed, the interdependence of supply chain partners is ignored. Average companies may also perform a root-cause analysis, but any corrective action is usually functionally based.

C.4.d: Map the Enterprise's Performance to the Desired State

Once again, this is a documentation and packaging step in preparation for step C.5. The information that has been compiled during the review of supply chain management planning and control activities and the supply chain management improvement methods and approaches that have been identified should be organized and documented for use in the next step of the quality process methodology.

C.5: Perform Gap Analysis

As the song goes, "This is it!" for the quality process methodology. The executive team must assemble all the material gained from this entire process methodology, organize it into a cohesive document, and develop an executive summary on the collective learnings. This executive summary should describe in a holistic manner the enterprise's current performance vis-à-vis customer demands and the desired future state.

The resulting document should closely resemble the "Journey to World-Class Quality in Supply Chain Management" (Exhibit 3-5). It should be used to feed information to the remaining transformation process methodologies. If the gap analysis reveals the presence of "low-hanging fruit" (that is, performance improvement opportunities that are considered "no-brainers"), take advantage of them! However, the transformation team should recognize the value of this step as a base document for the transformation process as a whole rather than see it as simply a means of achieving short-term gains.

C.6: Publish and Communicate the Results

The gap analysis document summarizing the enterprise's conformance to customer demands and expectations should be distributed to the enterprise's key stakeholders. In addition, the executive team should communicate whatever immediate corrective action has been implemented (such as establishing customer satisfaction measurement systems or taking advantage of opportunities to pluck "low-hanging fruit") and explain how it plans to proceed with the customer-centered supply chain management change process.

The executive team must remain committed to the change process and avoid taking the results of the gap analysis as personal embarrassments. The employees will be looking to the executive team for leadership that is committed to a change process. If instead they see executives who are not in control of the process and who want "heads to roll" for performance shortfalls, then they will be extremely conservative about taking risks. This retrenchment will make the change process that much more difficult to implement and create a lack of respect among employees for the executive team leading the change process.

C.7: Provide Results as Input for Transforming the Supply Chain

As mentioned in the discussion of step C.5, the results of the quality process methodology must be incorporated into the subsequent process methodologies. The "journey" document will provide wonderful input for future process steps. Remember the formatting and packaging steps! The actual transformation steps will proceed more quickly and with less confusion if they're based on consistent and thorough documentation.

Conclusion

To be successful, the customer-centered supply chain management change process has to produce real, tangible results. If the enterprise is to achieve long-term, lasting benefits, its business strategy must be linked with the actual transformation activities. The quality process methodology provides this link.

The team is now ready to start designing the transformation effort. Because the link between business strategy and the transformation effort must be solid, care must be taken to continually revisit the learnings gained through the foundation and quality process methodologies. The design phase of the transformation effort, discussed in the next chapter, will strengthen this linkage.

Chapter 4

The Transformation Journey Begins

Supply Chain Management Design

My meeting with the senior vice president of finance and administration for a Brazilian soft drink company started out as any normal consulting/client meeting. The client discussed his problems and critical issues, while I discussed our capabilities. The only rough spots in the meeting occurred when the client could not translate an English word and I could not help with my very limited Portuguese. (It continues to amaze me how many people around the world can speak two or more languages, yet many Americans can speak only one.)

The client then began to talk about his quality process, which seemed sound and was producing tangible results. The president of the company had recently attended a managing change seminar and now wanted his senior vice president to embark on a transformation effort. The senior vice president was at a loss. How could he embark on a transformation effort concurrently with his quality effort? Could he do both without risking the positive results his quality effort was producing? How could the two frameworks be blended together?

I have heard similar questions all over the world. How can two very positive and powerful efforts come together as one? Can such efforts be undertaken simultaneously without interfering with each other? The answer is fairly straightforward. As I mentioned in Chapter 3, if performed properly, these two processes can be complementary—and in fact, must be complementary if either one is to be totally successful. (Remember the comments of Robert C. Forrest of Corning

Exhibit 4-1. The customer-centered supply chain management change process.

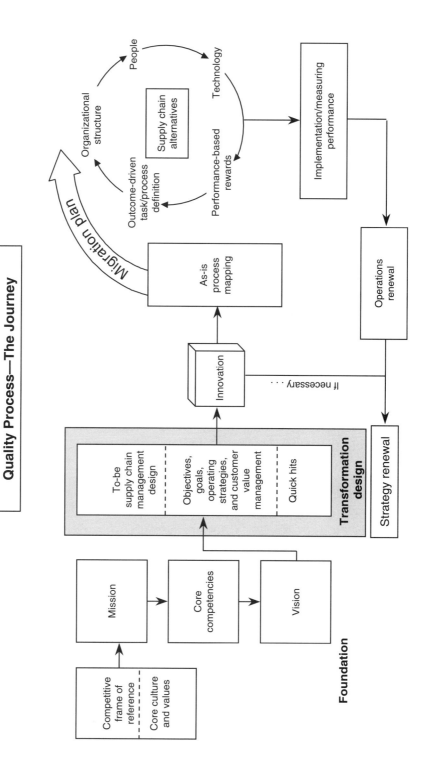

TPD concerning quality and business strategy at the end of the first part of Chapter 3.)

As for my Brazilian client, I mapped out an approach that blended the two processes into a single continuous effort. The quality process methodology in Chapter 3 and the design process methodology in the second part of this chapter mirror the mapping process I used for this Brazilian executive. As you will see, these two process methodologies are designed to integrate quality and transformation design as one complementary, extended effort.

Supply Chain Management and Transformation/Business Process Reengineering

The foundation and quality processes, discussed in Chapters 2 and 3, are actually the front end of the customer-centered supply chain management change process (Exhibit 4-1). The design phase of the transformation effort, covered in this chapter, involves the redesign of the supply chain, including the objectives, goals, and operating strategies necessary to support the redesigned supply chain.

My answer to our Brazilian client seemed to please him. It was obvious that he was being held accountable for his president's "silver bullets" and was nervous about his enterprise's ability to handle both his existing quality effort and a transformation effort. As I mentioned, the meeting ended with a discussion of how we could blend the two methodologies and position them in such a way that he could sell them to his president. The selling process would be easy, he said, since the two methodologies seemed naturally to be part of a holistic process. I told him I couldn't agree more. Part of my client's problem was that he didn't fully understand what the design phase of business process reengineering (BPR) includes. He is not alone. Let's take a look at what the design phase really means.

The Meaning of Transformation/Business Process Reengineering

Executives must respond to the changing visions of future states by continually rebuilding their order-to-cash supply chain bridges to ever-changing customers and marketplaces. This rebuilding of supply chain bridges was often called business process reengineering and has recently been referred to as transformation.

The terms *transformation* and *business process reengineering* are used rather loosely to describe three main types of business change efforts:

1. Business design
2. "Big" business process reengineering
3. "Little" business process reengineering

When translated into supply chain terms, these three change efforts have various meanings:

The Supply Chain and Business Change		
Business design	=	Restructuring businesses
"Big" business process reengineering	=	Transforming the supply chain order-to-cash cycle
"Little" business process reengineering	=	Transforming logistics functions (for example, transportation or warehousing)

The restructuring of a corporation from a total business perspective is often referred to as business design. Its purpose is to enable the corporation to exit, restructure, and/or enter businesses. For example, in 1997, PepsiCo announced the spin-off of its restaurants (primarily Pizza Hut, Taco Bell, and Kentucky Fried Chicken) and the sale of its food service logistics company (PFS). This move was designed to simplify its corporate structure to focus on soft drinks and snack foods.

One outcome of business design is a new business structure with fewer people—a combination that, it is hoped, will produce growth opportunities with a lower cost structure. However, business design is done rather frequently either to reduce costs or to close poorly performing divisions. The decision by Borden, Inc., a few years ago to restructure its operations and substantially exit the snack food business and the decision by Anheuser-Busch to exit the salty snack business are other examples of business design.

The next level of business change is called "big" business process reengineering, or "big" BPR. Processes at a high level, such as "finance" or "supply chain order-to-cash cycle," are redesigned to align the processes with the corporation's vision and business direction. A critical success factor is to achieve a customer focus throughout the process activities once the process is redesigned. Value-added activities are retained and enhanced, while non–value-added activities are eliminated. Unilever is merging its Lipton and Van Den Berg companies and is in the process of merging its finance and supply chains. This example involves both business design (the merger itself) and "big" BPR (the redesign of the resultant processes to reflect the new organization). According to Amy Reed, director of logistics strategy for Lipton, "The reengineering of the order-to-delivery supply chains will reduce costs and improve customer value for all Lipton/Van Den Berg products."[1]

The third level of business change is often referred to as "little" business process reengineering, or "little" BPR. For example, the "big" business process of the supply chain order-to-cash cycle is composed of several "little" business processes, such as order entry, customer demand allocation, manufacturing resource planning (MRP II), transportation, warehousing, production scheduling, distribution, and inventory management.

"Little" BPR need not be part of a "big" BPR effort. It can be performed independently from other functional efforts. Although the transformation of a "little" business process like transportation will produce vertical, functional efficiencies for a corporation, such a "little" BPR effort will often provide only limited, short-term benefits because of the lack of interdependent connectivity to other functional activities in the supply chain.

To convert extended enterprise supply chain theory into supply chain management reality, supply chain executives must focus on the "big" business process reengineering of the supply chain order-to-cash cycle. Redesigning the supply chain's order-to-cash process provides a solid foundation for the implementation of supply chain management. The key is the transformation design. As an example, let's consider an industry in which the issue of redesigning supply chains is especially pertinent.

The Food and Beverage Industry

The food and beverage industry is very large, with an estimated $700 billion in annual revenues for 1996 (see Exhibit 4-2), and is undergoing enormous change, which significantly impacts the design of its supply chains. This industry is made up of several segments and subsegments, including raw materials companies, food and beverage processors, and food and beverage wholesalers and retailers.

Every industry segment has its own unique characteristics and driving forces. The raw materials companies, like ConAgra and Cargill, are constantly at the mercy of Mother Nature as far as the supply, quality, and price of their commodities. We need to look no further than 1993 to see what havoc the floods in the Midwest or the drought in the Southeast wreaked on commodities like soybeans and 1996–

1. Conversation with Amy Reed, director of logistics strategy for Lipton, April 30, 1997.

Exhibit 4-2. Global food- and beverage-processing, services, and retailing industry.

	1996 Sales *($\times$ $1 million)*
Top 35 food companies	198,416
Top 7 beverage companies	44,725
Top 33 food and drug retailers	185,928
Top 11 food services companies	62,953
Subtotal	492,022
Add companies in other industries (e.g., Wal-Mart, P&G) and private food companies (e.g., Cargill)	207,978
Estimated total	700,000

Source: "Fortune's Global 500," *Fortune* (April 28, 1997), pp. F1, F45, F50–F53. Used with permission.

1997 to see the swing in weather fortunes. There was a terrible drought in the Southwest in 1996, damaging many crops and driving up commodity prices. In 1997, the upper Midwest and Southwest had so much rain that early crops were severely affected. The Southeast was very dry, and a late freeze impacted the availability and prices of early crops. El Niño of 1997–1998 continues this trend.

Although food- and beverage-processing companies have relatively high profit margins (see Exhibit 4-3), the growth in the demand for their products is slowing. The slowdown in the growth of the U.S. population and the consolidation in the retail industry are combining to put pressure on volume and retail price increases. In addition, private-label products are growing at the expense of higher-margin branded products. This slowdown in sales growth, coupled with the private-label/branded product mix shift, is creating intense pressure on profit margins for many companies.

Food and beverage wholesalers/distributors are struggling to

Exhibit 4-3. Food- and beverage-processing companies, 1996: Fortune 1,000 profitability snapshot.

	Revenues *($\times$ $1 million)*	*Profits* *($\times$ $1 million)*	*Profit Margin* *(%)*
Food (top 35 public companies)	198,416	6,586	3.4
Beverages (top 7 public companies)	44,725	5,162	11.6
Food services (top 11 public companies)	62,953	3,121	5.0

Source: "The 1,000 Ranked Within Industries," *Fortune* (April 28, 1997), pp. F45, F50–F52.

Exhibit 4-4. Food and drug retailers, 1996: *Fortune* 1,000 profitability snapshot.

	Revenues (× $1 million)	Profits (× $1 million)	Profit Margin (%)
Food and drug retailers (top 33 public companies)	185,928	3,539	1.9

Source: "The 1,000 Ranked Within Industries," *Fortune* (April 28, 1997), pp. F51–F52.

maintain their presence in the supply chain. The massive consolidation in the retail trade, coupled with manufacturers' desire to reduce costs, is creating manufacturer-retailer alliances that are excluding some wholesalers/distributors from their supply chains.

Food and drug retailers have historically had low profit margins (see Exhibit 4-4). These retailers have been hit hard by the growth in the club stores and supercenters, which have siphoned off the high-velocity items from the traditional food retailers, or grocers, leaving the retailers with lower volumes for an increasing number of line items. Lagging companies, like Borden, are retrenching.

The trend underlying all this change is that the food and beverage industry is in transition from a high-growth industry to a mature one. Leading U.S. companies are continuing to grow through global acquisitions and joint ventures, along with expanding their existing operations around the world. Their foreign counterparts show a similar pattern of growth. From 1984 to 1994, foreign direct investment in the U.S. food industry rose from $8.3 billion to $20.9 billion, driven by fluctuating currencies and the aggressive expansion plans of companies like Unilever and Nestlé.[2]

Given the accelerated pace of change, many industry leaders are anxious about how to stay competitive with limited resources. Several companies have established a supply chain effort, called Efficient Consumer Response (ECR), to address these concerns.

Efficient Consumer Response

Efficient Consumer Response is a grocery-industry effort that focuses on efficiencies in the grocery supply chain. ECR involves four strategies: efficient promotion strategies, efficient product introductions, efficient store assortments, and efficient replenishment. The ECR effort is being driven by the Grocery Manufacturers of America (GMA), the Food Marketing Institute (FMI), Food Distributors International

2. "Standard & Poor's Industry Surveys: Food, Beverages, and Tobacco" August 24, 1995, p. F20.

(formerly the North American Grocery Wholesale Association [NAGWA]), and other associations. In 1992, the Uniform Code Council, Inc., FMI, GMA, National Food Brokers Association, and American Meat Institute sponsored an ECR study, which was performed by Kurt Salmon Associates and resulted in the development of an ECR Task Force.[3]

The ECR Task Force is comprised of companies that represent the supply chain from manufacturing through retailing. The ECR vision includes timely, accurate, and paperless information flow throughout the supply chain, supporting a smooth, continual product flow matched to consumption.

The ECR grocery-industry effort was undertaken for competitive reasons. The retail grocery industry is a thin-margin business that has historically underspent on technology. Furthermore, business processes have historically meant very little to grocery retailers. Until the late 1980s, retailers bought most grocery products "on-deal." Manufacturers would create volume purchase "deals" to move unwanted merchandise or meet monthly sales quotas. The art of deal making pitted manufacturer against retailer, resulting in a silo-based supply chain.

Mass merchandisers, particularly Wal-Mart, started buying products on an annual, fifty-two–week, everyday-low-price basis. Their approach evened the flow of products out to match consumer demand, eliminating the peaks and valleys in product shipments from manufacturers to retailers that had resulted from the deal purchases. This approach reduced not only the inventory levels in the supply chain but also the infrastructure (in terms of people, warehouses, transportation equipment, and systems) that had been needed to support and manage the deals. Mass merchandisers thereby eliminated cost and time from their supply chain.

Another driving force behind ECR is the sheer size of the mass merchandisers. In 1996, the combined revenues of Wal-Mart and Kmart totaled $138 billion.[4] This size alone will drive efficiencies throughout a supply chain by creating truckload quantities from suppliers, large drop densities at stores that often include truckload deliveries, and higher velocity of throughput in the distribution centers resulting from the implementation of continual replenishment efforts.

Individually, members of the grocery industry have neither the financial resources nor the critical mass to duplicate the mass merchandisers' supply chain efforts. Collectively, however, they do.

3. Kurt Salmon Associates, "Efficient Consumer Response: Enhancing Consumer Value in the Grocery Industry," executive summary (January 1993), p. 2.
4. "Wal-Mart Stores and Kmart Corporation," *Value Line Investment Survey* (February 21, 1997), pp. 1652, 1664.

Benefits of ECR

According to the ECR study by Kurt Salmon Associates, ECR is estimated to have produced annual savings for the grocery industry of $30 billion.[5] According to the "ECR 1995 Progress Report," the grocery industry invested $3.2 billion in implementing ECR. The payback ranged from 1.94 years for grocery chains to 3.00 years for brokers. Regardless of whether the $30 billion figure is accurate, the 1995 ECR survey results show that ECR investments produce quick returns.[6]

Many grocery-industry executives attribute the size and speed of returns on ECR investments to the incredible inefficiencies that exist in the industry today. However, these savings do not simply appear magically. Furthermore, some industry executives question the value of ECR for their enterprises.

Do Food and Beverage Companies Need ECR?

Many industry executives privately question whether a lot of companies are ready to transition from a manufacturer-vendor adversarial relationship to a supply chain ECR partnership. They point to the continuing practice among retailers of selling space (slotting fees) as an indication that partnerships based on line-item profitability are slow to develop.

In my opinion, there is a need to separate organizational issues from operational and technological issues. The issue of organizing horizontally by product or like business (Quaker Oats, for example) needs to be an enterprise initiative, not a consortium issue. The operational opportunities of joining forces with other supply chain companies and sharing distribution channels exist without ECR. Many companies are actively pursuing shared distribution channel opportunities.

The technology aspect of ECR is critical. Very few companies have the financial resources to duplicate an internal telecommunications network like Wal-Mart's. I feel that ECR's largest value-added feature is the access to customer information through the use of technology and the application of this information to the supply chain fulfillment process.

The fact that Efficient Consumer Response even exists points to the need for individual enterprises along the food industry supply chain to behave organizationally as one "extended" enterprise. This

5. Kurt Salmon Associates, "Efficient Consumer Response," p. 3.
6. Kurt Salmon Associates, "ECR 1995 Progress Report," Joint Industry Project on Efficient Consumer Response (1996), pp. 32–33.

is a critical success factor in the design and definition of the "to-be" model of the desired future state. Let's begin the design phase of the transformation process with this "extended" enterprise concept in mind.

Developing the To-Be Model of the Desired Future State

Developing the to-be model of the desired future state of supply chain management is a critical step in the customer-centered supply chain management change process. This step includes the following activities:

- Benchmarking the industry's "best practices"
- Designing and modeling the desired future state
- Validating the future-state model to the foundation (that is, the enterprise's mission, vision, and business direction)
- Identifying potential "quick hits"

Suppliers and customers must be involved in these activities in order to ensure the success of the entire extended enterprise.

Benchmarking the Industry's Best Practices

The benchmarking of supply chain best practices is designed to determine how successful companies are managing their supply chains. The intent is not to duplicate the practices themselves but rather to learn how successful companies have approached the development and implementation of supply chain practices. Frito-Lay in the food industry, Dell in the electronics equipment industry, Toyota with its Toyota Production System in the automotive industry, and Xerox with its Integrated Global Supply Chain are examples of supply chain best practices. This step will provide the enterprise with a reference point as it begins to design the future state of its own supply chain.

Designing and Modeling the Desired Future State

Using the high-level design of an extended enterprise supply chain, the next step is to design, then model, the future-state operations. Modeling the supply chain's future-state operations will provide a snapshot of the performance results of the transformation. It will also

Exhibit 4-5. The generic value chain.

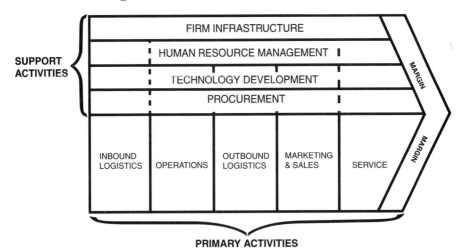

Source: Michael E. Porter, *Competitive Advantage* (New York: Free Press, 1985), p. 37.
Used with permission.

give the executive insight into what areas may pose particular problems as well as what areas are most sensitive from a critical-path standpoint.

Let's take a look at how to design a supply chain and examine an example of a food company that is active in this design phase.

Designing a Supply Chain

To design a supply chain, you must start with a basic outline of your enterprise's major, high-level activities, which will provide a structure for initiating the design phase of supply chain management. A solid example of such a basic outline is Michael Porter's "generic value chain."

Michael Porter's Value Chain   Michael Porter, a Harvard University professor, developed a version of supply chain management called the generic value chain (Exhibit 4-5). Porter's value chain consists of five types of primary activities (which involve the creation and delivery of products) and four types of support activities (which, as their name implies, support the primary activities).

Porter's version of supply chain management is called a value chain because it focuses on value. The primary and support activities are called value activities. According to Porter, value is measured by the amount customers are willing to pay for an enterprise's product or service. An enterprise will be profitable as long as it creates more value than the cost of performing the value activities. The creation of this value depends on the enterprise's ability to link and coordinate these internal activities. Porter also recognizes the linkages outside the enterprise as they relate to the customers' perception of value. However, we must complement this internal view with an external focus. The customers' perception of value must also be identified from the customers' perspective. Let's take a look at an approach for identifying perceptions of value from the customers' own standpoint.

Customer Value Management   AT&T Solutions has developed an approach called Customer Value Management to help companies create a business model that maximizes profitability through improvements in their customer portfolios. This approach includes:

- Developing a detailed understanding of the profit potential of the current and potential customer base
- Identifying the values of the desired customers that would motivate profit-enhancing behavior
- Providing product/service offerings that align with customers' motivations and values to maximize profitability
- Realigning supply chain processes, systems, and people strategies to meet the values of the preferred customers

Companies have only three ways to reach full performance potential with Customer Value Management:

1. *Acquire:* Grow the profitable customer base and retreat from unprofitable markets.
2. *Extend:* Increase the reward for longevity and/or increase the penalty for defection.
3. *Enhance:* Motivate behavior that generates higher returns through dynamic versioning of offerings.[7]

As I mentioned in the preceding subsection, Porter's definition of value measurement is the amount that customers are willing to pay for an enterprise's product or service. The AT&T Solutions Customer Value Management approach complements Porter's approach by furthering the definition of the customer values *and* the profitability of customer segments. By using this approach as a front end to Porter's generic value chain, a senior executive can design a supply chain in which true customer values and corporate profitability anchor the design.

7. "Customer Value Management," AT&T Solutions (Washington, D.C.: 1996), pp. 7–9.

(When we build our migration plan in Chapter 7, we will use a technique called responsibility charting, which will take the basic high-level primary and support activities, detail them down to the task level, and assign responsibilities for the completion of these tasks.)

Example: Quaker Oats Company   Quaker Oats is a good example of a company reorganizing by lines of business. As of January 1, 1993, Quaker Oats had reorganized into Quaker Europe, Quaker North and South America, and Quaker Gatorade Worldwide.[8] Here is how Quaker North and South America was organized at that time:

Lines of Business	Support Functions
Golden grain	U.S. grocery product services
Food services	• Purchasing
Pet foods	• Information systems
Breakfast foods	• Human resources
Frozen foods	Finance, customer services
Convenience foods	Research and development[9]

Each line of business is challenged to create economic value through sales growth, margin improvement, and improved asset utilization. Each of these business units, or "businesses," has profit-and-loss responsibility for its own products, and bonus compensation for its managers is tied to the unit's profit-and-loss improvement.[10]

Quaker Oats has termed the operations of the lines of business "Supply Chain Management."[11] The company's focus is to reevaluate each step in the value chain, from farmer's field to ultimate customer, with the goal of providing products to the market at the lowest possible cost and with the best possible service as well as achieving total integration of asset management.[12]

The Quaker Oats example seems to map well to Michael Porter's value chain, with the company's support functions mirroring the value chain's support activities and its business unit operations mirroring the value chain's primary activities. Quaker has connected the

8. "Quaker/91: Focused on Value Creation . . . ," The Quaker Oats Company 1991 Annual Report, p. 4.
9. The Quaker Oats Company 1992 Annual Report (Chicago: Quaker Oats Investor Relations), pp. 4–29, 31.
10. "Quaker/91," p. 4.
11. Ibid.
12. Ibid., p. 5.

activities within each business unit with a supply chain horizontal organizational structure, its people, and its rewards structure.

Quaker Oats has taken the very difficult but all-important first step toward effective supply chain management: the design of a supply chain process. In fact, the company has taken the second step and organized horizontally by like businesses to permit the implementation of supply chain management.

The jury is still out as to the effectiveness of Quaker's efforts. In its 1996 annual report, the company offered the following assessment of its progress: "Since 1992, purchasing, manufacturing, and distribution are managed as one integrated process—not a series of isolated activities. This 'supply chain' approach minimizes our costs and maximizes the efficiency of our system. In 1996, cost savings within our supply chain more than offset rising grain costs, aiding margin expansion in our U.S. and Canadian businesses."[13]

Although Quaker Oats has been struggling of late, due to the costly acquisition and disposal of Snapple and the compression in cold-cereal prices, the company should be recognized for taking these important steps toward more effective supply chain management. Quaker's collective learnings during the first four years of its effort will help increase the odds of continued success.

One way for any company to increase the odds of success in a supply chain management change effort is to develop the objectives, operating strategies, and goals of the redesigned supply chain, thus creating connectivity between concept and reality.

Validating the Future-State Model to the Foundation

During this transformation design phase of the customer-centered supply chain management change process, the objectives, goals, and operating strategies that were established during the design and modeling of the desired future state must be mapped to the foundation of the enterprise, or the vision and quality processes.

Business Direction: Objectives, Goals, and Strategies

The business direction of an enterprise—which consists of objectives, goals, and strategies—links its vision and quality processes with its day-to-day operations.

13. "What We're Made Of . . . ," The Quaker Oats Company 1996 Annual Report, p. 14.

Objectives   Generally, objectives are broad statements of what an organization is trying to achieve. The objectives must support and align with the organization's mission and vision.

An organization's vision might be to become part of an extended enterprise value chain. An objective could then be to achieve supply chain management in the organization's distribution channels. A complementary objective could be to achieve total customer satisfaction.

Goals   Goals are the quantifiable results that must be achieved in order to meet objectives. The goals that support supply chain management must be related to customer satisfaction. Examples of types of goals include order-fill rates, on-time deliveries, and other "value" activities as defined by the customers.

Goals should include time as well as metrics. For example, for fiscal year 1998, an enterprise may establish the goals of achieving a 99.5 percent order-fill rate and reducing the overall inventory level for suppliers, manufacturer, and retailers (as measured together).

It is important that goals for supply chain management be established in terms of the performance of the total supply chain. Goals that are set individually by function or enterprise may be suboptimal and may conflict with the performance of other functions or enterprises within the supply chain. For example, although a supplier might achieve a short-term reduction in its inventory carrying costs by minimizing inventory, such a move could produce long-term customer dissatisfaction with the supply chain as a whole by causing a manufacturer's order-fill rates to drop.

The optimal approach is for the participating functions and enterprises within the supply chain to establish joint goals that support overall objectives. For example, a joint goal of a 99.5 percent order-fill rate for customer orders would override any suboptimal goals of individual functions or enterprises (such as the supplier's inventory reduction effort) that would jeopardize achievement of the joint goal.

Strategies   Generally, operating strategies are broad statements of how an enterprise will achieve its goals and objectives. Our previously stated objective is to achieve supply chain management in an enterprise's distribution channels. Our examples of goals for fiscal year 1998 are a 99.5 percent order-fill rate and a reduction in the overall inventory level for suppliers, manufacturer, and retailers (as measured together).

The following strategies might be used to support the objective and goals:

- Regularly measure the customer order-fill rate.
- Consistently measure customer satisfaction from the customers' viewpoint.
- Routinely measure supply chain inventories.
- Transform supply chain processes once a year.
- Participate in customers' planning efforts with other supply chain partners.

The key to this step is executive alignment. The cooperative development of objectives, goals, and strategies that support the enterprise's mission and vision must be completed before the migration plan is developed.

Identifying Potential Quick Hits

All of us realize (or should realize) that any change process must be funded by operational savings or performance improvements in terms of customer satisfaction. Furthermore, transformation efforts often span six to eighteen months from organizational assessment through total implementation. In order to continue to secure senior management support and funding, transformation efforts need early successes, which I have termed "quick hits."

Quick hits generally represent opportunities that, with minimal investment, will yield large rewards. Delivering a product from the manufacturing plant directly to an end customer, bypassing the traditional warehousing step in the supply chain, would be an example of a quick hit. Such a move would produce savings in transportation, warehousing, and time, with no significant investment in capital equipment.

One major food company decided to consolidate less-than-truck-load (LTL) shipments for direct deliveries to retailers as a quick-hit project. This one project netted more than $1 million in annual savings and paid for the entire transformation effort!

The transformation design phase, which links the foundation of the customer-centered supply chain management change process to the implementation phase, is important because, without the proper design activities, the chances of implementing the transformation effort successfully are fairly low.

Developing objectives, goals, and strategies to support the supply chain design is what produces connectivity between design and implementation. When embarking on a change process, the executives and employees involved all need to know how they can tell when the desired results have been achieved. Objectives, goals, and strategies will enable everyone to determine when they are successful.

The following transformation design process methodology has been organized to establish connectivity from business strategy and quality to implementation. It also details the steps that should be taken to establish the objectives, goals, and operating strategies that will support the design phase of the customer-centered supply chain management change process.

Process Methodology Transformation Design

Some companies are successful in supply chain management (Frito-Lay, for example), some are achieving partial success (Quaker Oats), and others have not been very successful and are struggling for their very existence in the marketplace (Borden). As we can clearly see, results matter. Results are the direct outputs of the implementation of transformation designs. The transformation design phase must therefore be connected to activities that can be implemented and will produce tangible results.

The transformation design process methodology is a natural next step after the foundation and quality processes. As illustrated in the accompanying process flowchart, transformation design has two major components: developing the to-be model of the desired future state and identifying quick hits. The result of this process methodology should be the establishment of the strategic design for the supply chain management transformation effort.

D.1: Develop the To-Be Model of the Desired Future State

D.1.a: Perform Benchmarking of Industry Best Practices

The benchmarking of industry best practices is an expanded version of the mapping exercise that was performed in the quality process methodology. The executive team must incorporate the findings and collective learnings from the quality process into this step. However, the activities and practices to be benchmarked must be expanded to include internal functions such as sales and marketing, engineering,

THE SUPPLY CHAIN MANAGEMENT CHANGE PROCESS
Process Methodology
Design

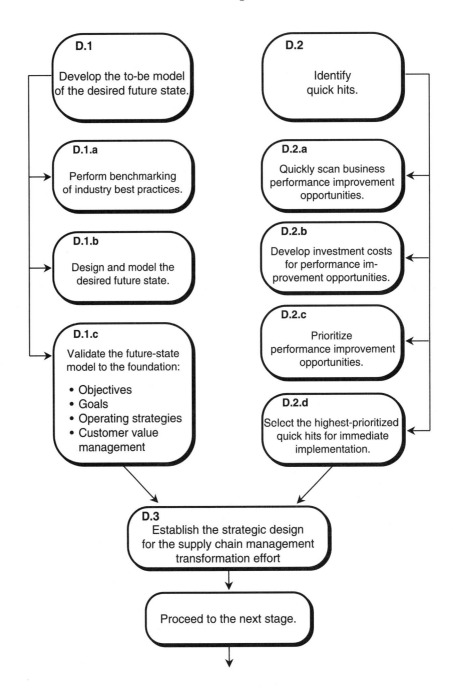

manufacturing processing/assembly, purchasing, and general and administrative functions such as finance and accounting.

Since these internal functions vary by enterprise and product group, it is critical to benchmark the *essence* of the best practices, which can be defined as the philosophy behind each practice together with the policies and procedures supporting the practice.

To complete this step, the executive team must first identify the industry's best practices in the functional areas that are within the scope of the transformation effort, conduct a benchmarking visit to the best-practice site (if possible), then summarize the *essence* of each best practice in a benchmarking document. The intent of this step is to determine not only what's possible but also what's being done today that is considered a best practice. Remember, if, in two years, you match today's best practice, you will probably be falling short of tomorrow's best practice.

D.1.b: Design and Model the Desired Future State

Designing and modeling the desired future state is the step that most executives anxiously await. It is also a very misunderstood step. A common expectation is that this step will produce a redesigned enterprise with world-class products and services that are low in cost, high in profit, and require a minimal amount of investment from a resource standpoint. Another common expectation is that a group of people (stakeholders and/or consultants) can collaborate to find a "silver bullet" that will make the preceding rosy scenario a reality. Unfortunately, transforming a supply chain does not involve magic. It does involve a significant amount of hard work, commitment, and common sense.

The common sense relates to the executive team's recognition of the function of this step within the overall change process. If the team reviews the results of the previous process methodologies, it will find the basic inputs for designing the enterprise's desired future state. Let's take a moment to review the results of those previous process methodologies.

In the foundation process methodology, the executive team defined the enterprise's competitive frame of reference by identifying the global competitors, global markets, stakeholder interests, and world-class performance standards. It also established, with stakeholder input, the enterprise's core culture and values, including its beliefs and principles. In addition, the team developed a mission statement, which defines why the enterprise exists, and a vision statement, which incorporates the core competencies of the enterprise while establishing the expectations regarding its future state.

In the quality process methodology, the executive team assessed customer satisfaction measurements of world-class performers in logistics in order to establish a baseline for the future performance of the enterprise's supply chain. It also evaluated the support activities of world-class performers in order to identify successful practices in the areas of organizational structure, employee empowerment, and the application of information technology, which could be used to guide the development of expectations for the business performance of the transformed enterprise. In addition, the team identified, and in some cases implemented, the needed customer satisfaction measurement systems.

The transformation team should take these results from previous process methodologies, combine them with the best-practice learnings from step D.1.a, and start designing and modeling the desired future state of the enterprise's supply chain. To begin the future-state design, the team can use a supply chain design along the lines of Michael Porter's generic value chain (discussed in the first portion of this chapter and illustrated in Exhibit 4-5). This initial design will be modified when we do the as-is process map (discussed in Chapter 6), so at this point, it's more important to capture the basic components of the future-state design than to get the future-state design "perfect."

D.1.c: Validate the Future-State Model to the Foundation

The desired future state is like the other side of the bay. There are two basic ways to get to the other side. The first is the long way, going around by land. This way is usually preferred by more risk-averse executives. The second is the short way, going across the water. With the building of a bridge, the short way becomes less risky. It also becomes faster and cheaper than the land route. To minimize the risk, however, you must build the bridge.

The objectives, goals, and operating strategies should be viewed as the first link in building the bridge to the future state. The executive team should recognize that this bridge is built from the future state to the present state. Thus, the objectives, goals, and operating strategies must be established with the end result, the future state, in mind.

As you may remember, objectives are broad statements of what an enterprise is trying to achieve. One possible objective mentioned earlier in the chapter was to achieve total customer satisfaction. Another possible objective could be to become the low-cost provider of products and services to the marketplace. The executive team should identify no more than six objectives for the transformed supply chain. These objectives must be documented and set aside for use later in the transformation process.

Goals were defined as quantifiable measurements that must be achieved to meet the objectives. The objective of total customer satisfaction may be expressed in terms of the following goals: order-fill and on-time delivery rates of 99.5 percent and an order-to-delivery cycle time of four days. If these goals are to carry any connectivity to customer satisfaction, they must be validated by the enterprise's key customers. Thus, the executive team must establish the goals supporting the objectives and then validate them with key customers.

Operating strategies were defined as broad statements of how an enterprise will achieve its goals and objectives. The implementation of an integrated order-entry, production-scheduling, shipping, and transportation system that tracks original customer orders through to customer deliveries is an example of an operating strategy that supports the aforementioned goals and objectives. Another operating strategy would be to develop a production to customer order (pull) manufacturing process as opposed to a production to inventory (push) manufacturing process.

The Customer Value Management exercise involves profiling the enterprise's preferred or profitable customers and identifying their values that would motivate profit-enhancing behavior. The transformation team should then review the objectives, goals, and operating strategies to verify that they support the values of the enterprise's preferred, profitable customers. Remember from the discussion of Customer Value Management earlier in the chapter that acquiring, extending, and enhancing are the ways to reach full performance potential. Alignment here is the key to maintaining a customer satisfaction focus throughout the transformation effort.

The results of the previous methodologies should also be reviewed to ensure connectivity. There is no sense in leaving loose ends, especially if any of the participants in the transformation process have changed or any time has elapsed between steps. The transformation process can move only as fast as the slowest-moving resource. When the resources in question are people, care must be taken to ensure that everyone participates in the calibration and communication efforts.

The executive team must then pull all these inputs together so that they can be mapped to the model of the desired future state. If this is done properly, the team has just started the process of building the migration plan.

D.2: Identify Quick Hits

D.2.a: Quickly Scan Business Performance Improvement Opportunities

From the start of the customer-centered supply chain management change process through the previous step, numerous performance improvement opportunities should have surfaced. For this step, the executive team should assemble and document these performance improvement opportunities, taking care to include only viable opportunities.

Validating the performance improvement opportunities involves identifying the benefits associated with each opportunity. These benefits must be expressed in metric form and involve reducing costs, improving quality, shortening cycle times, stabilizing the consistency of cycle times, or improving customer satisfaction. Performance improvement opportunities that cannot be expressed in these terms should not be included in the quick-hits list.

D.2.b: Develop Investment Costs for Performance Improvement Opportunities

For each performance improvement opportunity that is included in the quick-hits list, the executive team must establish and document the investment cost, which should include out-of-pocket expenses and capital needed to support the implementation of the opportunity.

In developing investment costs, the executive team must also be sensitive to the degree of difficulty of any proposed undertaking. Reracking a warehouse to improve its mixing capability and thereby minimize transportation costs might be a straightforward investment. However, if the warehouse is a rack-supported structure, both the investment and the degree of difficulty could be significant. Paying sufficient attention to the degree of difficulty can save the executive team tremendous embarrassment as it proceeds with the quick hits.

D.2.c: Prioritize Performance Improvement Opportunities

Once the tangible benefits and investment costs have been determined for each performance improvement opportunity on the quick-hits list, the executive team should proceed to prioritize these opportunities based on the greatest return to the enterprise. In other words, the opportunities should be ranked in terms of which ones offer the largest benefits at the lowest investment costs.

In prioritizing the proposed performance improvement opportunities, there is another critical consideration that the executive team must keep in mind—namely, how long it will take to realize benefits from each opportunity. The purpose of the whole quick-hits effort is twofold: (1) to develop a stream of savings that will offset the cost of the entire change process and (2) to provide and maintain momentum for the change process itself. The more quickly benefits can be realized, the greater the present value of those benefits, and the greater the chance for continued commitment to the change process on the part of the enterprise's stakeholders.

D.2.d: Select the Highest-Prioritized Quick Hits for Immediate Implementation

The highest-prioritized quick hits should be chosen for immediate implementation. The implementation and the results must be documented and communicated throughout the enterprise and to supply chain partners. The goals of the quick hits must not be forgotten. The savings stream from the quick hits that offsets the costs of the change process also reinforces the purpose of the change process: *to produce results!* Demonstrating a quick-hit success will prove the value of the change process in business terms even before the transformed process or business has been prototyped.

D.3: Establish the Strategic Design for the Supply Chain Management Transformation Effort

The development of the to-be model of the desired future state, coupled with the identification and implementation of the quick hits, provides the strategic design for the supply chain management transformation effort. The executive team is now ready to start the supply chain management innovation process (discussed in Chapter 5).

The documentation of all the steps supporting D.1 and D.2 should be assembled in a manner that clearly describes the strategic direction for the transformation effort. The to-be or desired future state—described in terms of objectives, goals, operating strategies, and customer values—provides a detailed blueprint for the effort. Implemented quick hits provide real-world examples of this strategic direction.

All information should be organized in such a way that it is easily accessible for future process methodologies. Also, when in doubt, *save your work papers!* It is always easier to discard no-longer-needed papers at the end of a process than to recreate prematurely discarded papers midway through the process.

Conclusion

The transformation design process methodology sets the stage for the next phase, innovation. It is critical for all team members to recall that they are in the middle of an integrated supply chain management change process, in which each process methodology builds on the preceding one(s). In order to ensure connectivity between the various process methodologies, executives must be consistent in their deployment of resources and personnel to the change process. This is especially true as the organization proceeds from transformation design to innovation.

Chapter 5
Inter-Enterprise Innovation

How Is Your Company Positioned?

Late in 1996, I visited with the president of a very large Latin American media and entertainment conglomerate. This individual was most impressive, both as a person and as the leader of a multibillion-dollar enterprise. His views on opportunities in the global marketplace were very acute and refreshing. He stated that he "attacks" the marketplace in three waves:

1. He has his people execute to the best of their abilities with the same intensity as if the business were their own. His motto for his employees is "Execute, execute, execute!"

2. He wants his senior executives to continually review the supply chains in which they participate. If they find value-added activities being performed by others, he wants to have his company either perform those activities or participate in joint ventures. If they find that his enterprise is performing low–value-added activities, he wants to pursue outsourcing or divesting those activities.

3. If other businesses outside of media and entertainment emerge from any of his enterprise's core competencies, he wants to review them quickly for potential investment.

Our discussion of supply chain management was centered on developing the flexibility of the extended enterprise to adapt quickly

Exhibit 5-1. The customer-centered supply chain management change process.

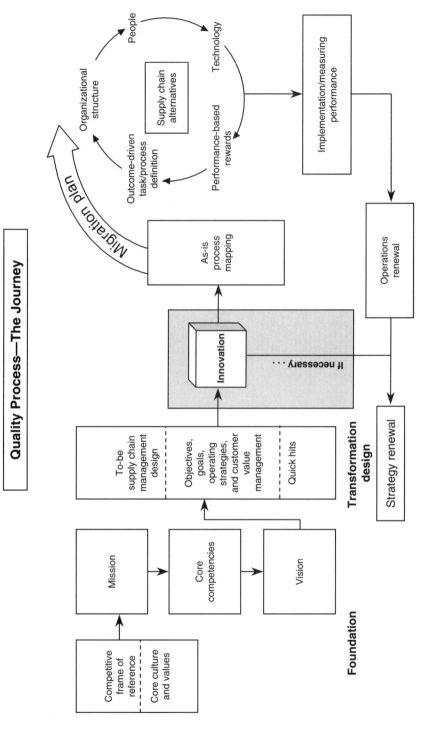

to changing marketplace needs. His example was his employees who are responsible for the programming for local cable TV operators. He said his people had to be flexible enough to purchase and resell programming and/or produce the programming themselves. These same people will also have to be flexible enough to do the same for cellular telephones if and when his enterprise wins a cellular operating license.

This flexibility must be based on process, people, technology, and performance measurements to balance operational efficiency and enterprisewide effectiveness. The key factor is to review the design of the supply chain against the innovation possibilities of the enterprise. Calibrating the supply chain design to the enterprise's innovation possibilities will strengthen the effectiveness of the implementation of the supply chain. It will also allow for the supply chain design to change and grow with the enterprise, withstand the test of time, and eventually be viewed as a competitive advantage enabler. Frito-Lay and Whirlpool are two examples of companies whose supply chain designs have evolved into competitive advantage enablers.

The Supply Chain Management Change Process and Innovation

The foundation and quality processes discussed in Chapters 2 and 3 are actually the front end of the customer-centered supply chain management change process (Exhibit 5-1). The design phase of transformation, covered in Chapter 4, focused on redesigning the supply chain, including the objectives, goals, and operating strategies necessary to support the redesigned supply chain. Before moving on to the as-is and implementation phases of transformation, covered in Chapters 6 and 7, it is necessary to complement the work performed to date with the process of innovation.

The Meaning of Innovation

As you'll recall, the rebuilding of supply chain bridges is often called transformation/business process reengineering (BPR). In Chapter 4, I identified the three main types of business change efforts as they relate to supply chain management. Now, we'll expand that list to show how each of these types of business change efforts maps to innovation and value creation:

The Supply Chain, Business Change, and Innovation

Business design	=	Restructuring businesses	=	Migrating value
"Big" business process reengineering	=	Transforming the supply chain order-to-cash cycle	=	Value creation
"Little" business process reengineering	=	Transforming logistics functions (for example, transportation or warehousing)	=	Value refinement

---

Balancing Inter-Enterprise Innovation With the To-Be Model of the Desired Future State

Once the to-be model of the desired future state of supply chain management has been developed, it is time to take an "outside-the-box" view of the inter-enterprise innovation possibilities. This is an all-important step for the supply chain design. When executives proceed to implementation with the supply chain design, they must be assured that the design is flexible and strong enough to adapt to the enterprise's innovation possibilities. *Failure to perform this step could result in the implementation of a supply chain design that either is too inflexible to adapt to change or is outdated by the time it is implemented!* There is too much at stake to allow this to happen.

This step, in which the executive team reviews the to-be model with "innovation levers," involves the following activities:

- Performing the innovation levers process
- Identifying and prioritizing value opportunities
- Reviewing the future-state to-be model in light of the value opportunities
- Modifying the future-state to-be model

Performing the Innovation Levers Process

The "innovation levers" process discussed in this chapter is based on AT&T Solutions' Value³Methodology,[1] an extract from which is shown in Exhibit 5-2. It is used in this book with permission from AT&T Solutions.

1. Copyright AT&T 1997.

Exhibit 5-2. AT&T innovation value opportunity process.

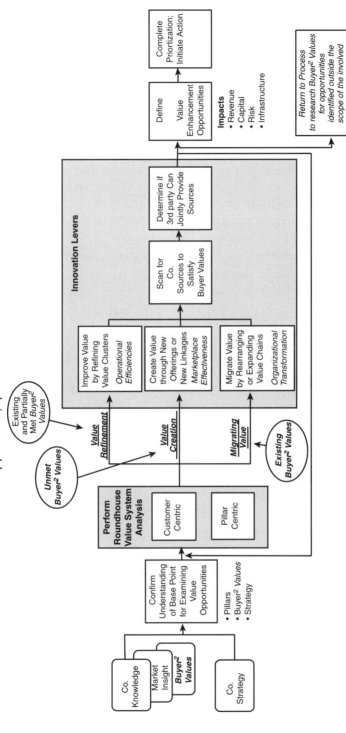

Source: AT&T 1997. Used with permission from AT&T Solutions.

Value Refinement: Operational Efficiencies

The purpose of the value refinement step is to find better ways to satisfy the values and needs of the supply chain's customers. Their basic supply chain values frequently involve order-to-delivery time, quality of deliveries, landed cost of the product, and related information that accompanies the deliveries. The transformation team must examine the relationships within the supply chain and focus on increasing the throughput of value to the customers. The key is to increase the efficiency of the current supply chain business model. An example of value refinement would be the use of dynamic scheduling models to reroute shipments real-time to shrink the order-to-delivery time and ensure a 100 percent order-fill rate.

Value Creation: Marketplace Effectiveness

Value creation is designed to break the industry mold or current business model. Unmet values of existing customers are reviewed and strategies developed to leverage competencies or infrastructures to satisfy those unmet values. For example, major trucking companies with private cellular networks can "share" their networks with key customers that also have private fleets. The shared use of the cellular network can enhance dynamic scheduling and create value through a new service offering. These types of value creation offerings also establish new linkages between supply chain partners.

Migrating Value: Organizational Transformation

Value migration involves thinking of ways to take over value-added activities within the supply chain and/or shed or outsource unprofitable activities currently being performed. For example, a retailer might use an Internet Web site to sell merchandise currently being sold in its stores, which would allow the retailer to ship from the manufacturer directly to the consumer and disintermediate the wholesaler. This would be *value refinement* and *value creation.* However, if this same retailer decided to use the Web site to sell merchandise not currently sold through its stores, then this would be *value migration:* The retailer would be migrating value out of other supply chains and into its own. Both examples impact the design and utilization of a supply chain.

The same holds true if this retailer decided to use the Web site to sell tickets to sporting events or arrange for tee times at golf courses all over the United States. TicketMaster has recently announced that it will use such a system to schedule tee times for anyone in the United States at any of the country's major public courses.

Example: Amazon.com   In July 1995, Jeff Bezos started an Internet Web site that allows consumers to search for in-print books written in English, then purchase the books on-line. The transaction is performed through credit-card payments, and the books are sent from the manufacturers directly to the consumers. The neighborhood bookstores and large distributors are, in effect, disintermediated through this Internet offering.

Revenues for Amazon.com were $16 million in 1996, up from only $500,000 in the last half of 1995. As Michael Krantz wrote in his *Time* magazine article on Amazon.com, "It was one of those ideas that are so inspired, you're amazed that no one thought of it sooner."[2]

This is an excellent example of migrating value. The value that had resided in the distribution and retailing of books was migrated to Amazon.com and the Internet offering. The development of this concept prompted the rearrangement of the overall supply chain for these books.

In early 1997, Barnes & Noble, the nation's largest bookstore, announced plans to sell books through its own Internet Web site. Although B&N's defensive move may succeed in slowing down Amazon.com, it doesn't address the core issue behind value migration. Barnes & Noble still must deal with the overhead of its bookstores, a component of the supply chain that Amazon.com has eliminated. However, Barnes & Noble's 1996 revenues were $2.45 billion, so it has the resources to put up a good fight with the fledgling Amazon.com.[3]

As executives review their supply chain design, they must answer the following question: "Will my design be flexible enough to adapt to changes like Amazon.com and encompass multiple reiterations of order-to-delivery possibilities?" Given the explosion of technological developments and the advent of global competition, world-class performance will require flexibility on demand within the supply chain. Without such flexibility, even established $2.45 billion companies can be threatened by $500,000 start-up companies in a matter of months!

Identifying and Prioritizing Value Opportunities

The transformation team must assemble the opportunities identified in the innovation levers process and group them by value dimen-

2. Michael Krantz, "Amazonian Challenge," *Time* (April 14, 1997), p. 71.
3. Ibid.

sion—that is, group them according to whether they involve value refinement, value creation, or value migration. For each group of opportunities, an analysis must be performed to answer two sets of questions:

1. Does the enterprise have the internal capabilities to take advantage of the opportunities (or thwart a competitor's threat)? If not, what acquisitions or alliances are available to expand the enterprise's capabilities?
2. What opportunities offer the greatest benefits (or pose the worst threats) to the enterprise?

The transformation team should then add the dimension of time to the answers to the two groups of questions. The result should be a ranking of opportunities by value dimension and by time.

Reviewing the Future-State To-Be Model in Light of the Value Opportunities

The next step is for the transformation team to take the ranking of opportunities by value dimension and by time and compare them to the to-be model developed in Chapter 4. A series of "what-if" scenarios should be employed to sensitize the to-be model to the newly developed value opportunities. Special focus must be placed on the impact these newly developed value opportunities will have on the primary and secondary activities of the to-be model *and* the customer values identified in the Customer Value Management exercise.

This effort should enable the transformation team to identify which components of the to-be model fall into the following three categories:

1. Those that are not materially affected by the value opportunities
2. Those that are minimally affected by the value opportunities
3. Those that are substantially or materially affected by the value opportunities

Modifying the Future-State To-Be Model

Depending on the results from the preceding step, the transformation team must proceed in one of two directions. When the results of the what-if scenarios identify no impact or minimal impact on the supply chain design/components, the transformation team should make the necessary minor modifications to the supply chain design and proceed to the as-is process mapping phase (Chapter 6). When the results of the what-if scenarios identify substantial or material impact on the supply chain design/components, then the transformation team should revisit the supply chain design phase (Chapter 4) to rework the supply chain design.

Many companies in emerging countries are having to rethink their supply chain designs due to the opening of their economies, the stabilization of their political and economic conditions, and the explosion in the type and availability of technologies. Let's look at one country that is leading the way in growth in the Western Hemisphere.

Brazil: The Country of Promise Has Arrived!

Brazil, long known as "The Country of Promise!" has seen several attempts at economic reform, only to have those reforms prove short-lived due to factors like political instability. All that changed in July 1994 with the *real* plan (the *real* is Brazil's monetary unit).

Since the election of President Fernando Henrique Cardoso and the implementation of the *real* plan, Brazil has enjoyed economic, political, and social stability. Inflation has dropped from 50 percent per month to 10 percent for all of 1996. The country's gross domestic product was estimated to be $976.8 billion for 1995. Brazil has a population of 160–165 million people, or roughly 60 percent of the population of the United States.[4]

The stability of the *real* against the U.S. dollar (the estimated conversion for 1996 was 1:1) and the low inflation rate have caused a surge of purchasing power for low- and medium-income wage earners. Consumer products companies have had to adapt from basically managing financial floats to managing supply chains.

In August 1994, I gave a speech at a leading Brazilian university concerning supply chain management and the *real* plan. Afterward, the managing director of a major global consumer products company told me that his whole sales force was geared to manage the financial float. In fact, he said his best sales tool was thirty-day payment terms!

In late 1995, I gave a similar but updated speech to selected leaders of consumer products companies in Brazil. The same managing director sought me out and told me that his company had to adapt from financial management to supply chain management based on the new consumer purchasing power. The market had shifted from

4. Central Intelligence Agency, "Brazil," Brassey's Edition (1997), pp. 67–70.

a push supply chain to a consumer pull supply chain in a matter of twelve months! The market continues to evolve in 1997 to adapt to consumer preferences and consumer purchasing power. In fact, consumers' selectivity has increased as unemployment has risen approximately 13 percent.[5]

Companies in Brazil have had to deal with value refinement, value creation, and migrating value issues in a short period of time. Although they may not use precisely those terms, the concepts are the same. In fact, many of these companies could be case studies in how to transform an extended enterprise within a compressed time frame. Of course, Brazil's economic developments provided the external stimulus to create such changes. However, many U.S. companies should adopt such a sense of urgency if they wish to remain competitive in the ever-changing global economy.

U.S. companies that are hoping to expand their market reach beyond North America should look to Brazil. They must, however, incorporate a Customer Value Management approach to the region to reflect the consumers' newfound purchasing power. They must also consider the MERCOSUR when mapping their supply chains.

The MERCOSUR   The MERCOSUR (or MERCOSUL in Portuguese) is the "NAFTA" (North American Free Trade Agreement) of the southern part of South America. Member countries currently include Brazil, Argentina, Paraguay, and Uruguay; Chile and Bolivia, which are now associate members, are soon expected to become full members. The MERCOSUR has a population of approximately 220 million people, or roughly 75 percent of the population of the United States. Trade in the MERCOSUR is dominated primarily by Brazil.

The impact of the MERCOSUR on supply chain management in these South American countries has been profound. For example, the Automotive Accord between Brazil and Argentina in early 1996 under the MERCOSUR umbrella promotes a balance of trade between the two countries. The maximum Argentine deficit is limited to $850 million, or 85,000 cars, which means that Argentine exporters can ship that amount within two years without having to import a similar volume. (Brazil has six times the population of Argentina and, as such, commands the larger consumer market between the two countries.) In addition, neither Argentina nor Brazil may import more than it exports to the rest of the world.[6]

---

5. AT&T Brasil Ltda., "Country Fact Sheet," developed with published data from Brazil's government agencies, pp. 9, 10.
6. "Automotive Accord With Brazil Until 2000," *Business Trends*, Vol. 31, No. 1522 (February 19, 1996), p. 6.

Thus, this accord supports those companies that have manufacturing plants on *both* sides of the Brazil/Argentina border. The penalties for shipping in automotive parts to a MERCOSUR country without having plants on both sides of the borders can reach a maximum of 40 percent of the cost of the parts! The result has been a building boom in both countries to comply with this accord and be competitive. GM completed the building of a car plant in Rosario, Argentina, in 1997, and is now operational. Fiat is building a plant in Córdoba, Argentina, while Toyota built a plant near Buenos Aires. Renault is building a plant in Paraná, Brazil, while GM, Ford, and others are boosting their existing presence in Brazil with billions of dollars in investments in new plants. There is also a rush by the major automotive manufacturers to develop local and regional parts suppliers to deal with the tariff and local-content requirements.

As these assembly and parts plants are being planned and completed, the supply chain infrastructure is being modified to adapt to the changes. The railroad in Brazil is being upgraded so it will eventually be able to provide reliable rail service from São Paulo to Buenos Aires and thus offer shippers a surface alternative to truck shipments. The port of Rosario is being converted to a deepwater port to provide an ocean-shipping alternative to the port of Buenos Aires. (The port of Rosario can be used to ship between Rosario and Córdoba in Argentina and São Paulo in Brazil.) Experts predict that the port of Rosario will offer a 40 percent reduction in costs and more reliable service than the port of Buenos Aires.

Consumer products companies and retailers have also adapted to the MERCOSUR. Companies like Kellogg's and Procter & Gamble in consumer products and Wal-Mart and Carrefour in retailing have either entered the emerging MERCOSUR markets or adapted their supply chains to account for the changes in purchasing power and MERCOSUR tariff regulations. In fact, when Wal-Mart opened its inaugural stores in Buenos Aires and São Paulo, each one eclipsed the company's previous all-time store-opening record.

In 1995, I had the pleasure of attending the opening of Wal-Mart's first new store in Buenos Aires, where opening-day sales topped $1 million. Arthur Emmanuel, then Wal-Mart's senior vice president for Latin America, said that the opening-day results surpassed all of the company's internal expectations. (He said this to me while helping cashiers bag purchases. The lines were so long that *everyone* on Wal-Mart's Latin American team pitched in to help the store's staff.)

If planned and implemented properly, entry into MERCOSUR countries like Brazil and Argentina can provide access to a large, high-growth marketplace. However, industries in these countries are changing very fast, as shown by the automotive, consumer products, and transportation examples I just discussed. Value refinement activities alone won't enable companies to stay ahead of the competition and take advantage of the growth opportunities offered by this region. To do it right, they will also have to explore value creation and migrating value. They will also find that flexibility in supply chain design and knowledge of the local markets are indispensable.

The outside-the-box view of the inter-enterprise innovation possibilities provides a good test of the strength and flexibility of the supply chain design. Again, failure to perform this step could potentially result in the implementation of a supply chain design that either lacks the flexibility to adapt to change or is outdated by the time it is implemented.

Regardless of what industry you are in, the threat of an Amazon.com type of company's taking value away from your supply chain is very real. The converse is also true: The possibility of creating an Amazon.com type of opportunity to migrate value to your supply chain is very real. In addition, emerging countries, which are being forced to transform themselves and their supply chains in a short period of time, offer attractive expansion opportunities for the U.S. companies that are flexible enough to keep pace with the dynamics of these markets.

The next portion of the chapter presents the innovation process methodology, which shows the executive team how to ensure that the supply chain design will be optimally flexible and responsive to changing conditions.

Process Methodology Innovation

Companies large and small have demonstrated the capacity to innovate and continually transform their enterprises. In Chapter 3, we saw how a large company (Motorola) redefines the industries in which it is involved; in Chapter 2, we saw how a large company (Intel) migrates value from other parts of the supply chain; and earlier in this chapter, we saw how a small company (Amazon.com) can redraw the industry supply chain rules through innovative applications of technology.

In the design process methodology (Chapter 4), I said that results are the direct outputs of the implementation of transformation designs. To enhance its transformation design, the executive team must review that design against a series of innovation process steps, illustrated in the accompanying process flowchart. This methodology has two major components: performing the innovation levers process and identifying and prioritizing the enterprise's value opportunities. The team will use the information generated through these activities as a basis for modifying the to-be model and/or reworking the supply chain design.

E.1: Perform the Innovation Levers Process

E.1.a: Review Opportunities for Value Refinement/Operational Efficiencies

In reviewing the enterprise's opportunities for value refinement, the executive team incorporates the Customer Value Management inputs from the design process methodology (step D.1.c in Chapter 4). These

THE SUPPLY CHAIN MANAGEMENT CHANGE PROCESS
Process Methodology
Innovation

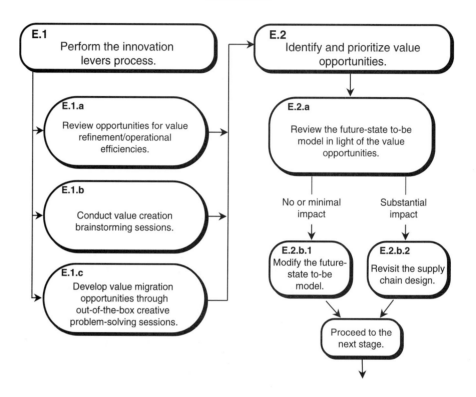

inputs are the buyer values that drive the purchase/loyalty behaviors of the enterprise's targeted and preferred customers. The traditional areas for operational efficiency improvements to better meet these buyer values are order-to-delivery times, quality of deliveries, landed costs of products, and related information to support the sale. As mentioned in the first portion of this chapter, the focus in this step needs to be on increasing the throughput of value to the preferred customers.

The transformation team should identify the traditional buyer values and assess the supply chain's ability to meet these values. The gap analysis performed in quality process methodology step C.5 (Chapter 3) and the resultant documentation of the findings of the quality process methodology prepared in step C.7 should be used as a basis for measuring the supply chain's performance in meeting these traditional buyer values. These values should then be categorized in three groups: met buyer values, partially met buyer values, and unmet buyer values. This information should be documented and held for use in the activities supporting step E.2.

E.1.b: Conduct Value Creation Brainstorming Sessions

Some executives find it difficult to participate in value creation brain-storming sessions because they equate the existence of unmet buyer values with "failure." The concept of unmet buyer values is greatly misunderstood. Although the fact that buyer values remain unmet can mean that management has failed in operational execution, it can also mean that buyers value characteristics of a product or service that the supply chain is just not providing. Nonexistence is different from failure of execution.

The transformation team should conduct a value creation brain-storming session with a select group of suppliers, customers, and members of each function or product organization within the enter-prise. This session should be facilitated and should focus on the en-hancement of existing products and services to meet the unmet buyer values that have been identified. The participants must be strategic thinkers. Warehouse-throughput ideas do not belong in this session!

This brainstorming session should include generating a diver-gence of ideas around each unmet value, developing a convergence of these ideas using valid qualifiers, and ranking the ideas. These converged, ranked ideas should then be documented and used in step E.2. This session can be expected to be difficult, so care must be taken to have it facilitated by someone who has conducted such sessions before.

E.1.c: Develop Value Migration Opportunities Through "Out-of-the-Box" Creative Problem-Solving Sessions

For an entirely different reason, some executives also find it difficult to develop value migration opportunities. Certain executives have risen through the corporate ranks because of their superior execution capabilities, not because of their creativity. This step involves identify-ing unmet buyer values within the supply chain that belong to another enterprise as well as unmet buyer values from other supply chains that involve a "pillar" or core competency of the enterprise.

The transformation team should conduct a migrating value brain-storming session with a small, select group of suppliers, customers, and members of each function or product organization within the enterprise. This session should be carefully conducted, focusing on which of the enterprise's current pillars or core competencies can be leveraged in another way.

For example, a bank may decide that the branch bank is not obsolete because of technology and electronic banking. It may view the branch as a "trusted" place that many of its customers feel comfortable visiting. The bank may look at offering additional value-added services at its branches, such as the virtual reality car show-room described in Chapter 1 or a virtual reality real estate center. This showroom and center could provide a one-stop shopping opportunity for the bank's customers to become totally educated on the options available for car or home purchases. The bank could, of course, also offer its customers car and mortgage loans!

The same holds true for retailers and electronic retailing. Retailers can establish an Internet Web site to sell any items, regardless of whether they offer these items in their store or catalog inventories. A wild idea could be The Limited selling automobiles. However, if The Limited focused on the types of cars that its targeted shoppers purchase (Saturns, for instance) and entered into an agreement with the dealer base that supports the car brands and selected lending institutions (like GMAC), this concept could take hold. What's more, these cars could be purchased through an on-site kiosk in their stores, increasing the traffic through each store.

Although, as I mentioned, this brainstorming session can be difficult to understand because of its uniquely imaginative and creative nature, it should result in a ranking of the migrating value ideas. These ranked ideas should then be documented and used in step E.2.

E.2: Identify and Prioritize Value Opportunities

After assembling the value opportunities surfaced in steps E.1.a, E.1.b, and E.1.c, the transformation team should evaluate each opportunity in terms of the size of the opportunity (or threat), the degree of difficulty in implementation, and the investment required. The team should then categorize these opportunities according to whether they involve value refinement, value creation, or migrating value and rank them.

In considering the degree of difficulty, the team should include the enterprise's internal capabilities to take advantage of the opportunities. In discussing the process of identifying and prioritizing value opportunities in the first half of this chapter, the first question I raised involved the existence of internal capabilities or, alternatively, the possibility of augmenting internal capabilities through external alliances.

The ranking of value opportunities should also include the dimension of time. When prioritizing the opportunities, the executive team should consider a balanced range of short-, medium-, and long-term opportunities and carefully avoid focusing only on short-term opportunities.

E.2.a: Review the Future-State To-Be Model in Light of the Value Opportunities

The transformation team should then take the highest-ranked opportunities by value dimension and by time and compare them to the to-be future-state model that was developed in the design process methodology. The what-if scenarios I discussed in the first portion of this chapter involve sensitizing the key variables behind the economics of each opportunity and matching these key variables to the to-be model.

This activity will enable the team to sort the components or variables of the to-be model into three categories: those that are not materially affected by the value opportunities, those that are minimally affected, and those that are substantially or materially affected.

The transformation team will then use the results of this review to make whatever modifications are necessary in the to-be model and/or the supply chain design.

E.2.b.1: Modify the Future-State To-Be Model

The transformation team must take the value opportunities that do not materially affect the to-be future-state design, or that affect it only minimally, and modify the design as needed. When performed in a creative, problem-solving way, this enhancement of the to-be model will allow for a strengthening of the solution. After completing step E.2.b.1, the transformation team should proceed to the as-is process methodology (discussed in Chapter 6).

E.2.b.2: Revisit the Supply Chain Design

The transformation team must review the value opportunities that appear to substantially impact the to-be design in order to make certain that these opportunities are priorities with the executive team and that they do in fact substantially alter the design of the future-state supply chain. If so, the team should revisit the design process methodology and rework the design to incorporate these value opportunities.

Conclusion

The innovation process methodology that you just completed will ensure that the supply chain management change process will involve more than just "paving the cowpath." The transformation process involves considerable time and resources, and for many enterprises, it makes the difference between being world-class, just surviving, or exiting a business. The last thing anybody needs is to complete a transformation process of this magnitude only to discover that the redesigned supply chain cannot support the new value opportunities facing the enterprise.

The as-is (current) process methodology, covered in the next chapter, is designed to help the transformation team assess the base for beginning the change effort. In mapping the current process, we will revisit some assumptions made in the innovation process methodology, such as the degree of difficulty expected in implementing value opportunities. Therefore, remember to document your work well for future reference!

Chapter 6

Understanding the Current (As-Is) State of the Supply Chain

Soon after the *real* plan took effect in Brazil, I was asked to visit a major Brazilian retailer. I toured one of its distribution centers, two of its stores, and its customs-clearing facilities at a Brazilian port. The tours were difficult because I could not follow the process flows very well. Although I have taken literally hundreds of such tours, these particular tours were challenging.

When I returned to the executive offices, I had planned to brief my executive sponsor on what I had discovered. He met me in the parking lot first, however, and before I could speak, blurted out, "Do you see what I am feeling? I don't know where my operations are or how to even address their inefficiencies. I know where I need to go, but I don't know how to start."

This retailer was feeling the pains of not having migrated his enterprise from a "manage the float" operation to a "manage the supply chain" operation. The activities and tasks in his supply chain were not anchored by any process design and were "allowed" to happen because they received no management attention. If we think in terms of Brazil's pre–*real* plan days, when inflation was so bad that money devalued at the rate of 2 percent *per day,* we can understand why the management focus was totally on managing the financial float.

The consolidation in the retail trade has hit retailers hard in the United States. When you combine a similar rapid consolidation with the aftershocks of economic stability following years of hyperinflation, you can get an idea of the compounded chaos faced by this Brazilian retailer. His greatest need was to map his current-state operations to gain an understanding of how to start an improvement process. Although this situation is by all accounts extreme for us in the United States, it does illustrate one premise: To build the bridge to a future-state design, an executive must have a firm understanding of the as-is state of his or her operations.

In the previous chapters, we completed the getting started, quality, foundation, design, and innovation process methodologies, which focused on business strategy, managing change, redesigning the order-to-cash supply chain, and creating value through innovation. In this chapter, I cover the development of the as-is, or current-state, model (Exhibit 6-1).

Defining the as-is state involves analyzing and mapping current processes, identifying organizational policies and procedures, detailing existing supply chain linkages, and establishing the current state of cost, quality, time, and customer satisfaction metrics. I have presented this phase of the transformation effort *after* the establishment of the to-be model, but it is often done before. Although there are advantages to either approach, it is better from a strategic standpoint to perform the to-be phase first. Doing so frees the executive and employees from a focus on existing practices that might limit the to-be solution.

Before we examine the process for defining the current state, let's consider a concrete example. The remarkable progress made by the U.S. textile industry in defining some of its supply chains with the aim of improving overall supply chain performance aptly illustrates many of the concepts with which we'll be dealing.

The U.S. Textile Industry and AMTEX

The textile industry is one of the largest U.S. manufacturing sectors, if not the largest, in terms of the number of jobs. Approximately 2 million jobs are associated with the textile industry, which represents $55.2 billion in gross domestic product. This is more than autos, paper, petroleum refining, or primary metals. The textile industry also represents $219 billion in consumer sales, one of the largest sectors in durable and nondurable goods.[1]

The U.S. integrated textile complex (ITC) includes manufacturers of fiber, textiles, apparel or fabricated products ("soft goods"), and retailers of soft goods. Despite the fact that employment in the U.S. ITC had declined from 2.3 million in 1970 to 1.6 million by 1996, it

---

1. "Questions and Answers," Demand-Activated Manufacturing Architecture, AMTEX Partnership (Cary, N.C.: Pacific Northwest Laboratory, 1995), p. 1.

Exhibit 6-1. The customer-centered supply chain management change process.

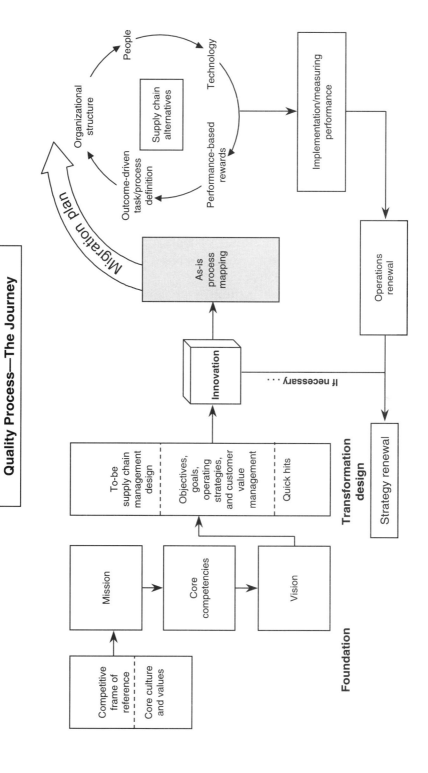

still represents 12 percent of all manufacturing workers in the United States. However, the drop in employment in 1994–1995 was 70,000, or 70 percent of all net manufacturing job losses for this time period![2]

The number of companies that support this employment base of 1.6 million workers is in itself significant. There are approximately 26,000 manufacturing companies in the ITC, about 40 percent of which manufacture fibers. There are approximately 4,000 producers of textiles and 21,000 companies that manufacture apparel and other fabricated products. There are also approximately 47,000 growers and processors of cotton and almost 300,000 retail establishments that sell ITC products to the ultimate consumers. If you do the math, it becomes clear that more than 90 percent of these companies employ fewer than 100 workers.[3]

The biggest threat to the employment base in the ITC is the negative trade balance in textiles. In 1994 (the most recent year for which these numbers were available at the time this book was published), the ITC exported $12 billion in products while importing $50 billion.[4] Many experts believe that the final cost of the landed product was the driving force behind this negative trade balance and that the factor underlying this lack of cost competitiveness was the ITC's time to market and non–value-added activities in the supply chain.

The losses in this critical sector of manufacturing spawned the Demand-Activated Manufacturing Architecture (DAMA) project under the umbrella of the American Textile Partnership, called AMTEX. "The DAMA Project is a unique opportunity to analyze and improve the ITC supply chain because it has brought together talented resources from the Department of Energy, national laboratories, industry, and several universities," says Jim Lovejoy, DAMA project director. "The project is working on behalf of the entire industry to reduce the time in the supply pipeline by 50 percent."[5]

AMTEX's DAMA project is of particular relevance to the present discussion because it has many parallels with the supply chain management change process. Let's quickly review the project's vision, mission, and goals:

Vision

By the year 2000, the DAMA project will have identified and demonstrated means for the U.S. Integrated Textile Complex to im-

2. Scandia National Laboratories, "Demand-Activated Manufacturing Architecture: 1996 Annual Report" (March 1997), p. 4.
3. Jim Lovejoy, "Textile Technology Through the AMTEX Partnership—A Technology Roadmap" (Cary, N.C.: AMTEX Industry Program Office), p. 1.
4. Ibid.
5. Voicemail message from Jim Lovejoy, May 6, 1996.

prove responsiveness to the consumer that can result in a 50 percent reduction in time for the ITC pipeline.[6]

Mission

DAMA's mission is to define and demonstrate new business structures and processes, and to establish the key elements of an electronic marketplace for the U.S. ITC to carry out major improvements leading to a 50 percent reduction in time for the pipeline.[7]

Goals

• *Pipeline improvements*—DAMA Partners and Laboratories will collaborate to identify, analyze, prioritize, and demonstrate process, procedures, and/or organizational improvements to eliminate excess inventory, reduce lead times, and move value added processes closer to the consumer. Produce 5 pilots showing measurable pipeline improvements by 1998.

• *Electronic Marketplace*—Identify, develop, and integrate intercompany and intracompany infrastructure and tools required to enable the ITC to reduce time in the supply chain pipeline. Pilotable tools and the supporting infrastructure will be developed by the end of [fiscal year 1998] to directly support the pipeline improvements goal.

• *Outreach & Commercialize*—Engage at least 30 percent of the U.S. ITC in the electronic marketplace through promotion of DAMA-developed tools and technologies by the year 2000, and facilitate the commercialization of DAMA tools.[8]

Except for mixing operating strategies with metric goals in the project's goals section, this front-end "foundation/design" work is very good. It looks even better when one considers that it was completed by a government-funded association dedicated to improving competitiveness and job growth in a key manufacturing sector. However, the association's work in mapping the process for the production of men's cotton slacks and men's nylon supplex parkas represents some of the best as-is process mapping I have encountered in the marketplace. (I have developed and reviewed hundreds of process maps of supply chains, and in my opinion, these two process maps rank with the best.)

---

6. "Demand-Activated Manufacturing Architecture: 1996 Annual Report," "Project Goals" section. Quoted with permission from the Textile/Clothing Technology Corporation.
7. Ibid.
8. Ibid.

Before we consider these process maps, though, let's look at the process used to define the current, or as-is, state.

Defining the Current (As-Is) State

Defining the enterprise's supply chain in its present form involves the following activities:

- Analyzing and mapping processes, technologies, organizational policies, and procedures
- Detailing existing supply chain linkages
- Establishing current- and future-state cost, quality, time, and customer satisfaction metrics

Analyzing and Mapping Processes, Technologies, Organizational Policies, and Procedures

The first step in defining the as-is state is to analyze and map the existing processes and technologies and identify organizational policies and procedures. This step includes gathering a significant amount of data through interviews with suppliers, customers, and key cross-functional personnel within the enterprise. It is important to validate the data as they are secured so that perceptions can quickly be separated from reality.

Once the data are collected, it is important to sort and assimilate them and represent the findings in the form of a process map. This converts the data into useful information that is presented in a process form. After the current processes are defined, the effectiveness of the technology that supports the business operations should be assessed in business terms. The users within the existing process represent the best evaluators of the effectiveness of the current technology.

The current organizational policies and procedures must also be reviewed in this step. A keen eye should be focused on the empowering or inhibiting effects of these policies and procedures. It is this review that will quickly surface any disconnects between the enterprise's value base and environment on the one hand and its policies and procedures on the other hand.

Detailing Existing Supply Chain Linkages

The next step in defining the as-is process is to detail the existing supply chain linkages within the process map. These linkages can be identified in the form of a matrix, which involves measuring the goods, information, and financial transactions that are flowing through the supply chain in terms of cost, quality, and time.

Supply Chain Management Design: Linkages in a Matrix Format			
	Cost	*Quality*	*Time*
Goods	————	————	————
Financial transactions	————	————	————
Information	————	————	————

Movement of Goods

The common focal point of company partnering is the movement of goods. Traditionally, the flow of goods between two companies is regarded as one complete transaction. For example, cereal might be shipped from the cereal manufacturer to a wholesale/distributor warehouse, with this movement being considered a complete transaction when the cereal is accepted by a warehouse representative.

The extended enterprise supply chain commands a view of the total value system's needs and marketplace demand. As the cereal manufacturer receives point-of-sale information and requests shipments, it in turn will relay the information to its suppliers to request the appropriate raw materials. The movement of cereal to the wholesalers/distributors must be viewed as one internal transaction along the continuum of transactions supporting the manufacture and delivery of cereal to the consumer (Exhibit 6-2). (Remember, in the "Journey to World-Class Quality in Supply Chain Management" [Exhibit 3-5], the world-class goal for "organizational structure" is horizontal integration internally and with customers and suppliers externally.)

The process map must include each step from raw materials to consumer purchase. As the cereal value chain example shows, it is the final delivery of product to the ultimate consumer that completes the value chain. The upcoming DAMA process maps present such a sequence of steps in greater detail.

Financial Transactions

When the movement of goods occurs between extended enterprise value chain participants, it generally represents a transaction that fulfills previously negotiated terms of agreement. These terms become

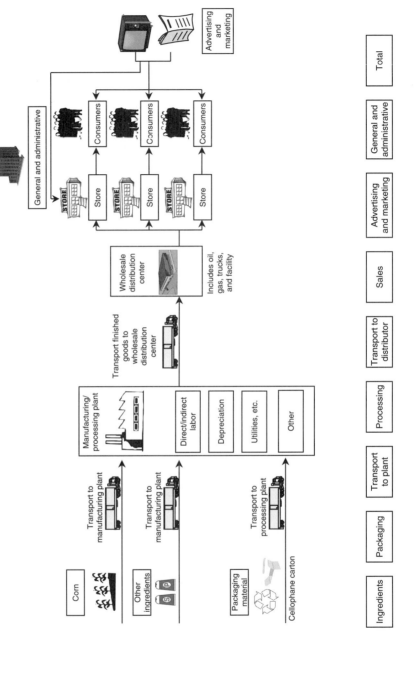

Exhibit 6-2. Customer supply chain for ready-to-eat cereal.

the basis for how supply chain participants are compensated for their efforts. They also determine how each company will behave organizationally within the value chain.

For example, regardless of whether the participants are food and beverage manufacturers, food and beverage wholesalers/distributors, or food retailers, the financial transactions involved with supply chain activities are crucial to the success of the supply chain. The traditional gamesmanship with payables and receivables should be replaced with consistent, predictable terms negotiated between participants.

Properly managed financial transactions must be the end result of the successful completion of a product or service transaction. Financial transactions must not represent an inhibitor to a partnership relationship between supply chain participants. To ensure that they do not, product purchase terms, freight payment terms, claims, returned goods, and value-added activities must be detailed, negotiated, and agreed upon before the first shipment of goods is made. Once agreement has been reached regarding these issues, the terms of the agreement must be complied with and trust must be present to make the process work. These items should be highlighted when the process map is developed.

Information

Information is an enabler for the successful movement of goods and financial transactions throughout an extended enterprise value chain. Information alone has limited value. To create significant value, information must be captured, sorted, and assimilated into the primary and support activities of the extended enterprise value chain.

As discussed in Chapter 4, we need look no further than the food industry wholesalers/distributors for an example of supply chain partners struggling for existence within their respective supply chains. If wholesalers/distributors are to justify the added cost they bring to the supply chain, they must add value above and beyond that cost. Furthermore, the value-added activities they perform must not be easily duplicated by manufacturers or retailers.

Many of these value-added activities are information-related. The use of point-of-sale data, category management, and quick response programs such as Efficient Consumer Response (ECR) are examples of information-driven value-added activities.

The food and beverage industry wholesalers/distributors that are surviving are doing so with a larger number of smaller customers. They are dealing with the added complexities of increasing line items and smaller delivery densities through customized information-driven services. The food and beverage industry wholesalers/

distributors that are not adapting to change are being removed from the supply chain by manufacturers and retailers.

Cost

Cost differences rest in the assessment of the performance of the extended enterprise supply chain by the marketplace buyer. The final cost of the product is the only cost of importance to that buyer. (Remember, in the "Journey to World-Class Quality in Supply Chain Management" [Exhibit 3-5], the world-class goal for "lowest landed cost" is the lowest landed cost of a product and service from raw material to the customer, period.) For example, the cereal manufacturer and the wholesaler/distributor must do their part to produce and deliver cereal to the overall "value system" that contributes to a competitive final price for the finished product. Thus, marketplace pricing should drive the extended enterprise supply chain, not cost-plus pricing.

The cost of each of the participants in the extended enterprise supply chain must be viewed in two ways. The first focus is external: At what cost must the participant perform the service or produce the work-in-process product in order to ensure that the final product is price-competitive in the marketplace? The second focus is internal: Can the enterprise generate a profit within the competitive price parameters of the marketplace?

Information enables participants in the extended enterprise supply chain to view their costs in a multidimensional way. It also enables companies and enterprise functions to determine their vertical costs within each activity, which helps them measure the efficiency of each activity over time and provides an internal budget. Information also enables companies to determine their costs horizontally across functions and across an extended enterprise supply chain. This measurement helps supply chain participants determine the effectiveness of their operations in fulfilling their commitments for their input to the extended enterprise supply chain's final product. The horizontal view will also help participants determine how competitive they are versus their competitors and how hard or how easy it would be to replace their enterprise in the extended enterprise supply chain.

Quality

The quality of raw materials contributes to the quality of a finished product. It is the supplier's responsibility to ensure that the quality of its raw materials meets the quality specifications for the finished product. Variations beyond quality specifications will result in waste, increased inventories to compensate for waste, increased costs in the supply chain, and ultimately customer dissatisfaction.

The quality of the financial transactions is a must. Participants in the extended enterprise supply chain must internalize the need to make the success of their supply chain partners their own. Prompt payment for products and services, expedited payment of claims, and a hassle-free environment in working through the financial implications of defects and complex, value-added activities are all critical. The goal is to eliminate any financial inhibitors to the partnership.

The quality of information is critical. In the ever-changing world of lean production, operations, administrative, and executive decisions must be swift and decisive—and these decisions are all based on information. (The work developed in the foundation process methodology [Chapter 2] and my "Journey to World-Class Quality in Supply Chain Management" [Exhibit 3-5] should be included in assessing the quality of information.)

Time

The measurement of time is extremely important to several industries. (Remember, in the "Journey to World-Class Quality in Supply Chain Management," the world-class goal for "compressed order-to-delivery cycle times" is to be number 1 in the industry.) As mentioned in Chapter 2, time-based competition has emerged from globalism, shorter product life cycles, and the need to drive excess costs out of the value system.

The original movement of raw materials from the supplier to the cereal manufacturer's plant warehouse suggests a mass-production, build-to-inventory process that involves buffer inventory. Today, this process is driven by lean production, which results in a minimum level of inventory to support a just-in-time delivery of raw materials and finished goods along a value chain that is driven by customer demand.

The DAMA project, mentioned earlier in the chapter, is dedicated to reducing the supply chain time from raw materials to consumer purchase by 50 percent. The belief is that to reduce supply chain time, non–value-added activities must be eliminated and the time required to perform value-added activities must be shortened. Both efforts will reduce the cost associated with each step in the supply chain. The timeliness of the financial transactions is also important. Whether payment is instantaneous (through an electronic transfer of funds) or involves a 30-day payment cycle, the keys are consistency and predictability. Cash flow is often referred to as the lifeblood of a company.

In the era of globalism, the workweek is quickly becoming twenty-four hours a day, seven days a week. Instantaneous transfer of information is replacing the old "upload to the mainframe" scenario. Time is waiting for no one. All participants in the extended enterprise supply chain must have access to the information they need when they need it.

Establishing Current- and Future-State Cost, Quality, Time, and Customer Satisfaction Metrics

The last step in this phase is to collect all the information gathered and determine where the supply chain is in terms of its effectiveness as a whole. This involves defining the metrics of importance, determining what the numbers are for the enterprise, and securing alignment and agreement on the metrics.

Benchmarking is included in this step. Knowing competitors' positioning within the industry relative to the supply chain performance metrics is critical. This competitive-positioning effort will allow senior executives to decide how much change the enterprise needs and how quickly that change should be implemented.

There is another reason why this step is important: The supply chain management change process has to produce results. In order to determine the impact of the overall effort, the transformation team must know where the current metrics are *and how to measure performance.* This step also provides a platform for making a first pass at the future metrics for the supply chain. By blending these metrics into the matrix presented in the "Journey to World-Class Quality in Supply Chain Management" (Exhibit 3-5), the transformation team can inform the executive about the as-is state of the enterprise's supply chain.

DAMA Process Maps

Using the "Journey to World-Class Quality in Supply Chain Management" matrix, it is important to detail how suppliers and customers interact with the enterprise's multiple functions, as well as how each of those multiple functions interacts with the other functions. A detailed depiction of how the various functions in the supply chain interact is called a process map. In this section, we'll examine what can be considered a showcase supply chain process-mapping effort.

The Demand-Activated Manufacturing Architecture (DAMA) project's process maps for men's cotton slacks, bedsheets, and men's nylon supplex parkas covered the production processes, business processes, and specific processes for production and replenishment. For men's cotton slacks, the supply chain was mapped from harvesting the cotton to the consumer's pulling the slacks off the display rack (Exhibit 6-3). For the bedsheet, the supply chain was mapped from harvesting the cotton to the consumer's buying the bedsheet (Exhibit 6-4).

These process maps included the movement of the goods and the conversion steps through which the goods passed, the information behind each step, quality checkpoints, and time elements for each step. The cost component sections were outlined but not completed because the focus of the process maps was on reducing supply chain time. The financial transaction linkages were not identified but could easily be mapped.

In 1997, the detailed pipeline analysis for the men's parka product line was completed with DAMA partners L. L. Bean, Glen Raven Mills, and Du Pont. Specific opportunities for improvement in pipeline performance were identified. Three of the forty-five weeks in the supply chain have been eliminated, along with two of fifteen inspections. In addition, several of the "just-in-case" inventories throughout the supply chain are being reviewed with the intention of either reducing or eliminating them.[9] Based on this detailed pipeline analysis and process-mapping effort, the DAMA project has already begun building the "bridge" to transform its supply chain! (In the next chapter, we'll examine the process for building such a bridge.)

Jane Macfarlane, formerly of Lawrence Berkley National Laboratory, was the leader for these supply chain mapping efforts. She says that the key issue was to focus on the critical decisions made by the people within the supply chain. According to Macfarlane:

> These critical decisions drive the operational performance of the supply chain. They are usually based upon the financial conditions supporting the linkages between the supply chain partners. They are also made frequently without the necessary information to make the optimal decisions for the supply chain as a whole. The as-is process mapping effort will provide the base from which to identify the information needs that will improve these critical decision points. The drill-down efforts of the winter jacket pipeline analysis will help produce the results that AMTEX is looking for from these mapping efforts *and* [that] the country needs for job preservation.[10]

9. Voicemail message from Jim Lovejoy, May 6, 1996.
10. Discussion with Jane Macfarlane, May 4, 1997.

Exhibit 6-3. Process steps for men's cotton slacks.

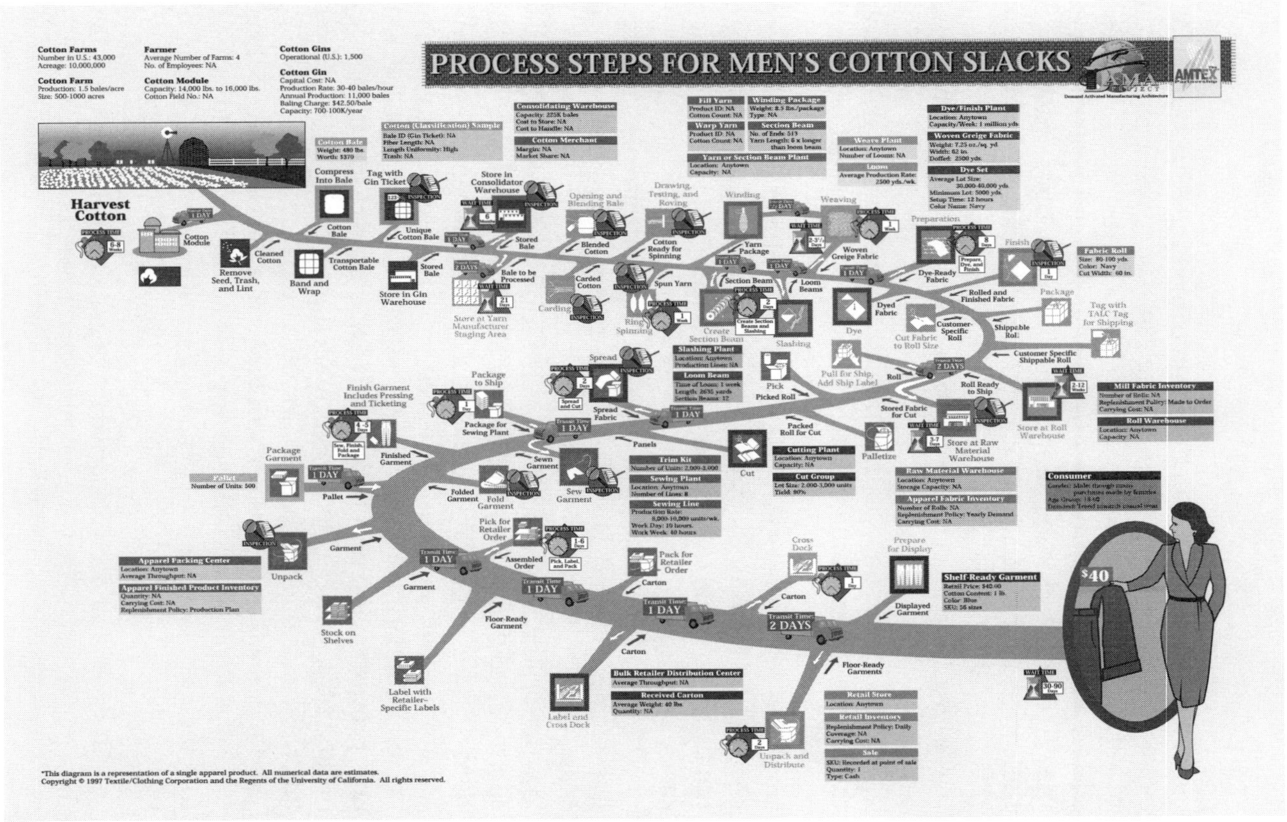

Exhibit 6-4. Process steps for bedsheet.

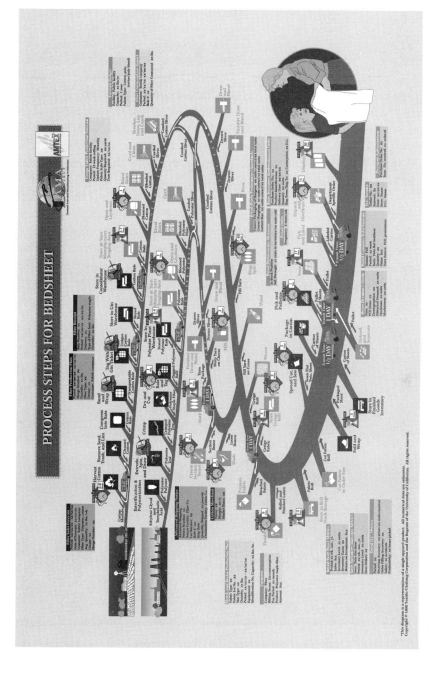

In its mapping of the as-is supply chain processes, does the transformation team have to create a process map as detailed as the DAMA maps, or will a less detailed map such as the one shown earlier in the chapter for the cereal supply chain suffice? The answer depends on how committed the executive team is to the transformation effort. By using a highly detailed as-is process map and combining it with the design of the to-be future state, the transformation team can readily identify non–value-added activities that must be eliminated and begin redrawing the as-is process map so it will become the new to-be process map. Although a less detailed as-is process map can be used, it will tend to be less effective. The result of mapping the current process will be a natural flow into the development of the bridge to implementation of the redesigned supply chain (discussed in Chapter 7). But first, let's work through the as-is process methodology.

Process Methodology
As-Is

As I have said several times, results are the direct outputs of the implementation of transformation designs. The process methodology for mapping the current (as-is) supply chain involves analyzing and mapping existing processes; identifying organizational policies and procedures; detailing existing supply chain linkages; establishing the current state of cost, quality, time, and customer satisfaction metrics; and then updating the transformation design accordingly. The result should be a modified as-is process map, or a to-be process map, that begins the building of the "bridge" to the enterprise's transformed supply chain.

This process, illustrated in the accompanying process flowchart, has two major components: defining the current (as-is) state and completing the to-be process map.

F.1: Define the Current (As-Is) State

F.1.a: Analyze and Map Processes, Technologies, Policies, and Procedures

The transformation team must analyze the existing processes, technologies, and organizational policies and procedures with two objectives in mind: (1) to determine what formal "rules" of the enterprise govern organizational behavior and (2) to determine the connectivity of the organizational policies and procedures to the organization's core culture and values (see foundation process methodology step B.2 in Chapter 2).

This step involves gathering data through interviews with raw materials providers, transport providers, suppliers, employees, and

THE SUPPLY CHAIN MANAGEMENT CHANGE PROCESS
Process Methodology
As-Is

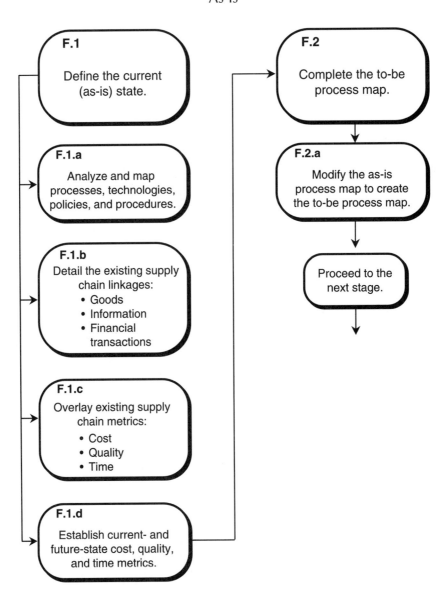

customers. Validation of data is important. The transformation team must document what policies and procedures are in force and actively guiding the behavior of the enterprise and the supply chain. The team must also identify what policies and procedures are "in print" but largely ignored by the enterprise. It is important for the team to assess whether these policies and procedures are ignored due to inappropriate demands by executives, a lack of effective communication, or a lack of managerial competence.

Once the policies and procedures have been reviewed and separated into "in-force" and "in-print-but-ignored" groups, the team must document their impact on processes and technologies. This is critical to the upcoming process steps. As the transformation team proceeds into implementation, it must know whether results are inhibited due to inefficient processes and technologies, inappropriate policies and procedures, or ineffective communications. The answer may in fact include all three factors.

At this point in the overall supply chain management change process, the transformation team has the luxury of knowing the design of the desired future state. Thus, the results of this step should be sorted into three separate groups of policies, procedures, and technologies:

1. Those that should be preserved
2. Those that should be modified
3. Those that should be eliminated

Armed with this knowledge, the transformation team should start building its process map of the basic supply chain steps, including all activities from raw materials to the end consumer. This should be done as a multifunctional and extended enterprise activity. At this point, you should just draw icons to represent each activity without concerning yourself about the details behind each linkage. These details will be determined in subsequent steps.

F.1.b: Detail the Existing Supply Chain Linkages

Step F.1.a involved reviewing the "soft" influences on organizational behavior and drawing the high-level process map. In step F.1.b, we'll identify the actual physical flows through the supply chain, which include the flows of goods, information, and financial transactions.

To begin mapping the physical flows, the transformation team should use the expanded view of the supply chain, which involves a series of transactions dedicated to providing a final finished product to the ultimate consumer. This approach forces each supply chain participant to focus on both its immediate transaction partners and the supply chain's end customer.

The transformation team needs to document the movement of materials between supply chain participants and represent that movement graphically, using an approach similar to that used in the DAMA process maps. After the movement of materials has been documented and a first-draft process map has been created, the supply chain participants involved in the movement of the materials should validate the map.

The movement of information is linked to the movement of goods. Customer orders, collaborative materials and finished goods forecasts, and production schedules are three examples of information that supports the movement of goods. The transformation team must not only document the movement of information but also assess the necessity, timing, and value of that information.

This aspect of the step is critical, because the movement of materials is directly dependent on the movement of information. The transformation team should document the movement of information in written form, capture and/or collect all the necessary documents (such as customer order on-line screen printouts or production schedules) that support the movement of information, and reference all the material to the associated supply chain steps. Once again, the supply chain participants involved in the movement of information should validate the documentation.

The movement of goods and information causes the movement of financial transactions. For the external, or extended enterprise, supply chain participants, these financial transactions are actual payments for materials and services. For enterprise functions, these financial transactions are frequently internal debits and credits involving individual budgets. The team must document these terms of payment and include them in the documentation supporting the movement of information.

This aspect of this step is also crucial. Policies and procedures influence organizational behavior internally, but the agreements surrounding financial transactions influence the behavior of all supply chain participants. By understanding the terms of payment between supply chain participants, and examining the enterprise's policies and procedures, the transformation team can identify the driving forces behind supply chain behavior.

The as-is process map must now be enhanced to include the movement of goods, information, and financial transactions among the various supply chain participants. The transformation team should continue to refer to the DAMA process maps for examples of how to depict these linkages on the map. At this point, we are ready to address the issue of supply chain metrics.

F.1.c: Overlay Existing Supply Chain Metrics

The documentation of the movement of goods, information, and financial transactions among supply chain participants must involve the metrics of cost, quality, and time. These metrics should surface at the time data were gathered for step F.1.b.

The cost metric should include all costs allocated to the final finished product. An easy way to develop this information is to take the price of the goods and services that the downstream participant pays the upstream participant. This way, the cost metrics are bundled and easier for everyone to understand.

The quality metric should include the quality checks of the product at various stages of manufacture, the quality of information, and the quality of the financial transactions. Product defects, reworked customer orders, and multiple reconciliations of supplier payables are examples of quality problems in the movement of goods, information, and financial transactions.

The time metric should be the time it takes to complete each step in the supply chain. For sophisticated, time-sensitive supply chains, time should be measured in hours and perhaps minutes. Otherwise, time should be measured in days.

The transformation team must now combine the output of steps F.1.a and F.1.b and enhance the as-is process map to reflect cost, quality, and time. The result should be a process map that includes each metric for each step and a cumulative running total for time and cost.

F.1.d: Establish Current- and Future-State Cost, Quality, and Time Metrics

The transformation team must take the output from the previous three steps, combine it with the output from quality process methodology step C.1.d (Chapter 3), and produce a summary document of the current-state cost, quality, and time metrics. The team should also prepare a working document that summarizes the future-state cost, quality, and time metrics. The outputs of the design and innovation process methodologies should give the transformation team an idea of "what's possible" for each step in the supply chain. The future-state metrics should be shown as "no-brainer" metrics and "stretch" metrics.

F.2: Complete the To-Be Process Map

F.2.a: Modify the As-Is Process Map to Create the To-Be Process Map

The as-is process map should now be modified using the output from the previous steps and from the design and innovation process methodologies. Linkages and activities that do not add value should be eliminated. The remaining linkages and activities should be either preserved or modified as appropriate. Those that are modified must align with the vision of the future state and support the design and innovation work performed to date. The goal must be the movement of goods, information, and financial transactions through the supply chain at the lowest cost and fastest speed and with the highest quality.

The output from steps F.1.a through F.1.c that relates to policies and procedures should be summarized in a working document, which will provide input to bridge process methodology step G.2.a ("Define outcome-driven tasks and processes") in Chapter 7.

Modifying the as-is process map to develop the to-be process map need not be boring. In fact, it can even be fun! A former colleague of mine used an approach called "I am an order" to create the to-be process map from the as-is process map. He would assume the role of an order and walk through the maze of people representing functions, suppliers, and customers. For each supply chain representative, he would review a series of transactions to determine the to-be linkages of the supply chain. By the end of the process, he would have developed a solid definition of the to-be process. (He would also be covered with Post-it notes as a result!)

Conclusion

The as-is process map is where the transformation team can start picking up momentum in the supply chain management change process. The graphic depiction of the as-is process, coupled with the previous work in the design and innovation process methodologies, will help accelerate the graphic design of the to-be process map. This is why I said it wasn't important to make the graphics perfect when designing the future state in the design process methodology.

The elimination and modification of linkages, policies, and procedures that occur in the course of reworking the as-is map into the to-be map provide a natural flow to the bridge process methodology, presented in the next chapter. Remember, save your work papers and be organized. Implementation is just around the corner!

Chapter 7

Converting Theory Into Reality

Building the Bridge to Transform the Supply Chain

Recently, I visited with a senior executive of a large consumer products company. His company had just acquired another company, and he was in the process of deciding what to do to create a new supply chain.

After discussions with other company executives and several consultants, this executive chose not to design a to-be model. In fact, he decided to develop only a spartan as-is model and ignore building a transition, or migration, plan. He told his staff to start implementing a new supply chain immediately.

His staff was totally confused. When his director of logistics asked him why they were going to proceed without the proper planning, he told her to "just do it!" Her answer was simple: "But with the merger, we don't even know where we're at today!"

Apparently, when the company's first-quarter results came in, the reality fell short of expectations. This executive had a personal philosophy, which he shared with me that day:

- Employees are paid to do what he tells them to do. When he says "change," they must change or be terminated.
- Companies should cut out this transformation "stuff" and "just do it." (No, he doesn't lead a major sports shoe manufacturing company.)
- Employees should not be involved in changing the way the business is run. Employees might pay too much attention to the transformation process and neglect their "real" day-to-day operations jobs.
- He did not want to "fail."

As an observer to his conversation with the director of logistics, I felt both bewilderment and sadness for this executive. My bewilderment centered around his position and how his organization and his board of directors could continue to support him. Sooner or later, the competitive position of his company (number 2 in a consumer products segment) will suffer from his leadership style and his resistance to managing change. My sadness centered around the fact that this individual either is threatened by change or does not know how to change.

In referring to his fear of failure, this executive was obviously reminded of individuals who had been ousted by their board of directors for not managing change, not properly redesigning their operations to meet changing consumer demands, and/or not producing positive, ongoing results. Not changing and not taking risk in today's fast-changing global environment is a surefire way to find yourself (and your company) in a declining competitive position.

This executive is very well known and could easily end up on the cover of *Fortune*. However, it won't be for trying to renew his company by transforming his supply chain. Throughout this chapter, as we examine the factors that are critical for success, remember this executive's comments and consider his philosophy of leadership and employee empowerment in light of these success factors. If you follow my process, you may come to share the bewilderment and sadness that I felt in response to his comments.

Refining the To-Be Process Map

In the previous chapters, we completed the getting started, quality, foundation, design, innovation, and as-is process methodologies, which focused on business strategy, managing change, redesigning the order-to-cash supply chain, creating value through innovation, and mapping the current state. In this chapter, I present the migration plan for moving from the as-is state to the to-be state (Exhibit 7-1). In other words, this chapter focuses on building the "bridge" that will enable successful implementation, which is the driving force behind producing results.

The transformation team starts by further defining the to-be process map for use in the migration-planning step. This involves the following activities:

- Analyzing the to-be process map versus the to-be model
- Analyzing the gap between the as-is and to-be process maps
- Simulating the to-be process
- Assessing the results and reworking the to-be process map

Exhibit 7-1. The customer-centered supply chain management change process.

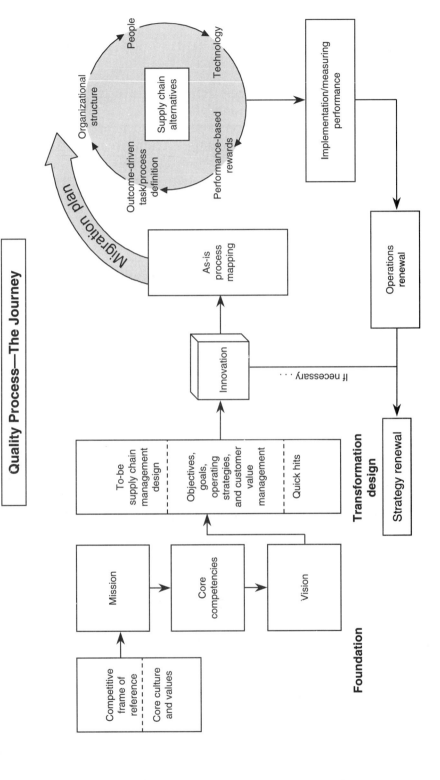

Quality Process—The Journey

Migration plan

People

Technology

Organizational structure

Supply chain alternatives

Performance-based rewards

Outcome-driven task/process definition

Implementation/measuring performance

As-is process mapping

Innovation

If necessary . . .

Operations renewal

Strategy renewal

Transformation design

To-be supply chain management design

Objectives, goals, operating strategies, and customer value management

Quick hits

Mission

Core competencies

Vision

Competitive frame of reference

Core culture and values

Foundation

Comparing the To-Be Process Map to the To-Be Model

The gaps between the to-be vision of the future-state supply chain and the to-be process map must be analyzed in order to ensure consistency and alignment. By the end of the as-is process methodology, we had determined the linkages, policies, and procedures that were to be maintained, modified, or eliminated. We now need to review this information, validate it once more, and sort it by supply chain component and by the linkage matrix.

Analyzing the Gap Between the As-Is and To-Be Process Maps

The transformation team must be able to answer the following question: Can we get there from here, and how long will it take? As mentioned in the preceding subsection, the gaps between the current and future states should be measured in terms of the linkages (movement of goods, information, and financial transactions) and in terms of cost, quality, and time. The "journey" matrix (see Exhibit 3-5, "Journey to World-Class Quality in Supply Chain Management") developed in the quality and as-is process methodologies provides an additional source of input to complement the information generated in the as-is process methodology and summarized in the preceding step.

Simulating the To-Be Process

Simulating the to-be process can range from a sophisticated computer simulation to the "I am an order" process described at the end of the last chapter. However it is done, the simulation must be performed with the involved personnel and with real-world constraints to emulate the future-state supply chain's probable impact and results. Of course, the real world always produces surprises when implementation actually occurs. However, a strong process simulation will help the company avoid preventable mistakes.

Assessing the Results and Redrawing the To-Be Process Map

The results of the simulation should be incorporated into the to-be process map. At this stage, the transformation team should be in refinement mode. If not, then there have been omissions in the preparation work performed to date. The detail behind this refined to-be process map will be developed through the establishment of the migration plan.

Building the Bridge: Establishing the Migration Plan

The bridge, or migration plan, for getting to the future (to-be) state involves many separate plans:

- An operational plan, which provides for functional tasks that build into supply chain activities. Goals must be established that provide incentives for cross-functional behavior rather than functional suboptimization.
- A technology plan, which supports the operational plan. This includes the technology architecture and systems applications necessary to support the redesigned business operations.
- The change management plan, the last but perhaps most crucial of these plans, which encompasses the operational and technology plans and maps out the organizational structure and behavior necessary for successful migration.

The migration plan is the cornerstone of the implementation phase. It must be strong yet flexible enough to be a living document. This plan should be subdivided into five sections:

1. Definition of outcome-driven tasks and processes
2. Organizational structure
3. People
4. Technology
5. Performance-based rewards

If this phase is completed properly, the enterprise will be ready to begin implementation of the new supply chain design.

Definition of Outcome-Driven Tasks and Processes

The outcome-driven tasks of an enterprise must be designed to support the to-be, or future, state. Specifically, these tasks must focus on activities that add value to the product or service from the customer's perspective. Because these activities must produce outcomes that move the enterprise toward its objectives, goals must be established for each activity.

Richard Beckhard, a leader in developing organizational change methods, has developed a "responsibility chart," which helps executives design outcome-driven tasks (Exhibit 7-2).[1] The responsibility chart is set up in the form of a matrix. For every task, there is a series of activities that must be performed, which are listed vertically on the chart. Every task also involves employees—or "actors," as Beckhard calls employees—who would potentially be involved with the completion of the activities. The transformation team should take the high-level activities from the supply chain design that was developed in Chapter 4 and begin breaking them down into the tasks necessary to complete each activity.

The power of responsibility charting is twofold. First, only the necessary value-added activities need to be placed on the chart. By default, the activities left off the chart are deemed non–value-added and eliminated. For each activity, the employees, or actors, determine as a team who's responsible (R); who should have approval (A), or the right to veto; whose support (S) is needed; who should be informed (I); and who's not involved. If performed in a nonthreatening and empowered atmosphere, the responsibility-charting exercise causes decision-making responsibility to be "pulled" down to the lowest levels possible.

Care must be taken to measure the difficulty, breadth, and frequency of activities to be performed. Enthusiasm can quickly turn into despair if a group misjudges the true effort needed to perform redesigned activities.

Organizational Structure

The organizational structure of an enterprise summarizes how work is allocated. It also summarizes the roles and responsibilities of employees, how functions are integrated, and how power is dispersed within the enterprise.

The responsibility chart in Exhibit 7-2 also depicts how roles and responsibilities can be transformed. By working horizontally on the responsibility chart, we can determine how tasks will be completed. By working vertically, we can summarize the responsibilities of each employee. When all activities within an operation are transformed through responsibility charting, the summation of the vertical responsibilities by job title is the duties and responsibilities for each position. In other words, the task definitions and job descriptions are developed concurrently.

Responsibility charting can have an even more powerful effect. As mentioned in the preceding subsection, if responsibility charting

---

1. Richard Beckhard, *Managing Change in Organizations* (Reading, Mass.: Addison-Wesley, 1985), pp. 42–46.

Exhibit 7-2. Responsibility chart.

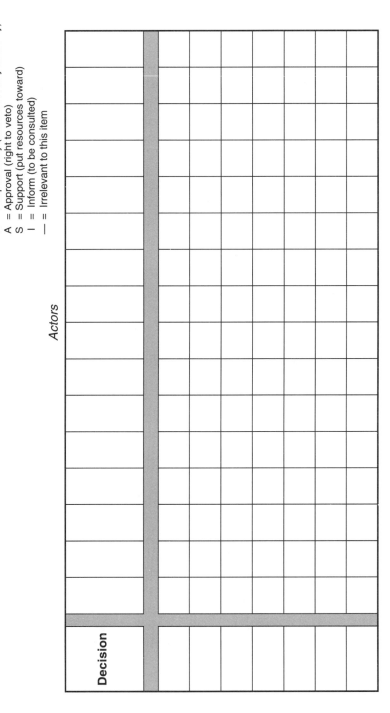

R = Responsibility (not necessarily authority)
A = Approval (right to veto)
S = Support (put resources toward)
I = Inform (to be consulted)
— = Irrelevant to this item

Actors

Decision

Source: Richard Beckhard, *Managing Change in Organizations: Participant's Workbook* (Reading, Mass.: Addison-Wesley, 1986), p. 45. Used with permission.

is performed in a nonthreatening environment, decision making tends to be pulled to employees at all levels, so there may be no need to make a special effort to push decision making down to the lowest possible level. The responsibility-charting effort should free up the time and energies of the middle and senior levels of the organization to pursue strategic opportunities like supply chain management.

The responsibility-charting process should renew itself every time a win-win supply chain opportunity develops. This continual improvement process blends well with the quality process, discussed in Chapter 3. Expanding the connectivity of activities within processes to include suppliers, vendors, customers, and internal functions strengthens the flow of materials, information, and financial transactions from raw materials to store shelf.

People

Once the tasks and processes are redefined, the organizational structure is developed, and roles and responsibilities by position are determined, the next step is to compare the existing employees with the transformed positions. Although very difficult, this task is critical to the success of the transformation effort and supply chain management.

Transformed positions often include expanded job duties and responsibilities. In addition, these new positions often involve greater autonomy and decision-making authority, due to responsibility charting and the reduction in the number of management layers. Thus, the technical and overall business skills required for each position will have increased.

The horizontal focus of supply chain management adds another skill set needed by employees: interpersonal skills. Employees must be able to interface with and influence people in other functions within the company and people in other companies. Interpersonal skills are vastly different from the command-and-control directive management skills that were successful in the functionally focused business world of the previous three decades.

In short, the skill sets and desires of existing employees must be reviewed to determine their "fit" within the new positions and organizational structure. This review will result in an array of decisions regarding promotions, lateral transfers, demotions, outplacements, and outside hirings designed to place the most qualified people in the redesigned positions and structure.

Training and development is a key step in the placement of people. Since existing employees may have the basic abilities needed to meet the challenges of positions involving expanded responsibility, they should be afforded the opportunity to develop those abilities through appropriate training programs.

The process of assessing employees and their abilities can be strengthened through the use of training to help their development. By providing access to training, employers can assess two other critical areas. The first is the employees' ability to perform in expanded roles. If employees have the basic ability, then training should enhance their development, thereby providing evidence of that ability. If they lack the basic ability, training will not enhance their development, thereby surfacing this deficiency.

The second critical area is desire. The training process will showcase how employees respond to the new structure. The lack of desire must weigh heavily in the process of selecting employees for the new organizational structure.

Selection decisions *must* be based on an accurate assessment of people and their abilities. Training programs help differentiate and enhance employees' abilities. They also enable senior management to assess desire to adapt to the redesigned structure.

The sensitivity of this activity cannot be overemphasized. I mentioned in Chapter 2 that transformation efforts must be anchored on a strong value base to produce the trust and integrity needed for a successful effort. People must feel that, no matter what the outcome of the transformation effort, the company will treat them fairly.

In the case of outplaced employees, care must be taken to exhibit empathy. In addition, experts often recommend a strong separation package that includes outplacement services. These employees have often served the company well and deserve to be treated as the senior managers themselves would want to be treated.

How an enterprise treats its outplaced employees does have an impact on the remaining employees. It is important for those who remain to be focused on their new positions with a renewed sense of responsibility. A badly handled outplacement effort could quickly shift the focus of the remaining employees to fear of the next round of layoffs.

In a transformed environment in which the duties and activities of every position have been expanded, diluting the employees' focus could have a dramatically negative effect on results. My recommendation is to make the necessary changes swiftly, treating the outplaced people as you yourself would want to be treated. Then, treat the fewer, remaining employees like royalty. After all, people are the greatest asset of any enterprise.

As mentioned earlier in this section, employees must interact with and influence people in multiple functions and companies. This

Exhibit 7-3. Toyota production system.

Purpose of the System: Maximize Profits Through the Total Elimination of Waste

Types of Waste	Systems Used	Method to Implement	Results
Inventory Conveyance Overproduction	"Just-in-Time"	Leveling Kanban Quick Setup	Make Only What You Need
Correction	Autonomation	Clear Standards Prevention/Detection Line Stop	Good Quality Products
Motion Processing Waiting	Workplace Management	Standardized Work Workplace Org. Kaizen (C.I.)	Safe Workplace High Productivity
Inventory Conveyance Overproduction	"Just-in-Time"	Leveling Kanban Quick Setup	Make Only What You Need

Source: NUMMI plant tour presentation overview, February 1993.

task would be extremely difficult if employees were focused on what's wrong with their company versus what opportunities are available for the supply chain. Senior managers must secure the right people with the necessary skill sets for the transformed tasks, processes, and structure. How this is handled is critical to the success of the whole supply chain management change process.

Example: NUMMI

The General Motors Corporation/Toyota joint venture plant in Fremont, California, is called New United Motor Manufacturing, Inc. (NUMMI). Opened in 1985, the NUMMI plant produces the GEO Prizm and Toyota Corolla. The plant has frequently been ranked among the top ten in terms of the fewest defects per hundred cars. As the key to NUMMI's success, many observers point to the Toyota production system (Exhibit 7-3), which has proved to be a model for other automotive companies.[2]

2. NUMMI plant tour presentation overview, Technical Liaison Office, New United Motor Manufacturing, Inc., February 1993, pp. 22, 23.

However, when I toured the NUMMI facility a few years ago, the employees and supervisors pointed to an even greater driver of NUMMI's success, known as the four cornerstones of NUMMI:

1. Mutual trust and respect
2. Fairness and equity
3. Teamwork
4. Involvement[3]

The employees feel that NUMMI's senior management incorporates the four cornerstones into every activity at the plant. They feel involved with the plant and openly support the company's *kaizen*, or continuous improvement, philosophy. In fact, the NUMMI plant's suggestion program produced 14,750 suggestions in 1992, more than 70 percent of which were adopted by management. The level of employee involvement is demonstrated by the 94.3 percent participation rate in the program.

More than 50 percent of the NUMMI employees are UAW (United Auto Workers) members from the old General Motors operation that ran the same facility until 1983. The old GM plant had one of the industry's worst records for employee relations. It experienced four shutdowns in twenty years, earning the nickname "The Battleship" in the process.[4]

The majority of employees with whom I spoke embrace the NUMMI philosophy and would not go back to their old plant philosophy even if they had an opportunity to do so. This is truly amazing, since these employees have significantly greater responsibilities and involvement at NUMMI than at the old GM plant. The NUMMI example shows that an operation redesigned around a solid value base can produce significantly greater results and higher employee morale.

Technology

The application of technology must support the redesigned tasks, activities, and processes as well as enhance communications among functions and among companies. Supply chain technologies like the SAP, i2 Technologies, Oracle, and Manugistics systems applications must be reviewed to support the redesigned tasks, activities, and processes. The transformation team must also perform an analysis of the

3. NUMMI plant tour presentation, Fremont, California, February 6, 1993, p. 49.
4. Michael Ray and Alan Rinzler, "The New Paradigm in Business: Emerging Strategies for Leadership and Organizational Change" (New York: Putnam, 1993), p. 159.

type of architecture (open systems, distributed processing, or mainframe) needed to support the transformed supply chain. Since this is a huge area, help from a third-party systems adviser may be needed.

Enhanced communications can take the form of telecommunications. It can also take the form of sharing timely information on the movement of goods, the status of orders, and the processing of financial transactions through intranets or private satellite-based cellular networks.

The key is to acquire only the technology needed to support the to-be vision. No one wants to be "high-tech, high-cost"! A solid example of the utilization of technology to support a best-in-class supply chain is Wal-Mart.

Example: Wal-Mart

Wal-Mart is widely recognized as a leader in supply chain management excellence. At the heart of that excellence is the design of its logistics process. According to many logistics experts, Wal-Mart's logistics process is what many companies are trying to emulate and adapt to their enterprises.

Wal-Mart's 1996 revenues were approximately $105 billion. Its incremental growth in revenues has averaged $1 billion a month for the past few years! At the end of 1996, Wal-Mart had an approximate total of more than 2,700 retail stores as well as 27 general merchandise distribution centers and 5 food distribution centers.[5]

The focus of the Wal-Mart supply chain is the retail store. The average Wal-Mart store has less than half as much square footage in back-room storage space as the average for the retail industry. The philosophy behind this design is to force merchandise onto the retail floor and in front of the customer. (It seems so simple. If the product is not on the shelf for the customer to buy, it won't sell.)

The Wal-Mart logistics process starts with the retail store replenishment signals. Wal-Mart "associates," or store workers, use handheld computers to manage their floor space and shelf space. Wal-Mart uses computer models (like Apollo) to assist associates in optimizing merchandise combinations that yield maximum profitability per square foot and cubic foot of selling space. Associates key information into the handhelds concerning shelf space decisions and local sales programs. The information from these handhelds is combined with

---

5. Jay Finegan, "The Continuously Improving CEO," *Inc.* magazine, February 1993, pp. 72–74. The information about Wal-Mart in the *Inc.* article was updated, verified, and/or modified for me by Mike Duke, Wal-Mart's senior vice president of logistics, on May 13, 1997.

point-of-sale (POS) information and uploaded several times a day to Wal-Mart's headquarters in Bentonville, Arkansas (Exhibit 7-4).

The point-of-sale and handheld information travels over Wal-Mart's private, satellite-based telecommunications network. When the information arrives at corporate headquarters, it is sorted and assimilated into Wal-Mart's supply chain system. At this point, Wal-Mart utilizes multiple supply chain processes to move its merchandise from its suppliers to its stores.

One of these supply chain processes is the Wal-Mart vendor-managed, or supplier-managed, quick response process. This process is focused primarily in softlines, which have the responsibility for receiving information from stores and rapidly replenishing their merchandise.[6] The supplier-managed quick response merchandise is shipped directly to the stores, bypassing Wal-Mart's twenty-seven distribution centers.

Another supply chain process is the Wal-Mart–managed quick response process. Merchandise is shipped from the suppliers to either the stores or the distribution centers, with Wal-Mart dictating to the suppliers how the merchandise will be routed. The merchandise that is shipped from the suppliers to the distribution centers is "cross-docked" and not inventoried at the distribution centers.

A third supply chain process is the Wal-Mart just-in-time (JIT) process, which involves the fastest-moving line items (totaling more than 1,000). These items are inventoried at the distribution centers, and the merchandise is automatically shipped to replenish store shelves, triggered by point-of-sale information. Approximately 85 percent of merchandise shipped by suppliers to Wal-Mart moves through Wal-Mart's distribution centers.[7] The remaining 15 percent is shipped from suppliers directly to stores through the supplier-managed quick response process.

Wal-Mart also has multiple delivery options available to its stores from the company's distribution centers. One option is daily delivery. Another is twice-a-week delivery with dropped trailers. These trailers can provide a limited amount of storage space when seasonal or labor-scheduling demands call for flexibility. An additional option is reserved for stores located close to distribution centers or for emergency shipments. For these and other delivery options, each store can elect to have either daytime or nighttime deliveries.[8]

The Wal-Mart supply chain process is continually redesigned to ensure that the right merchandise is on the right store shelves at the right time. It is the discipline within this process, coupled with the

6. Ibid., p. 76.
7. Ibid.
8. Ibid., p. 80.

Exhibit 7-4. Wal-Mart's logistics process.

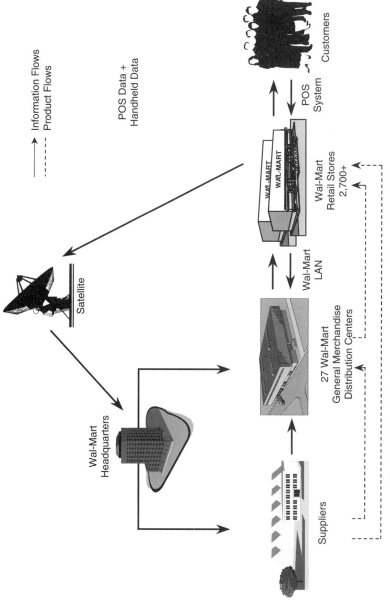

Information Flows
Product Flows

POS Data +
Handheld Data

Satellite

Wal-Mart
Headquarters

Customers

POS
System

Wal-Mart
Retail Stores
2,700+

Wal-Mart
LAN

27 Wal-Mart
General Merchandise
Distribution Centers

Suppliers

Vendor-Managed Quick Response/Direct Store Deliveries

Used with permission.

empowerment of employees and suppliers to execute within the system and the expectation that they will do so, that is at the center of Wal-Mart's success.

Performance-Based Rewards

The reward system of supply chain management must be designed with group rewards for supply chain members and individual rewards for employees of the separate enterprises. To be most effective, the group rewards need to be structured around the supply chain's ultimate customer.

An example of supply chain group performance measurements would include those items identified in the "Journey to World-Class Quality in Supply Chain Management" (Exhibit 3-5)—for example, customer satisfaction ratings as measured by the customer, customer order-fill rates, inventory reductions, and on-time customer deliveries. The supply chain members would receive a collective rating for each area and would be compensated by their enterprises based on joint goals.

Individual rewards would reflect the performance of the specific enterprise and function. In addition, the individual rewards would recognize the traditional performance areas of leadership, employee development, commitment, and loyalty to the enterprise.

The complexity of matricing horizontal group rewards with vertical, individual rewards demonstrates the intricate balance of effort needed for supply chain management. The group performance-based rewards reinforce the need for all supply chain participants to focus on the ultimate customer. However, each enterprise must operate at a profit that meets or exceeds stakeholder expectations.

Rewards can be monetary, as in an employee's compensation. They can be intrinsic, as in recognition and promotions. Regardless of their mix, rewards must provide incentives that encourage the behavior needed to implement supply chain management successfully.

Remember the executive I described at the beginning of the chapter? His command-and-control directive style, his failure to promote employee empowerment, and his risk-averse actions seem very archaic, a throwback to the management style of the 1950s. In a global environment in which successful companies need fewer, more productive employees, his style will ultimately produce negative ongoing results.

The following bridge process methodology focuses on the development of the migration plan—the blueprint for moving the enterprise from the current (as-is) state to the future (to-be) state. It is also designed to help readers avoid heading down the same path that the executive of the consumer products company was taking.

Process Methodology Bridge

The result of the as-is process methodology was a modified as-is process map, or a to-be process map, that began the building of the bridge. This first-draft to-be process map will be the primary document for building the bridge to the previously defined future state of the supply chain. Remember, we began this process with the end in mind, then proceeded to modify the present-state, as-is process map. In this section, we will further define the to-be process map and build the migration plan to begin the implementation process.

This process, illustrated in the accompanying process flowchart, has two major components: refining the to-be process map and building the bridge/establishing the migration plan. The third component, preparing the prototype for start-up, is actually an assimilation step using the outputs of the first two steps.

G.1: Refine the To-Be Process Map

G.1.a: Analyze the To-Be Process Map vs. the To-Be Model

The modified as-is, or to-be, process map developed in as-is process methodology step F.2.a (Chapter 6) should now be further defined using the output from the previous steps and from the design and innovation process methodologies. The modified linkages and activities must align with the vision of the future state and support the design and innovation work performed to date. This is a critical step, because the to-be process map must be complete in order to establish the migration plan.

Using the modified future-state model developed in innovation process methodology step E.2.b.1 (Chapter 5), the following policies, procedures, and technologies must be analyzed:

- Those that should be preserved
- Those that should be modified
- Those that should be eliminated

The required action (if any) should be taken with regard to these policies, procedures, and technologies, and the to-be process map should then be modified as appropriate. Any modifications should be minimal at this point, because step G.1.a is really a review of as-is process methodology step F.2.a (Chapter 6). This review is essential because, except for any final changes from step G.1.b, this planning document will be complete after this step. The to-be process map will now become an implementation map rather than just a planning map. As such, it must be the best process map possible and align with all previous work performed by the transformation team.

G.1.b: Review and Analyze the Gap Between the As-Is Process Map and the To-Be Process Map

The to-be process map should now be analyzed against the original as-is process map developed in as-is process methodology step F.1.c (Chapter 6). This step should be easy because of all the work that has been performed between steps F.1.c and G.1.a. However, now is the time to take a last look at the size of the gaps between the as-is and to-be process maps.

Sometimes, the gaps are too big for the to-be process map to be considered real-world. Although everyone would want to duplicate the Wal-Mart telecommunications and logistics processes, very few companies in the world can provide the resources necessary to do so. Then there is the issue of economic returns. Thus, a gap analysis must be performed to temper the to-be process map in areas that just will not be implementable.

The to-be process map should receive one final reality check before being considered a finished planning document. After this document is complete, the transformation team is ready for simulation.

G.1.c: Simulate the To-Be Process

In order to make the transition from a planning document to an implementation document, the to-be process map—complete with the defined linkages, policies, and procedures—needs to be simulated. This simulation can be as simple as the "I am an order" exercise or as

THE SUPPLY CHAIN MANAGEMENT CHANGE PROCESS
Process Methodology
Bridge

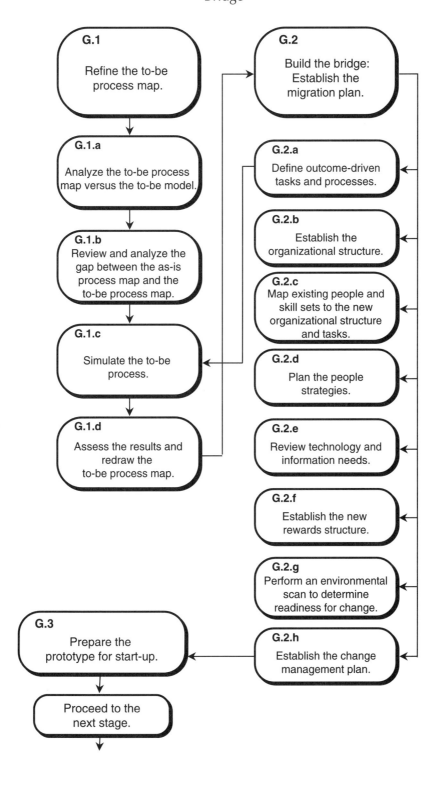

G.1
Refine the to-be process map.

G.2
Build the bridge: Establish the migration plan.

G.1.a
Analyze the to-be process map versus the to-be model.

G.2.a
Define outcome-driven tasks and processes.

G.1.b
Review and analyze the gap between the as-is process map and the to-be process map.

G.2.b
Establish the organizational structure.

G.2.c
Map existing people and skill sets to the new organizational structure and tasks.

G.1.c
Simulate the to-be process.

G.2.d
Plan the people strategies.

G.1.d
Assess the results and redraw the to-be process map.

G.2.e
Review technology and information needs.

G.2.f
Establish the new rewards structure.

G.2.g
Perform an environmental scan to determine readiness for change.

G.3
Prepare the prototype for start-up.

G.2.h
Establish the change management plan.

Proceed to the next stage.

sophisticated as using Enterprise Resource Planning (ERP) tools and constraint-based modeling tools and systems applications. The transformation team must determine how complex the company's environment is and what is truly needed. For example, discrete manufacturers have multiple supply chains merging together to form one large, integrated, and complex supply chain. The supply chains for many chemicals actually involve multiple supply chains for multiple chemicals that are "work-in-process" for the ultimate product. The process manufacturing supply chain for cereal, on the other hand, is much simpler.

Whatever method it uses, the transformation team needs to "test" the to-be process map/model in a real-world setting. The team must also determine the results that the transformed supply chain will produce. Remember, results matter! That is what the whole transformation effort is all about. The information collected during the simulation should then be summarized, with sensitized variances highlighted for the next process step.

G.1.d: Assess the Results and Redraw the To-Be Process Map

The summarized information from step G.1.c should be assessed, with a focus on how the key variables performed. The sensitized variances should be evaluated for impact on supply chain performance. If the variances are too great, the to-be process map should be modified and the simulation run again. If the variances are small, then the to-be process map should be modified, and the team should proceed to step G.2.

G.2: Build the Bridge: Establish the Migration Plan

G.2.a: Define Outcome-Driven Tasks and Processes

The transformation team now gets into what people refer to as "real work." This is where the team will be defining what tasks have to be completed to support the to-be process map. This step must incorporate all the work that has been done up to this point. (I hope you all have your work papers in order. This is where you'll need them the most!)

The transformation team must separate itself into work groups along the supply chain's functional or component lines. For example, order entry, inbound raw materials transportation scheduling, and production scheduling could be separated into a "demand-planning" work group, while finished goods warehousing, transportation, and customer service could be separated into a "customer care" work group.

The individual work groups should then initiate a responsibility-charting exercise. As I mentioned in the first half of the chapter, responsibility charting involves designing the outcome-driven tasks. The responsibility chart (Exhibit 7-2) should be used as a guiding document for this exercise.

The first job of each work group is to list all the tasks to be completed for each activity. Only the necessary tasks are to be included! For example, the tasks for order entry might be defined as follows:

1. Receive order (electronically or by paper, telephone, or some other method).
   - Verify order and/or enter it into order-entry system.
2. Run validation check (right date, right items to be ordered, proper delivery dates and addresses, correct financial/credit information, and so forth).
3. Submit order into system.
   - Receive confirmation of order from system.
   - Send/communicate confirmation information to customer (if necessary).

For each task, the work group must determine which employee is responsible (R) for the task, which employee has the right to veto (V) the task, who's to provide support for the task (S), who should be informed (I) about the task, and perhaps most important, who should not be involved (—).

When completed, the responsibility chart provides the team with two valuable items of information:

1. A summary of how tasks are to be completed, which can be obtained by moving horizontally across each task and assessing which employee is involved with the task and at what level of responsibility
2. A summary of the job duties and responsibilities for each employee, which can be obtained by moving vertically down each column for each employee and for each task

The transformation team must guide the work groups to ensure that they accurately measure the difficulty, breadth, and frequency of tasks to be performed. If a work group underestimates how much effort the transformed tasks and activities will actually require, its enthusiasm can evaporate rapidly.

G.2.b: Establish the Organizational Structure

The transformation team should closely evaluate the responsibility charts developed in step G.2.a and develop an organizational structure that supports employee empowerment. The enterprise should contain fewer, more expanded positions. In addition, a greater percentage of positions should have customer "touch points," or be involved with the customer service activities.

The executive team is needed in this area as well. Perhaps outside counsel is required to evaluate the executive talent versus the remaining positions. It is very important to perform this step properly and retain the desired executives at all costs.

One key success factor is to focus the organizational structure around the customer and not by function. The Quaker Oats example I discussed in Chapter 4 follows this philosophy. I know of a vice president of "supply" who is responsible for the activities from order entry to warehouse shipment. This same company has a vice president of customer service who is responsible for deliveries, sales, marketing, and research and development. Whatever the structure, it must be focused on the customer and make it easy for the company to respond to customer inquiries, complaints, and compliments!

G.2.c: Map Existing People and Skill Sets to the New Organizational Structure and Tasks

I have heard many executives lament, "The good employees leave, the bad employees leave, and the mediocre employees stay!" Often, this is true. This step, which consists of overlaying existing employees with the transformed positions, is critical for the success of the change effort and supply chain management. Unfortunately, politics often overrule logic, and the people process becomes less than optimal.

The transformed positions frequently include expanded job duties and responsibilities that involve increased decision-making authority and empowerment. These expanded positions require greater technical, business, and interpersonal skills than comparable positions prior to transformation.

The executive team, with the help of human resources professionals, must review each new position vis-à-vis the existing employees and determine which employees match the new positions and which do not.

Using the organizational charts supporting the new positions, the executive team should begin penciling in the names of the employees who match the new positions. After this initial exercise, the executives will know the size of the "people task" that confronts them and what people strategies need to be developed.

G.2.d: Plan the People Strategies

Employees who match the new positions fall into three categories: promotions, lateral transfers, and demotions. Extreme care must be exercised and empathy must be demonstrated in all cases, with adequate training and development offered to all employees.

The employees who do not match the new positions represent a different challenge. For some people, retraining for different positions and careers within the company is an option; for others, it is not. How to proceed with the employees who do not fit the new positions can be complex and legally troublesome. Legal counsel and professional human resources guidance are needed to handle this process carefully.

I have three recommendations regarding this process:

1. *Start at the top.* The most senior executive should ask the board to review his or her capabilities against his or her new position. If there is one thing that creates poor employee morale during a transformation process, it is the appearance that transformation efforts are for employees *below* the executive level.

2. *Give people a chance.* It is better for the company to let its existing employees have a shot at the new positions than to assume they cannot perform and hire from the outside. Although not every employee who takes a new position will succeed, this approach will boost morale among all the remaining employees.

3. *Keep politics out of the selection process.* Nothing devastates employee morale worse than blatant politics that preserves jobs for underperforming but well-connected employees. Remember, the existence of underperformers will force others to pick up the slack. If the transformation process is performed properly, there will be no slack!

G.2.e: Review Technology and Information Needs

As mentioned in the first half of the chapter, the application of technology must support the redesigned tasks, activities, and processes. Supply chain technologies like the SAP, i2, Oracle, and Manugistics systems applications must be reviewed to ensure that they will provide the necessary support. Selecting an integrated supply chain suite of systems applications must be done with caution. After investing tens of millions of dollars in these types of systems, many companies have discovered that only certain modules work in their environment.

In addition, technology must enhance communications among functions and among companies. Expanded, autonomous, and empowered positions demand faster and better information. Furthermore, they do not need endless reports or data dumps that offer very little value. The employees in the new positions should review what information they need versus what information they have and identify any gaps. The information needs should be categorized in three ways: essential to run the business, needed to manage the business, and nice to have. These information gaps should then be prioritized by the internal chief information officer (CIO) and acted upon in an expedited fashion.

Sometimes, the best strategy is to stop issuing selected reports and wait for a response. Dead silence or minimal complaints provide clear evidence that the reports contained no useful information. (Be careful with this recommendation, though! There are certain legal and financial reports that *must* be prepared, regardless of their perceived value in the eyes of employees.)

G.2.f: Establish the New Rewards Structure

The new rewards structure must be set up to be both work group–based and individually based. To be effective, the group rewards structure in a transformed supply chain must be based on customer satisfaction and costs. Individual rewards should be based on leadership, employee development, teamwork, team results, and loyalty to the enterprise.

The executive team must develop a mix of group and individual rewards that are performance-based. Employees should have joint ownership in the establishment of the targets. In addition, the measurement system must be simple.

One recommendation is to recognize the expanded roles that each position commands. *Pay for performance!* Do not try to reduce salaries for your most critical positions unless the pay structure was too high before this process. Even then, it may be advisable to hold off on reducing salaries. For many employees, changing from a seniority-based rewards system to a pay-for-performance system is traumatic. Once again, experts should be consulted in this area.

G.2.g: Perform an Environmental Scan to Determine Readiness for Change

The executive team must decide how much change employees can handle. This determination should be made with input from the transformation team leaders, who have experienced the employees' reactions throughout the change process. The leaders' recommendations, together with the size of the personnel challenge that has been identified in step G.2.d, will determine how quickly or slowly to proceed.

The transformation team must also decide how much change the enterprise can absorb and still maintain its day-to-day operations. Customer service must not suffer. After all, customer satisfaction is what the change process seeks to improve. The transformation team should enlist the opinion of the employees responsible for implementation before making this determination.

There are many sophisticated "environmental scan" processes and tools on the market. My recommendation is to keep things very simple and not overwhelm employees with questionnaires, surveys, or formal meetings. With their new positions, they will have more tasks to perform in the same or less time, and there may be increased anxiety if employee turnover is high. In addition, if opinion surveys are lengthy or ill-timed, their effect can be the opposite of what was intended.

G.2.h: Establish the Change Management Plan

The information gathered in steps G.2.a through G.2.g should be gathered and summarized. The environmental scan in step G.2.g will enable the transformation team to determine the time frame within which the change effort should be undertaken. When this information has been pulled together, the team should use it to develop the operational plan with the outcome-driven task and process definitions, a technology plan that includes informational needs, and a change management plan that includes people/responsibility charting, organizational structures, and newly created performance-based rewards structures.

This master document represents the heart and soul of the enterprise's supply chain operations. At this point, only a few copies of this plan should be made. It has significant value to competitors, and the team must still implement a live test through a prototype.

G.3: Prepare the Prototype for Start-Up

The prototype represents a live but controlled pilot for implementation. A prototype location should be high-performing, with proactive employees and a continual learning environment. In essence, the selected location should have a good chance for successful prototype implementation.

The transformation team must prepare the prototype location completely for start-up. Tasks, activities, processes, and change management enablers must all be included. In addition, customers, suppliers, and the community must be involved in the prototype planning. Modest goals must be established. Exceeding those goals, no matter how modest, is important to maintain the momentum of the change process.

My only advice is to spare no expense in preparing the prototype. All eyes will be on the performance of the prototype. Invest in it accordingly. At the end of this, all that should be needed is to start. If the prototype is done properly, the actual implementation may be a nonevent!

Conclusion

The entire supply chain management change process is focused on providing the enterprise with an integrated process that will produce growth, lasting change, and positive results. Since producing positive results must be complemented by the ability to implement and measure those results, the next chapter addresses implementation and measuring performance. Remember, results matter!

Chapter 8

Results Matter!

Measuring Performance After Implementation

After graduate school, I started my professional experience with Yellow Freight System in Overland Park, Kansas. Yellow Freight is currently the largest less-than-truckload (LTL) trucking company in the United States. Within two years of starting with Yellow Freight, I was asked to manage an internal audit group that focused on the operational and financial activities of the company's field locations.

One of my first challenges in the new position was to pull together my group's weekly activity report. Since it was my first "official" report, I spent considerable time customizing the format and articulating the content to make the report a showcase document. When I submitted my activity report to my director, I felt the pride of authorship that many executives feel after finishing a solid presentation or proposal.

The next day, my director called me into his office. My initial thought was how to accept the upcoming compliment on my activity report. What I actually received was the activity report back again—covered with highlights and comments! I don't remember a lot of those comments, except the phrase "Results, not activities!" Not only did the director repeat this phrase several times in his remarks, but it was written all over my showcase document.

I left the director's office frustrated and upset. How could I have missed the mark by such a wide margin? How could my director not have liked my activity report? If he had wanted a "results report," why did he ask for an "activity report"? Always seeking challenges, I set out to redo the document as a results report with the same intensity as I had exhibited in preparing it originally as an activity report.

Within a couple of working days, I submitted my results report and patterned all subsequent reports after this results-focused format. After several weeks, I ran into the company treasurer (my director's boss) in the hallway. He said in passing, "Nice reports! Well done!" and winked at me. He obviously knew about my first "activity" report and the process I went through to convert it to a "results" report.

When I look back on this incident, I regard it as a very positive growth experience. The clear message was that activities must be results-based. In addition, it is important to be able to link activities, articulate them, and then communicate them in the form of business results. The higher an executive ascends in an enterprise, the more critical this capability becomes.

Transforming the supply chain is no different. The redesigned tasks and activities must produce the expected results in order to justify the associated time, expense, and disruption in ongoing operations. As we will see in the following section, this "return on the transformation effort" is by no means guaranteed.

I still do not understand why many companies continue to require "activity" reports from their executives, directors, and managers. My advice to clients is to rename these reports: Call them "results" reports and request that all activities be linked to these results. (This is actually my second request. My first request is to eliminate the reports if possible.) My old director-boss would be proud to see me being a proponent of results-based activity reports. I often wonder how many MBA graduates he put through this process. I know I'm glad he put me through it. Results do matter!

At this point in the customer-centered supply chain management change process, we have completed the getting-started, foundation, quality, transformation design, innovation, as-is, and bridge process methodologies. It is now time to implement the transformation process and establish how our efforts will be measured (Exhibit 8-1).

The performance results process methodology, presented in this chapter, involves three main steps: identifying, defining, and developing process measurements; identifying, defining, and developing metric measurements; and establishing the necessary management reporting/executive information system feedback process.

Getting the Performance Results You Want From the Transformation Effort

Before discussing the issues of measuring and providing feedback on the results of your transformation effort, let's consider what actions

Exhibit 8-1. The customer-centered supply chain management change process.

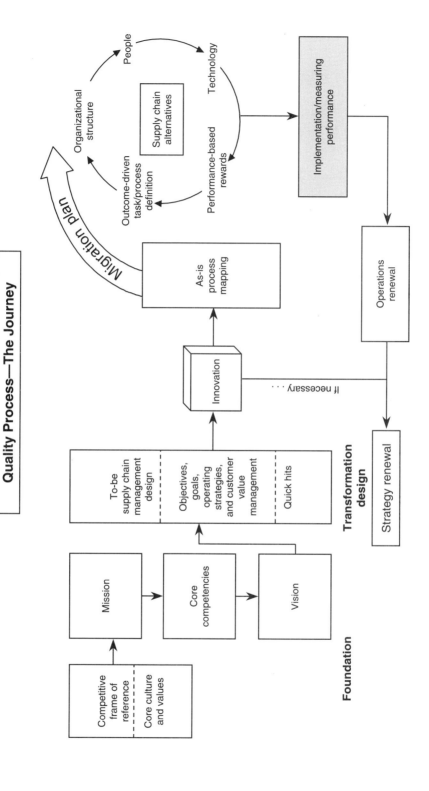

you can take at this point to ensure that those results live up to your expectations.

The AMA Studies

At the risk of being redundant, I'll repeat it one more time: After all is said and done, results matter! Transforming the supply chain is no guarantee of improved performance results. Many factors surrounding the transformation dictate the success, or lack thereof, of supply chain management, depending on whether those factors are included in or excluded from the process.

According to a 1992 American Management Association (AMA) study involving 500 companies that had laid off employees since 1987, more than 75 percent reported a decline in employee morale, and less than half realized an improvement in profits.[1] In a separate 1991 survey, 52 percent of senior executives said that their reengineering efforts had failed to produce the expected or desired results.[2]

Since the 1992 study, other AMA surveys have produced similar findings. Thus, the significant number of transformation efforts producing less than the expected or desired results dictates the need to focus on selected key measurements for the transformation effort. To ensure accuracy and credibility, these key measurements must be defined prior to the start of the transformation effort. In addition, a process must be established to measure the results of the transformation effort on a timely basis.

I often wonder how many of the executives polled in the AMA study would reinvest in a transformation effort if they had it to do all over again. The message is that transformation represents an investment of time and resources as well as some disruption in day-to-day activities. The return on this investment must be sufficient to justify the effort to the enterprise's stakeholders. Let's take a look at an approach that connects the process of transforming the supply chain with performance results.

Refining the To-Be Design

The prototype or pilot offers the enterprise an opportunity to gain valuable learnings prior to total implementation of the migration plan—learnings that can be used to refine the to-be design. Conduct-

1. Bernard Baumohl, "When Downsizing Becomes 'Dumbsizing,'" *Time*, March 15, 1993, p. 55.
2. "Perspectives," *Chain Store Age Executive* (November 1991), p. 29.

ing a prototype or pilot will also give employees a chance to provide operational, day-to-day input to the process beyond the simulation exercises, thus building ownership in the final supply chain design.

The transformation team should monitor the pilot or prototype at regular intervals and make assessments, which should be categorized in three groups:

1. What's working and should be continued or expanded
2. What's partly working and requires modification before it can be continued or expanded
3. What's not working and needs to be stopped until further analysis can be performed

Based on the information and learnings from these assessments, both the pilot and the to-be design of the supply chain and the migration plan should be modified accordingly.

Developing and Implementing the Rollout Plan

After the time frame scheduled for the pilot test, the pilot should be formally reviewed. The company should hold off on making any changes to the objectives, goals, and operating strategies for the pilot and/or the transformation effort itself until this formal review. The actual performance of the pilot should be reflected as a "variance" to the original goals/measurements.

The migration plan should then be reprioritized with respect to which sections of the supply chain to implement first. Readiness for change and impact on the enterprise should be monitored continually during this reprioritization. In addition, unmet and partly met buyers' values identified through our Customer Value Management process should carry significant weight during the reprioritization process.

The implementation rollout should be monitored carefully. Day-to-day business operations cannot be discontinued for the duration of the rollout. Several years ago, there was a merger between two now defunct trucking companies: Ryder Trucklines (no relation to Ryder Corp., headquartered in Miami) and Pacific Inter-Mountain Express (PIE). Although the financial processes and systems for the new, merged unit (Ryder/PIE) were not strong enough to support the new unit's operations, the old processes and systems were discontinued as soon as the new unit was operational. The company suffered from day one of the merger. Many company insiders as well as experts in the trucking industry cite the failure of the financial systems and processes as *the* reason for the merged carrier's demise.

Measuring the Supply Chain's Performance Results

In Chapter 3, "The Quality Commitment," I introduced the "Journey to World-Class Quality in Supply Chain Management" process (Exhibit 3-5), in which I outlined four measurements in the "logistics operations" and "results" sections. For the purpose of measuring the effectiveness of the implementation of a supply chain management change effort, I have sorted these four measurements into process measurements and metric measurements:

Process Measurements

- Customer satisfaction
- Quality of customer deliveries
- Order-to-delivery (cash) cycle time

Metric Measurements

- Supply chain costs

These measurements will assist executives in designing, implementing, measuring, and redesigning the order-to-cash supply chain for their company. To accomplish this, it is important to understand the driving forces behind these measurements and how executives can proactively respond to changes in these driving forces.

Customer Satisfaction

In Chapter 3, I outlined three progressive approaches to measuring a company's overall performance in customer satisfaction: Measuring customer complaints provides a good start for companies with no formal customer satisfaction measurement program. Using customer feedback questionnaires allows the company to hear the voices of its customers—provided that the questionnaires are returned. Involving customers in product and process performance reviews on a timely and consistent basis represents the best way to integrate customer needs into performance measurements.

Let's take a moment to review the seven R's of customer satisfaction, originally presented in Chapter 3:

1. The right product
2. Delivered to the right place
3. At the right time
4. In the right condition and packaging

5. In the right quantity
6. At the right cost
7. To the right customer

In the following subsections, we'll examine these seven R's (in a slightly different order) and consider how the supply chain's performance should be enhanced in each category.

Right Customer

Understanding and anticipating customer needs helps the enterprise connect with the customer. More important, it helps the enterprise connect with the customer's customer! For example, a packaging materials supplier to Frito-Lay may in fact have Wal-Mart as its customer's customer. Recognizing this connection enables the enterprise to help its immediate customer be more successful with its own customers, thereby setting the stage for measuring the supply chain's performance on an extended basis. Thus, the "right customer" may be one or two companies removed from the enterprise's direct customer.

Example: Major Food and Beverage Company   A *Fortune* 500 food and beverage company ships its products exclusively to distributors. These distributors, in turn, sell and deliver the products to retail outlets in their designated geographic areas.

Although this company's product brand names are nationally recognized, and its marketing is done from a national level, it is highly dependent on the success of its distributors in the marketplace. This company has invested in an internal consulting group that is designed to help its distributors become more successful in their marketplace.

The focus of this internal consulting group is on product purchasing, order forecasting, warehousing, delivery, customer service, and administrative activities. This company's philosophy is that the more successful its customers are, the more successful the company itself will be. The group's performance has exceeded the distributors' expectations, resulting in a significant backlog of requests for its services.

The customers' customers have also responded. Major retailers have become involved in the efforts of the food and beverage internal consulting group, resulting in several instances in which the processes of the food and beverage manufacturer, the distributors, and the retailers were transformed together as a single process.

This company has a successful track record of increasing market share and profits year in and year out. It represents a good example of integrating the customers' needs into its own product and process reviews. It also represents an example of proactively responding to these needs, continually improving the performance of the supply chain process as a whole. The "buyer value" for this company's distributors truly transcends a simple product purchase transaction.

Right Product and Right Quantity

To measure the success of customer deliveries, it is critical to measure order-fill rates, because customers expect their orders to be filled perfectly. All participants in the supply chain have an impact on the ability of the supply chain as a whole to achieve perfect order-fill rates.

There are many ways to measure the order-fill rates for customer deliveries. What is important is to measure those rates in the customers' terms. The two quality gurus I discussed earlier in the book, Joseph M. Juran and W. Edwards Deming, would have different approaches to this objective. Joseph M. Juran's approach would be to measure the actual rates statistically. W. Edwards Deming's approach would be to measure only the exceptions and eliminate the cause of the problem. The company can assess how well its deliveries meet customers' expectations for perfect order-fill performance by asking customers the simple question, "Was your delivered order 100 percent complete?"

Right Place

The location to which customer deliveries are made is becoming increasingly critical for delivery success. A single automotive assembly plant may have multiple receiving locations. Even if a delivery is made to the right plant, the assembly line may still be forced to shut down if that delivery is directed to the wrong receiving location at the plant. The company can assess its effectiveness in getting deliveries to their intended destination by asking its customers, "Were the products delivered to the right location?"

This question can also be used to measure the company's success in performing value-added activities expected with customer deliveries. Such activities include placing product directly into inventory, rearranging product retail floors or shelves, and stacking products in a particular order that helps customers use them.

Right Condition and Packaging

For obvious reasons, the condition of the products delivered to customers must be measured. Damaged products are oftentimes of little value to customers. Furthermore, damaged products create added cost in terms of handling, administrative activities, and expediting the shipment of replacement products. If excessive damage is occurring, a root-cause analysis can determine the reason, whether it be packaging, a specific carrier or carrier location, or any other factor. To assess the condition of the delivered products, the company can ask its customers another simple question: "Were the products delivered in good condition?"

Right Time

The timeliness of customer deliveries must be measured on the customer's terms. The Diamond Star delivery window for GATX Logistics' deliveries is measured in minutes. The delivery of grain to a silo may be measured by working day. There may be a one-hour delivery window for getting the same grain to a process manufacturing plant.

The measure for timeliness of customer delivery must reflect performance vis-à-vis customer expectations and needs. Any timeliness measure that is not based on customer expectations and needs runs the risk of measuring the supply chain's performance inaccurately. The simple customer question used to assess the timeliness of delivery is: "Was the delivery on time?"

Right Cost

The right cost for the customer is a cost that is price-competitive for the value of the product or service. It should go without saying that the customer wants to get the most value for the lowest cost, whereas the manufacturer wants to charge the highest price it can while still creating a demand for the product or service. This delicate balance is commonly termed "the art of the sale." (Cost is such an important measure that I have treated it as a stand-alone, metric measure.)

The seven R's of customer satisfaction are focused on the value of the product or service as the customers perceive it. The first step is to listen to the voice of the customers and measure their overall satisfaction level. I outlined three ways to accomplish this in my "Journey to World-Class Quality in Supply Chain Management" (Exhibit 3-5). The second step is to institute measures that internally link tangible activities of the enterprise with customer expectations or drivers of customer satisfaction. Three measures that link enterprise supply chain activities with customer satisfaction are quality of customer deliveries, order-to-cash cycle time, and supply chain costs.

Quality of Customer Deliveries

Successfully delivering a product to a customer involves meeting the customer's expectations and producing buyer value. These customer expectations often include perfect order-fill rates as well as delivery of the products to the right location, in good condition, and in a timely manner.

Deliveries of goods throughout the supply chain are all critical to the final delivery of the finished products to the supply chain's ultimate customer. The performance measurements for supply chain management must therefore include these deliveries in addition to the final delivery.

Measuring the quality of customer deliveries can be simple but effective if performed properly. The sample customer delivery measurement system presented in this subsection will help you get started.

Many companies have tried to be very sophisticated in their measurement of customer delivery performance. Although their attempts to measure performance represented a step in the right direction, the performance measurements themselves often became complex and cumbersome to use. One major food industry company has such a complex delivery performance measurement system that its managers are always explaining the measurement process variances and not the company's true performance results!

The intent of delivery performance measurement systems is to measure actual performance versus customer expectations. If the nature of the measurement process causes the logistics managers to interpret, massage, or adjust the results, then it is much too complex to produce meaningful information. Furthermore, a successful transformation of the logistics order-to-cash cycle is designed to eliminate non–value-added activities. Interpreting, massaging, and adjusting performance numbers adds no value to an enterprise's customers.

Exhibit 8-2 shows a sample customer delivery performance measurement feedback questionnaire that is straightforward enough to produce meaningful information. The five questions it asks focus on six of the seven R's of customer satisfaction. (Right cost is not included on the form.) This questionnaire requires simple yes/no answers and can be completed by the customer in less than one minute. The many companies that use paperless distribution systems can have these feedback forms filed electronically.

These five questions also focus on one main premise: Your customer either was or was not satisfied 100 percent. Since, as noted in Chapter 3, 96 percent of dissatisfied customers never complain di-

Exhibit 8-2. Sample customer delivery performance measurement feedback questionnaire.

Customer:	ABC Corporation Dallas, TX	Delivery date:	5/01/99
Customer order no.:	0123456789	Order date:	4/29/99

	Yes	No
Was your delivery on time?	☐	☐
Were your products delivered in good condition?	☐	☐
Were your products delivered to the right location?	☐	☐
Was your delivered order 100 percent complete?	☐	☐
Was your delivery satisfactory?	☐	☐

If you have any comments or problems, please call 1 (800) 555-0000 immediately!

rectly to the company that provided the unsatisfactory product or service, it is imperative that the company make it easy for customers to communicate their dissatisfaction.

The extra step of providing a toll-free number on the feedback form allows the customer to go beyond marking the form and talk to a customer service representative immediately. This is very important, because, as was also noted in Chapter 3, each dissatisfied customer will tell an average of ten other people about his or her problems with your enterprise's performance. If customers are going to tell someone, they might as well tell you first!

If the feedback process is to be successful, supply chain managers must respond to every negative questionnaire response. The goal must be perfect order execution. Performing a root-cause analysis on each negative response will quickly surface areas of opportunity.

Executives who think that this process involves additional time and resources are absolutely correct. However, these responses are from the enterprise's customers—the people who provide its revenues. To ensure the success of the supply chain management change effort, the enterprise must give the highest priority to investing in the measurement and assurance of customer satisfaction. When the quality of deliveries comes so close to perfection that the negative-response rate can be expressed in terms of one in several thousand, then the feedback questionnaire will have become redundant and can be discarded.

Order-to-Delivery (Cash) Cycle Time

The order-to-delivery part of the order-to-cash cycle measures the time that elapses between a customer's placing an order and receiving delivery of the order. There are various ways, many of them sophisticated, to measure this cycle time. Exhibit 8-2 illustrates a simple approach, in which the customer order date and delivery date are included in the customer delivery performance measurement feedback questionnaire. Electronic methods can measure this time to the minute and second.

First of all, it is important that cycle time be measured. Order-to-delivery cycle time can produce a competitive advantage in the marketplace. Ralph Wilson Plastics Company, which produces high-pressure decorative laminates, captured its industry's leadership position on the strength of being the fastest from customer order to customer delivery.

It is also important to measure not only speed but accuracy. Early deliveries can be just as disruptive as late deliveries. In the mid-1980s, Frito-Lay marketed a packaged cookie that could not be delivered for two weeks after packaging. The delay was needed for enzymes to finish "curing" the cookie. To help prevent early delivery, the packaged cookie cartons were marked "Do Not Ship Until [date]." This is not uncommon in the food industry.

An automotive assembly plant using a just-in-time process cannot accept early deliveries. Neither can a retail store operating on a quick response basis. Thus, it is important to measure both the order-to-delivery speed and the order-to-promised date/time accuracy.

Another serious concern is that the starting point for measuring the order-to-delivery cycle time be determined correctly. Unless the customer transmits its order on-line through an intranet, the Internet, or electronic data interchange (EDI), there most likely will be a time lapse between when the customer places the order and when the order is entered into the enterprise's order entry system. *The time that counts with the customer is the time when he or she places the order.* Although simply using the order-entry time as the starting point for measuring the order-to-delivery cycle time may be convenient, executives thereby run the risk of measuring customer delivery performance inaccurately. Why measure performance in the first place if the measurement is inaccurate?

Supply Chain Costs

The measurement of supply chain costs frequently represents the area of greatest interest for executives. It is also an area that often includes a complex series of activities that makes accurate measurement difficult for most companies. There are two steps that executives must take to ensure that supply chain costs are accurately measured: They

Exhibit 8-3. Bread customer supply chain.

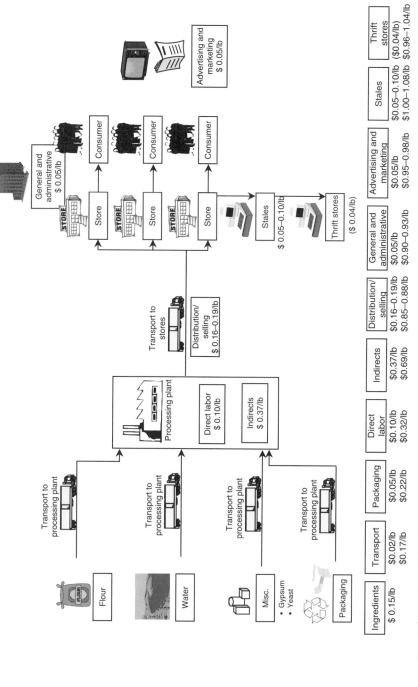

Note: Cost information is based on research performed in March and April 1997.

must first design the supply chain cost structure and then design the system to measure and report those costs.

Designing the Supply Chain Cost Structure

The design of the supply chain dictates how supply chain costs should be reported. Let's review a bread customer supply chain, which is similar to the cereal customer supply chain presented in Chapter 6 but includes cost factors applied to each supply chain component (Exhibit 8-3). Developing the cost factors for each supply chain component could be difficult, depending on the sophistication and accuracy of your costing systems. However, the process of developing supply chain costs will prove beneficial in many ways.

It is important to build up the costs for each component and document the activities that each component entails. This "decomposition" of supply chain costs will allow for quick resolution of what the costs represent. It will also provide a base from which to benchmark costs using like or similar activities.

The vertical or component costs within the supply chain must be sensitized to identify which area represents the largest impact on costs. This may mean either the largest cost component or the largest influence on costs. This sensitizing of supply chain costs, along with the linkages within the supply chain, will identify the supply chain "leverage points." It is these leverage points that executives must exploit to produce maximum results with limited resources.

For example, a bread company executive may want to increase manufacturing costs by one cent per pound to reduce obsolescence, or "stales," costs by two cents per pound. This might be accomplished by limiting production runs to direct customer orders. Because of the variable cost nature of the incremental production volume, the "run-out" philosophy of completing production runs may seem like a sound strategy to the production manager. However, this approach may be producing bread that exceeds demand and is destined to be sold as stale bread in thrift stores. By successfully implementing this trade-off, the bread company could gain one cent per pound, or one margin point. Using a supply chain cost model will enable executives to identify areas of interdependent activities that could potentially lead to true leverage points.

There are many leverage points throughout a supply chain. It is critical for executives to focus on those that offer the biggest potential gain for the organization. As we did in the as-is process methodology, mapping the supply chain and its related costs is an effective way to identify leverage point opportunities for improvement.

Activity-Based Costing: A System for Measuring and Reporting Costs

Many of my executive friends just roll their eyes when questioned about the effectiveness of their accounting and financial systems. Some very polished executives have been known to use a series of colorful expletives when asked to rate their company's financial reporting capabilities. Clearly, what's needed after transforming the supply chain is a supporting approach to provide accurate and timely costing data. In this subsection, we'll take a look at activity-based costing (ABC) as one way to obtain these data.

The successful implementation of supply chain management relies on both interfunctional and intercompany cooperation to reduce overall supply chain costs. The costing approach to supply chain management must support and encourage optimal supply chain behavior rather than suboptimal behavior that masks true productivity efforts.

The costing approach needed for supply chain management must be horizontally focused across internal functions and integrated by product and like businesses. It must also have connectivity to the corporation's general ledger and profit and loss. At this point, short of a full-scale SAP (a popular enterprisewide planning system that has financial modules for tracking costs by activity and by product) implementation that could cost tens of millions of dollars, activity-based costing comes the closest to meeting the costing needs of supply chain management.

The activities of a supply chain enterprise must add value to the production and delivery of goods and services to the supply chain's customers. These logistical activities consume resources. An activity-based costing system provides the mechanism for relating the activities to the need for the activities and the resources consumed by the activities.[3] The goal of ABC is to link all costs directly to their output, product, service, channel, or customer.

History of ABC   Some industry experts claim that the origins of activity-based costing can be traced back to the writings of Alexander Hamilton Church in the 1920s. From the standpoint of ABC's use as a formal company program, its origins can be traced to 1963, when General Electric attempted to develop a way to stop the growth of its indirect costs through its "cross-functional activity analysis" or ABC initiative. Its "ABC team" found that the majority of indirect costs occurred in the supply chain. For example, engineering deci-

---

3. Margaret L. Gagne and Richard Discenza, "Accurate Product Costing in a JIT Environment," *International Journal of Purchasing and Material Management* (October 1992), p. 29.

sions made during a product's design phase caused indirect costs in parts ordering, stocking, and so on.[4] Thus, it was General Electric's efforts in the 1960s that spawned what is known today as activity-based costing.

ABC and Supply Chain Management   The series of logistics activities that comprise supply chain management are all interrelated. These activities have a series of drivers that, when identified, can be linked with other activities created by these drivers. The goal is to develop accurate cost information that will enable supply chain managers to make effective decisions regarding network planning and the development of logistics alternatives. Trade-off decisions are becoming increasingly important for supply chain managers. For example, assuming that maximizing customer satisfaction is the number one goal, does the supply chain manager build extra warehouse space to store emergency (just-in-case) inventories or utilize premium transportation (air freight, for example) and incur additional transportation costs to ensure meeting customer delivery expectations?

Most accounting systems handle an enterprise's direct costs reasonably well, but they frequently misallocate its indirect costs, such as those that General Electric addressed in the early 1960s, using volume-based allocation factors that do not vary with the indirect costs. In addition, the selling, general, and administrative costs are frequently expressed as period costs on the enterprise's profit-and-loss statements and not traced back to customers or business-sustaining cost receivers that cause these costs to exist.

The logistics activities within the supply chain must all support the end customer. The costs associated with these activities must support the product portfolio strategies and pricing strategies within the given customer base. Accurate cost information can help an enterprise avoid bad product and customer decisions.

Activity-based costing must not be viewed as an accounting system but rather as an executive operational and financial system. Successful ABC users claim that it even serves as an organizational change management system since it equips managers with fact-based data that enable them to build stronger business cases and develop consensus more quickly.

Here are the answers to four frequently asked questions about ABC that will broaden executives' understanding of what it is and how it might help them measure the results of supply chain management:

---

4. H. Thomas Johnson, "It's Time to Stop Overselling Activity-Based Concepts," *Management Accounting* (September 1992), p. 27.

Exhibit 8-4. How ABC differs from traditional costing approaches.

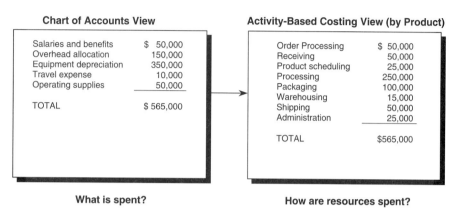

Chart of Accounts View		Activity-Based Costing View (by Product)	
Salaries and benefits	$ 50,000	Order Processing	$ 50,000
Overhead allocation	150,000	Receiving	50,000
Equipment depreciation	350,000	Product scheduling	25,000
Travel expense	10,000	Processing	250,000
Operating supplies	50,000	Packaging	100,000
		Warehousing	15,000
TOTAL	$ 565,000	Shipping	50,000
		Administration	25,000
		TOTAL	$565,000
What is spent?		**How are resources spent?**	

Source: Gary Cokins, CPIM.

1. *Question:* How does ABC differ from traditional costing approaches?

    Answer: ABC restates costs based on how the supply chain consumes resources, whereas the traditional costing approach uses a chart of accounts organized by vertical responsibility center. (See Exhibit 8-4.)

2. *Question:* As an executive, how can I use ABC to achieve operational gains?

    Answer: You can use ABC to leverage cross-functional activities without penalizing the leveraged functions. You can also perform root-cause analysis on high-cost activities.

3. *Question:* How can I use ABC to achieve financial gains?

    Answer: ABC will accurately assign cost activities not only to products but also to the shipping container sizes and shapes as well as to the specific channels and customers that uniquely cause or disproportionately consume the various work activities. This will help you determine the real profitability of the products and subsequent investment strategies within the enterprise's product portfolio.

4. *Question:* What are some of the benefits of ABC?

    Answer: It enables you to:
    - Rationalize your product portfolio
    - Determine customer and product profitability
    - Develop effective marketing and infrastructure investment strategies
    - Eliminate waste
    - Work with one set of financial numbers

The Importance of Differentiating Between ABC and ABM   The executive must differentiate between activity-based costing (ABC) and activity-based management (ABM). Activity-based costing is a method for measuring the cost and performance of process-related activities and cost objects. ABC assigns cost activities based on their use of resources and assigns cost to cost objects, such as customers.

According to Gary Cokins, CPIM, who is considered an expert in activity-based costing:

> ABC is like an imaging system, like sonar or CAT scans. It provides the data to measure costs accurately. Costs measure effect more so than the cause. ABC also recognizes the relationship of cost drivers to activities. It provides the supply chain managers a full image of the cost drivers, starting with customer demand and linking consumption all the way back to the enterprise's checkbook.[5]

Activity-based management is the discipline that focuses on managing process activities to produce value to the customer and profit to the enterprise. (Sounds like the supply chain management change process to me. As this whole book explains, this process transformation can be beneficial but somewhat complex.)

Executives must identify the value of ABC in supply chain management and proceed to blend in an ABC system to support the implementation of supply chain management. They must avoid the trap of procuring a bundled ABC/ABM system and service offering. Many ABC vendors offer ABM as a way to expand their service offerings beyond the accounting department. In the absence of a supply chain management change process, their approach is correct. Transformation must complement, yet precede, ABC. However, transformation is much deeper than the standard ABM approach and has a greater chance of success if performed properly.

In closing this discussion of ABC and ABM, I'll say it again: Results do matter! Establishing a horizontal costing structure and adopting a supporting costing system will produce the metric measurements that the executive needs in order to lead the enterprise through a successful implementation of supply chain management. However, once the metrics are known, it is time to renew the process to improve the supply chain's performance continually.

The key to long-term success in supply chain management is the con-

---

5. Discussion with Gary Cokins, director of industry relations, ABC Technologies, Inc., May 23, 1997.

tinued prototyping or piloting of transformed primary and secondary activities and the measurement of performance results. Adopting this continual improvement approach to supply chain management ensures a constant alignment of supply chain activities to evolving customer needs and demands. This continual improvement/pilot approach may include process improvements like throughput efficiencies in warehouses or reductions in transportation cost per mile; it may include opening, closing, or changing the configuration of plants and warehouses in the supply chain; or it may include a little of both.

Executives must have a renewal process to maintain the competitive advantage gained through the implementation of a supply chain management process. With change occurring so rapidly in the business of manufacturing, companies must renew their operations just to survive. The world-class performers won't wait for change. They will change themselves.

The renewal process that executives institute must be driven by accurate performance measurements. The following process methodology will enable them to measure the performance of their supply chains.

Process Methodology Performance Results

Accurate performance measurements that support a transformed supply chain don't just happen. They must be designed and implemented throughout the supply chain management change process. This process methodology revisits my "Journey to World-Class Quality in Supply Chain Management" (Exhibit 3-5) and leverages all the work performed to date by the transformation team.

This process has three major components, shown in the accompanying process flowchart: identifying, defining, and developing process measurements; identifying, defining, and developing metric measurements; and establishing the necessary management reporting/executive information system feedback process.

H.1: Identify, Define, and Develop Process Measurements

H.1.a: Identify, Define, and Develop the Customer Satisfaction Measurement Process

The transformation team must obtain the work performed with the "Journey to World-Class Quality in Supply Chain Management" (Exhibit 3-5). A significant amount of information on customer satisfaction expectations should have been gathered, even though this information is probably focused on industry measurements and customer satisfaction techniques.

The team should summarize this previously compiled information and use it as a framework for approaching the enterprise's customers. In selecting customers to interview, it is critical to obtain a representative sample, which should include at least 10 percent of the customer base plus the top five customers. This group should

THE SUPPLY CHAIN MANAGEMENT CHANGE PROCESS
Process Methodology
Performance Results

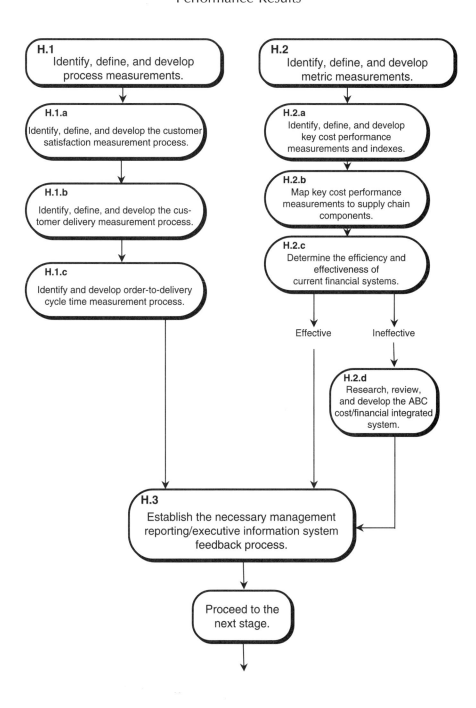

contain large and small customers, frequent and infrequent customers, and previously defined satisfied as well as dissatisfied customers. The team must avoid "loading" the customer interview group with customers who are shown to like the enterprise.

The interview questionnaire must be designed to ask hard questions concerning customer expectations. The questions must assess what performance level is needed in each category both to retain existing customers and to secure new customers. The team must avoid structuring the interviews to assess whether the customers like the enterprise—a frequent pitfall of these types of interviews. Remember, running a profitable business is what we are all after, not winning a popularity contest.

Once the interviews have been completed, the team must first summarize and categorize the answers to the interview questions and then document this information for use in developing the customer satisfaction measurement process.

This document should provide the information needed to determine which customer satisfaction areas should be measured and how often. For example, quality of customer deliveries should be measured at least every week and preferably every delivery. The team should also define how the results will be reported, to whom, and how often. This task cannot be "pushed" into the operating groups. To be effective, it must be "pulled."

The transformation team must now develop the measurement process and ensure that it is practical. The input up to this point might be so complex that the measurement process could take on a life all its own. It's up to the team to design a process that is simple but still supports the transformed supply chain effectively.

The development of the measurement process should begin with all the customer "touch" points. In other words, anytime customer contact is made (for example, customer quotations, customer inquiries, and order processing), there is a need to measure performance.

In the quality process methodology (Chapter 3), we reviewed (and established) three customer satisfaction measurement techniques as part of the "Journey to World-Class Quality in Supply Chain Management" (Exhibit 3-5): customer complaints, customer feedback questionnaires, and customer performance reviews. These techniques, which were established early in the transformation process using primarily high-end industry information, must now be enhanced with specific customer expectations identified during the present step.

The team needs to recommend the development of systems to secure and process this information and disseminate it to the right work groups. These systems must be developed with the aim of minimizing the amount of manual effort that will be involved in producing the reports, running on time, and disseminating the information on a schedule that has been agreed to with the user groups. Actual results, variance from targets, and variance from optimal performance (for example, 100 percent order fill) should be used in these reports.

Once the customer satisfaction measurement process is developed, the transformation team must take it back to the work teams for concurrence and final modifications. Once concurrence is obtained, the process should be set up for implementation in step H.3.

H.1.b: Identify, Define, and Develop the Customer Delivery Measurement Process

As discussed in Chapter 3 and reiterated in the first half of this chapter, the two measures at the heart of customer delivery satisfaction are customer order-fill rates and on-time delivery performance. It should be possible to obtain much of the needed information from the original customer order, which should contain the delivery date, time, and location. If the order itself does not show this information, then the customer file that the order accesses should have agreed-to delivery dates, times, and locations.

It is important to note that the customer order should be "frozen," or captured in its original form, when received. *It must not be manipulated or modified before it is frozen or captured.* The customer order in its original form is as close to the measurement of customer demand as the enterprise can get in this way. Manipulation of customer orders, especially to match internally available inventory stocks, renders the information useless for measuring customer satisfaction. You have gone this far with the supply chain management change process, so why settle for internally manipulated data from a measurement system? Your competitors may have *real* customer order-fill rates and may be working to satisfy *real* customer demand.

The team should develop a customer delivery measurement form that captures the order-fill and on-time delivery performance for each delivery. This form should be on-line whenever possible and should be easy for customers to use. Please refer to the "Quality of Customer Deliveries" subsection in the first half of this chapter, which presents a sample customer delivery measurement system, together with a sample customer delivery form.

H.1.c: Identify and Develop the Order-to-Delivery Cycle Time Measurement Process

Another key measurement of customer satisfaction and supply chain performance is order-to-delivery (or cash) cycle time. In quality process methodology step C.1.a (Chapter 3), we identified the order-to-delivery cycle times in the industry. This step identifies the order-to-delivery (or cash) cycle time as a *key* customer satisfaction and internal process performance measurement. Remember the Demand-Activated Manufacturing Architecture (DAMA) process maps presented in Chapter 6? Those maps focused on reducing cycle times!

The speed and consistency of the cycle time must be incorporated into the measurement systems of each work group. The date of the order should be captured by the order-entry system, and the delivery date should be captured at the time of delivery. A system should be developed that measures the difference between the two. A summary document should be assembled for multiple shipments. This will allow service to specific customers to be measured in terms of average performance and consistency of performance.

Also, it is important that the "order date" not be the date that the order was put into the system but rather the date that the order was received by the enterprise! The order side of the cycle time is what starts the clock ticking from the customer's standpoint.

The transformation team must once again collaborate with each work group to ensure that the right measurement system is developed. The team must also make sure that the system it designs captures the actual date and time when customer orders are submitted.

The delivery side of cycle time should be the actual date and time when customer deliveries are made. Companies such as UPS and Federal Express have very sophisticated delivery systems to capture this information. Many other companies are not as fortunate. I have personally seen companies use trailer loading times, accounts receivable billing dates (on prepaid shipments, no less), and manifesting dates as "delivery" dates. None of those dates matters to the end customer. To measure cycle times from the customer's perspective, actual customer delivery times must be used.

The cash side of cycle time is the point at which a delivery results in actual cash being transacted. This can occur when payments are made to suppliers or when cash is received from the end customer. Order-to-cash is an internal enterprise measurement. The customer, for the most part, only cares about order-to-delivery cycle times.

The system must be easy to administer. It must also be designed from a customer perspective. Otherwise, it is not worth the effort. Although it sounds simple, measuring supply chain effectiveness in terms of customer satisfaction, customer delivery satisfaction, and customer order-to-delivery times must include the customer.

H.2: Identify, Define, and Develop Metric Measurements

H.2.a: Identify, Define, and Develop Key Cost Performance Measurements and Indexes

The cost performance of the supply chain represents an area of great interest for most executives. In this step, the transformation team determines what performance measurements and indexes will be used to measure supply chain costs.

Many executives want costs to be measured in terms of units. Cost per pound manufactured, cost per unit purchased, and cost per hundredweight transported are a few measurements commonly employed in the marketplace.

However, there are stronger measures to be used for supply chain performance. Landed cost per product line item and economic value added (EVA) are two measures used by proactive supply chain executives. The team rewards structure should be based on team measurements. Measuring the landed cost per product line item encourages multifunctional teams to work together to achieve the lowest cost possible. Measuring the costs associated with individual functional activities may lead to suboptimal behavior to achieve the lowest cost per functional activity without necessarily lowering the total supply chain cost.

The transformation team must collaborate with the key work groups to develop the appropriate measurements and indexes to assess supply chain performance. My recommendation is to create multifunctional work teams to review and approve these measurements and indexes. This cross-functional involvement and approval process will spur awareness and ownership of each other's goals along the supply chain.

H.2.b: Map Key Cost Performance Measurements to Supply Chain Components

The design of the supply chain and the definition of tasks and activities through responsibility charting will determine the supply chain components to be used in cost reporting. As mentioned in the first half of the chapter, determining the costs associated with the tasks and activities in each supply chain component will allow executives to quickly identify the leverage opportunities within the supply chain.

My recommendation is to establish both vertical and horizontal cost structures. The vertical or functional costs can be used to associate costs to a specific supply chain component. The horizontal costs can be used to associate costs to specific product line items or product groups.

Let's go back to the bread customer supply chain (Exhibit 8-3). The key supply chain components are ingredients, inbound transportation, packaging, manufacturing (direct labor and indirects), distribution/selling, general and administrative, advertising and marketing, and thrift stores. Although each component has an associated cost, the total cost ($.96–$1.04 per pound) represents the landed cost for a branded loaf of bread. Let's say that a private-label loaf of bread costs $.80. With both functional and horizontal cost performance measurements available, an executive may determine that the difference lies in ingredients ($.02), advertising ($.05), distribution/selling ($.08), and stales ($.01 to $.03). Thus, the executive may decide to provide retailers with a distribution/selling program that encourages backroom deliveries versus store-door deliveries and share in the cost savings accordingly.

H.2.c: Determine the Efficiency and Effectiveness of Current Financial Systems

Once the transformation team has identified the key cost performance measurements and the key supply chain components with related costs that will be used for supply chain management, it must then define the necessary cost-reporting and financial systems. It is critical to define the systems that will be needed to meet the requirements of both the supply chain employees and the executives. All too often, companies acquire off-the-shelf systems that meet only a portion of the employees' and executives' needs. Less-than-optimal off-the-shelf systems can force the company to manipulate results manually, employ multiple sets of numbers, and work with inaccurate data. It is precisely these types of activities that transformation is dedicated to eliminating.

The transformation team must secure two lists of employee and executive demands for cost-reporting and financial systems. The first should be a wish list of every type of report and information they would want in the new, redesigned supply chain. The second should include only the reports and information that are absolutely necessary to operate the supply chain on a day-to-day basis.

The overriding goal has to be one set of numbers. The cost-reporting and financial systems must be flexible enough to measure efficiencies in functional activities and effectiveness of supply chain performance for specific product line items or product groups. Integration and compatibility among the systems themselves and with the tasks and activities within the redesigned processes are essential to achieve one set of numbers. The accuracy of this one set of numbers as well as the timeliness of its delivery are also essential to successful supply chain management.

The transformation team should poll the work group teams to determine the efficiency and effectiveness of the current cost-reporting and financial systems. Users of these systems should rate the systems as either "effective" or "ineffective" for the new, redesigned supply chain environment. There should be no middle ground in this review.

For the fortunate enterprises whose systems receive an "effective" rating from users, the transformation team should proceed to step H.3. For the unfortunate enterprises (perhaps the majority) whose systems receive an "ineffective" rating, the transformation team should proceed to step H.2.d.

H.2.d: Research, Review, and Develop the ABC Cost/Financial Integrated System

The use of a value chain approach to determine supply chain costs relies on the premise that costs should be measured as the activities consume resources. This approach should result in the ability to leverage cross-functional activities without penalizing the leveraged functions. In addition, executives should be able to perform root-cause analyses on high-cost activities and determine the real profitability of their enterprise's product portfolio.

Activity-based costing is a financial and accounting system that is designed to support the preceding scenario. In developing ways to improve the enterprise's existing cost-reporting and financial systems, the transformation team must determine whether ABC is applicable to the improvement effort.

If the existing systems are ineffective, yet only in selected areas, then the team should proceed to upgrade only those selected areas. If the existing systems are ineffective on a broad scale, then the team should proceed to replace the company's existing systems with an activity-based costing system.

Once the applicability of ABC has been determined, the team should immediately start developing the ABC cost/financial integrated system. Under the guidance of an executive sponsor, the team should seek assistance from professional associations and experienced consultants to help it select, develop, and integrate this system.

This system should be implemented in phases to avoid disrupting day-to-day operations. I know of several companies that have rushed into the implementation of supply chain systems (remember silver bullets?) only to find that they have spent millions of dollars on the wrong systems. I know of one manufacturing company that hastily implemented ABC and lost thirty days' receivables *and* many of the operational records supporting those receivables. Focusing on the user groups' system "necessities" will help avoid the confusion that a "wish list" might create during the definition of requirements.

(For a more in-depth analysis of ABC, the transformation team should consult *An ABC Manager's Primer*, a publication on the basics of activity-based costing developed for the Consortium for Advanced Manufacturing International.)[6]

H.3: Establish the Necessary Management Reporting/Executive Information System Feedback Process

The results from steps H.1 and H.2 should be consolidated and summarized to provide input for defining the requirements for an overall management reporting and executive information system. An ABC system will allocate the costs, while the management reporting system will present the operational information in a meaningful format. The management reporting system should provide feedback on the day-to-day performance versus indexes, while an executive information system will help senior executives measure trends and variances to performance measurements.

There are many good companies that have extensive experience with the creation of management reporting and executive information systems (Oracle, IBM, and so on). Again, the transformation team, with the guidance of the executive sponsor, should review the systems providers and select the most appropriate system for the redesigned supply chain.

Once the management reporting and executive information system is operational, care must be taken to use the information from

---

6. Gary Cokins, Alan Stratton, and Jack Helbling, *An ABC Manager's Primer*, Consortium for Advanced Manufacturing International/Cost Management Systems, Institute of Management Accountants, 1993.

that system for its intended purpose. This information should not be used to micromanage the supply chain employees. In other words, the sudden availability of quality cost information should not tempt management to circumvent the behavior that was instilled through the responsibility-charting effort! Access to quality cost information should reinforce the enterprise's culture and value base by helping the employees at the lowest levels to be more productive.

Conclusion

Creating positive results by transforming the supply chain must be complemented by the ability to measure those results! This ability doesn't just happen. It must be built by proceeding from the definition of the process through the definition of the requirements to the selection, implementation, and integration of the systems. Results matter, but those results must be measured and reported in a way that enables the transformation team to use them effectively.

Chapter 9

Supply Chain Alternatives

Imagine for a moment that you are driving your car along an interstate and are about to enter an automobile assembly complex. You drive through the entrance gate, park your car in the visitors parking area, and board the waiting tour bus. Your tour guide, a seasoned professional, is prepared to discuss the movement of material into the assembly plant and the supply chain strategy for dealing with suppliers.

As you look out the window of the tour bus, you notice a steel mill and a glass factory within sight of the assembly plant. The tour guide informs the visitors that all parts and subsystems are furnished by suppliers that are located within a twenty-mile radius of the plant and deliver these parts and subsystems to the automotive assembly line on a just-in-time basis. Everything seems to come together as an automotive assembly operation should function in the mid- to late 1990s.

When the tour bus stops, you look out the window and notice that the automobiles the plant is assembling are not late 1990s cars but Model Ts! You glance at the newspaper on the seat next to you and discover that it's dated 1931! The bus has taken you back in time, and you've just toured Ford Motor Company's River Rouge Plant in Detroit, Michigan.

Henry Ford had a vision in the late 1910s and early 1920s: He sought to achieve a fully integrated automotive organization, with complete supply chain integration and control of materials and parts for his assembly operations. Between 1927 and 1931, the River Rouge Plant complex was completed, and Ford realized his vision.

The River Rouge Plant had its own steel mill and glass plant. Henry Ford owned his own parts companies, most of which were located either on-site or in close proximity to the plant in communities like Highland Park. He even owned the railroad that served the River Rouge Plant—the Detroit, Toledo, and Ironton Railroad.[1]

Executives frequently ask me which companies have achieved a fully integrated supply chain that delivers almost all parts and subsystems to an assembly plant on a just-in-time basis. Although there are several modern examples I can cite, I always include Henry Ford's River Rouge Plant as well. He also did it with a distinct competitive advantage. In 1931, Ford had perfected mass-production techniques before his suppliers did. Thus, by being totally vertically integrated, he could achieve a significant cost advantage by doing everything in-house.

Recently, I asked a couple of university professors who are recognized "gurus" for the automotive industry whether they believed that Henry Ford would be successful in the mid- to late 1990s. Their answers were very lengthy (remember the lectures your college professors sometimes gave?) and surprising. I have incorporated their observations here along with my own. As you read this chapter, see whether *you* think Henry Ford's operation would thrive in today's business environment.

At this point in the customer-centered supply chain management change process, we have completed the getting-started, foundation, quality, transformation design, innovation, as-is, bridge, and performance results process methodologies. It is now time to review the enterprise's core competencies and examine the option of outsourcing and supply chain alternatives (Exhibit 9-1).

The subject of core competencies was introduced in Chapter 2 and reviewed in the transformation design process methodology (Chapter 4). This preliminary review should have identified what stakeholders *perceive* as the core competencies of their enterprise. The work that has been done thus far with the customer-centered supply chain management change process, together with the process methodology presented later in this chapter, will enable the executive to review the enterprise's supply chain management activities in depth and identify its *real* core competencies.

Once the enterprise's core competencies are clearly identified and agreed upon by executives and stakeholders, a powerful next step awaits the transformation team: The team must analyze the gap between the enterprise's actual core competencies and the core competencies (and associated necessary value-added activities) needed in

---

1. John Bell Rae, *The American Automobile Industry* (Boston: G. K. Hall & Company, 1984), p. 39. James P. Womack, *The Machine That Changed the World* (New York: Macmillan, 1990), pp. 38–39.

Exhibit 9-1. The customer-centered supply chain management change process.

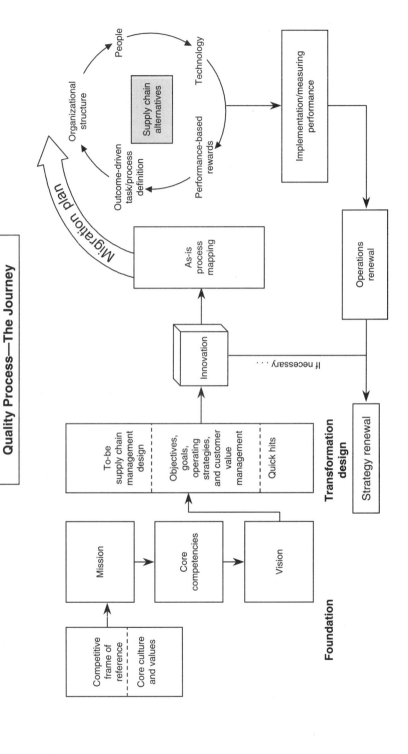

the marketplace. I have structured this chapter and its process methodology to help executives analyze this gap and explore the available alternatives for closing any gaps that are identified.

In this chapter, I discuss core competencies in greater detail, provide an overview of the global automotive assembly industry, discuss third-party logistics within the supply chain, and present company examples of supply chain outsourcing within the automotive industry. In addition, I have designed a two-phase process that supply chain executives can follow to determine whether outsourcing is right for their enterprise and, if so, select the most qualified third-party supply chain provider.

Core Competencies

Core competencies are the individual and collective learnings of an organization. These learnings tend to focus on production skills, logistics skills, and the integration of multiple sources of technology. Core competencies also focus on the organization of work and the delivery of value.[2]

The journey to supply chain management and world-class performance has companies relying on core competencies for leadership. As I stated before, Honda's core competency is in engines and power trains, which gives Honda a competitive advantage in automobiles, motorcycles, and small-engine equipment. The Home Depot, the largest U.S. home center retailer, relies on its customer service core competency to guide do-it-yourself customers through their home improvement projects. This core competency allows The Home Depot to sell a wide assortment of products. Its critical mass gives the company the scale to leverage its purchasing power and offer its products at everyday low prices.[3] The core competency of United Parcel Service (UPS) is fast, efficient service, which allows UPS to provide both surface transportation and air freight services.

Test for Core Competencies

Here are three criteria for determining whether an enterprise's competencies qualify as core competencies. Core competencies must:

2. C. K. Prahalad and Gary Hamel, ''The Core Competencies of the Corporation,'' *Harvard Business Review*, May–June 1990, p. 82.
3. ''The Home Depot 1991 Annual Report,'' The Home Depot, 1992, p. i.

1. Provide access to a wide variety of markets
2. Make a significant contribution to the perceived customer benefits of the end product
3. Be difficult for competitors to imitate[4]

The competencies of Honda, UPS, and The Home Depot pass the test in all three areas.

General Motors, Allison Gas Turbine Division (Allison), and EDS

The old Automotive Components Group Worldwide, a division of General Motors (now called Delphi), sold its Allison Gas Turbine Division to the division's managers, employees, and the Wall Street firm of Clayton, Dubilier & Rice in February 1994. The new firm, called Allison Engine Company, now focuses on its core competency—making engines for helicopters, military aircraft, and aerospace markets.[5] In 1996, GM spun off EDS and sold the defense business of Hughes Electronics to focus on its core competency—the manufacture and assembly of automobiles.

If we look at the test for core competencies, we can see the driving need for General Motors to divest itself of these businesses. Let's consider the case of Allison Gas Turbine Division. The first item on the core competency test, providing access to a wide variety of markets, applied to Allison.

The second item on the core competency test, making a significant contribution to the perceived customer benefits of the end product, did not apply. The perceived customer benefits of Allison's engines were defined by General Motors, helicopter and aircraft manufacturers, and their ultimate customers, the buyers of helicopters and military aircraft. Although GM had hoped to enhance its collective learnings about engine manufacture through its ownership of Allison, the acquisition made no significant contribution to GM's automobile business. In fact, the reverse happened: Allison was a significant money loser, in part because of the high automotive wage structure it used. In addition, the losses at Allison forced GM to funnel capital into Allison at a time when its own core business, automobile assembly, was desperately in need of cash.

The third item on the core competency test, being difficult for competitors to imitate, applied only in part. Insiders agree that Allison

4. Prahalad and Hamel, "Core Competencies of the Corporation," pp. 83–84.
5. "GM Sells Allison Back to Management for $310 Million," *Aerospace Propulsion* 4, no. 25 (December 9, 1993): 3.

does make an excellent aircraft engine. However, its high cost structure made it vulnerable to lower-cost competitors.

Current trends in the automotive industry allow little room for companies to make investments that divert resources and executive time away from their core competencies. Let's take a brief look at the automotive industry, its trends, and the application of third-party outsourcing within the supply chain.

Overview of the Global Automotive Industry

There are thousands of statistics that measure the automotive industry. However, one glaring statistic hangs over the industry like a dark cloud: Industry experts conservatively believe that worldwide capacity will grow to almost 80 million vehicles per year by the year 2000. Worldwide production was approximately 48.4 million vehicles in 1996. Stated another way, the industry will have the capacity to produce almost two vehicles for every one vehicle of demand by the year 2000 if demand does not increase above 1996 levels![6]

What all this means is that, overall, supply exceeds demand, productivity of the best-in-class companies is accelerating, and quality standards are getting higher and higher. In essence, automobile assemblers must produce high-quality, low-cost automobiles and get them to market quickly in order to compete in a highly competitive industry.

Industry experts estimate that roughly two-thirds of the total landed cost of an automobile is sunk by the time the parts and subsystems are delivered to the automotive assembly plants. The "upstream" activities of procurement, inbound transportation, warehousing, subassembly of parts into subsystems, and just-in-time delivery to the automotive assembly line combine with health care to produce the vast majority of the two-thirds sunk costs. Many of these supply chain activities are "logistics" activities.

Automotive Industry Core Competencies and Logistics

Automotive assembly companies are increasingly focusing on their core competencies—assembling automobiles. Although "order-to-assemble" activities, or upstream logistics activities, are necessary for the whole automotive assembly supply chain, these activities do not

6. Standard & Poors, "Autos and Auto Parts," Industry Surveys, *Monthly Investment Review,* Vol. 165, No. 37, Sec. 3 (September 1997), pp. 8–9.

represent core competencies for *automotive assembly* companies. Automobile assembly companies are therefore increasingly turning to third-party logistics providers and outsourcing their order-to-assemble activities.

Third-Party Logistics

Every day, all manufacturing executives, including those in the automotive industry, face the challenge of offering the breadth and depth of supply chain services to their organizations. As companies strive for global leadership in their respective industries through supply chain management, there is intense pressure to create a core competency in logistics. Logistics executives are increasingly challenged to develop this core competency quickly or look to third-party providers to fill the void.

Third-party logistics has received an incredible amount of press coverage in trade journals and magazines in the past few years. Transport carriers, freight forwarders, public warehousing companies, wholesaler distributors, and even manufacturers have ventured into the third-party logistics business. The marketplace seems crowded with third-party logistics providers.

There are dynamics within supply chain management that are creating the perceived need for companies to enter the third-party logistics business. Globalism is changing the tonnage patterns of the existing freight movements. Innovations like the global use of E-mail for advance customs clearance and the use of double-stacked containers are changing the balance of tonnage within modes of transport. Thus, with all the marketplace changes and innovations, several existing players within the logistics value chains recognize a need to expand their base of business to survive.

In conversations with several executives of third-party logistics companies, it is interesting to note that *third-party logistics* is defined differently within each company. Before you attempt to outsource to a third party, it is critical to understand what third-party logistics is.

The concept of outsourcing in the supply chain is really not new. When a logistics professional calls a transport carrier to transport goods, this activity represents a form of outsourcing. Another example of outsourcing is the use of third-party payment services like Cass Bank in Saint Louis to process freight payables.

The thought of outsourcing other logistics activities, like warehousing and procurement, may produce anxiety and fear of loss of control in many executives. These feelings are normal. If an enterprise is thinking of outsourcing its logistics operations, it is critical to approach the decision to outsource in an objective, strategic manner.

When an enterprise is considering the use of third-party logistics providers (or other supply chain outsourcing of activities), two major phases are involved: determining the advisability of outsourcing and (if the enterprise decides to proceed with outsourcing) actually selecting the most qualified third-party provider.

Determining the Advisability of Outsourcing: The Outsourcing Strategic Decision Process

To help you focus objectively and strategically, I have developed the outsourcing strategic decision process, which has five components:

1. Reviewing the competitive frame of reference and core culture and values (determined in the foundation process methodology, presented in Chapter 2)
2. Reviewing the mission and vision (also determined in the foundation process methodology), as well as the core competencies
3. Reviewing the objectives, goals, and operating strategies (determined in the transformation design process methodology, presented in Chapter 4)
4. Performing a current assessment of internal capabilities
5. Analyzing the strategic options

If this process is followed properly, it will result in a sound decision on whether a company should consider outsourcing. As you can see, the foundation and transformation design process methodologies of the customer-centered supply chain management change process anchor the outsourcing strategic decision process.

Reviewing the Competitive Frame of Reference and Core Culture and Values

The competitive frame of reference and core culture and values, introduced in Chapter 2, must be revisited during the outsourcing strategic decision process. It is critical for third parties providing outsourcing services to become business partners, not vendors. To accomplish this, the outsourcing partner must buy into the customer's needs and calibrate its service offerings to those needs. However, third parties cannot accomplish this until their customer solidifies its own needs around its competitive frame of reference and core culture and values.

In other words, the more the company spells out and defines in terms of strategic direction, the less room there is for guesswork. The result should be a greater chance for a successful partnership.

Reviewing the Mission, Vision, and Core Competencies

As indicated in Chapter 2, the mission statement should answer the question "Why does your enterprise exist?" It should also support the core culture and values. The core competencies discussed in the first section of this chapter should serve as the cornerstone for building the corporation's vision. The vision statement should tie in to the corporation's strengths, weaknesses, opportunities, threats, and leadership. This vision statement should also serve as a bridge between the competitive frame of reference and core culture and values and the corporation's objectives, goals, and strategies.

This linkage is important for third-party providers. These providers will spend most of their time within the objectives, goals, and operating strategy areas. However, the success of the third-party providers must be measured in terms of the business success of the enterprise that they support. In order for this linkage to occur, their objectives, goals, and operating strategies must be connected to the business strategy of their enterprise client. Without this linkage, the old story of the woodcutter in the forest may apply: Although the woodcutter may be making progress clearing a path in the dense forest, the woodcutter may be laboring in the wrong forest!

Reviewing the Objectives, Goals, and Operating Strategies

The objectives are generally broad statements of what the organization is trying to achieve. The goals are quantifiable measures that must be met to achieve the objectives. These measures should include time and metrics. Operating strategies are statements of how the company will achieve its goals and objectives.

If the company is following the customer-centered supply chain management change process, it should already have defined its objectives, goals, and operating strategies. If any appreciable time has elapsed between when they were defined and when the outsourcing decision is being made, a review of the objectives, goals, and operating strategies may be advisable.

Executives must be consistent if they are to empower third-party outsourcing providers to be true partners. If the third-party outsourcing provider is to be measured on the success of the enterprise's business performance, it must share the same strategic plan and supply chain design as the enterprise. True third-party partnerships appear seamless to the participants in an extended enterprise supply chain.

Performing a Current Assessment of Internal Capabilities

Once the competitive frame of reference and core culture and values; mission, vision, and core competencies; and objectives, goals, and operating strategies have all been identified and reviewed, it is time to look within and assess the enterprise's capabilities. This assessment can be performed by answering the following focused questions:

- Does your enterprise have the people to support its vision? Do these people have the logistics skill sets needed to meet the expected performance standards?
- Is logistics a core competency of your enterprise?
- Is it essential that logistics become a core competency in order for your enterprise to become a world-class performer?
- Most important, can the logistics professionals adapt to change quickly and lead, not inhibit, the enterprise?

Many of the answers to these and other questions will surface throughout the process. These answers will provide the basis for analyzing the strategic options available to the enterprise.

Analyzing the Strategic Options

At this point in the process, an enterprise has three basic strategic options:

1. Doing nothing/insourcing
2. Partial outsourcing
3. Total outsourcing

Each option has merit, depending on the enterprise and the strength of its logistics capabilities. Let's review each one.

Doing Nothing/Insourcing   If, during the current assessment stage, an enterprise's logistics function is determined to be strong and flexible, then there is virtually no operational need to outsource. Wal-Mart continues to insource its logistics activities and is recognized for its logistics excellence.

Outsourcing is not for all enterprises. Even if the decision is to insource, this whole review process is valuable to enable continuous improvement and alignment within the enterprise.

Partial Outsourcing   In some instances, it may be advantageous to outsource some of an enterprise's logistics activities. GATX Logistics' Bloomington, Illinois, operations provide third-party services for a few of J. I. Case's operations. Ford Motor Company has outsourced its inbound logistics activities to its engine plants to Roadway Logistics Services. These are two examples of partial outsourcing, in which certain logistics processes and/or operations are outsourced while others remain insourced.

Total Outsourcing   For selected enterprises, total logistics outsourcing may be the best alternative. The gap between the current assessment of the enterprise's internal capabilities and its balanced business strategy might be so large that logistics will clearly inhibit the enterprise's progress. The rate of change within the enterprise's industry might be so rapid that it could be beneficial to let a third party keep up with it all. There are also numerous financial ploys involving assets and the use of cash. The list of reasons for total outsourcing is extensive.

Every outsourcing situation is unique. If you are considering outsourcing, there should be a selection process to ensure a customized solution for your enterprise.

The outsourcing strategic decision process is valuable as a way to assess the advisability of outsourcing the enterprise's logistics activities. Alignment with the customer-centered supply chain management change process is critical to the development of value in logistics activities.

If, as a result of the decision process, the enterprise concludes that outsourcing is advisable, it should proceed with the selection process.

Selecting a Third-Party Logistics Provider

Once the outsourcing strategic decision process has confirmed the advisability of outsourcing, the enterprise must select the right third-party logistics provider. The process for doing so consists of:

1. Identifying the core competencies needed
2. Establishing a short list of qualified companies
3. Conducting "virtual-company" team evaluations
4. Selecting the most qualified company
5. Developing and implementing the transition plan

Identifying the Core Competencies Needed

The balanced business strategy and leadership/business direction steps of the outsourcing strategic decision process should have surfaced the breadth and depth of logistics activities needed to support the enterprise's vision. The current assessment step should have surfaced the enterprise's existing logistics core competencies.

Overlaying the enterprise's existing logistics core competencies on the breadth and depth of logistics activities needed to support the vision will reveal core competency "gaps" or "voids." The logistics activities within these gaps or voids are the logistics core competencies *needed* by the enterprise.

Establishing a Short List of Qualified Companies

The needed competencies that have just been identified become the criteria for selecting qualified third-party logistics providers. For example, Company A may have an excellent purchasing and procurement department. It may also have an inflexible and costly warehousing infrastructure. This company should focus its third-party selection criteria on core competencies in warehousing while preserving its own core competency in purchasing and procurement.

The list of third-party logistics companies is extensive for such a young and emerging industry. The top ten companies as of February 1997 are shown in Exhibit 9-2.

Exhibit 9-2. Top ten third-party logistics providers.

Company	Net Revenue ($000,000)	Employees
Ryder	867	7,000
Penske	560	10,000
Circle	468	3,025
Fritz	356	7,000
Schneider	340	4,200
Exel	321	6,000
Caliber	275	2,700
GATX	250	3,500
CTI	205	2,400
Expeditors	202	2,800

Source: "Who's Who in Logistics?" *Armstrong's Guide to Third-Party Logistics Providers and Dedicated Contract Carriers, 3rd. ed.* (Stoughton, Wisc.: Transportation Education Specialists, A Division of Armstrong & Associates, Inc., February 1997). pp. 10, 11.

Conducting "Virtual-Company" Team Evaluations

The traditional method of soliciting bids from third-party logistics providers is to work up a detailed request for proposal (RFP), then distribute the RFPs to the short list of qualified companies. Although this approach is effective in forcing the responses to follow a standard format (thereby allowing apples-to-apples comparisons), I feel it misses the mark.

Forcing a short list of qualified providers to respond to an RFP in a standardized format all but eliminates the providers' ability to showcase creativity and uniqueness—qualities that may provide added value to the outsourcing solution beyond the detailed request for proposal. This added value could be the marketplace differentiation that distinguishes the enterprise from its competition.

I recommend a "virtual-company" team evaluation. Members of key enterprise functions are selected to be on the evaluation team. A real, live business case is presented to the team, or virtual company, for review and recommendations. Each third-party logistics provider on the short list is invited into the virtual company and asked to provide the logistics support in the areas of core competency "voids."

The third-party logistics providers are then measured on the following:

- Creativity, uniqueness, and value-added of solutions
- Teamwork with logistics professionals
- Synergy with other, insourced enterprise functions
- Ability to be customer-focused and market-driven
- Ability to map technology to business solutions

A key success factor in any strategic alliance is the ability of two companies to join forces and behave organizationally as one company. To accomplish this, it is critical for each company to have professionals with the necessary interpersonal skills to motivate and influence others without direct control. The core cultures and values of the two companies should allow this interaction to occur. However, it is up to the individual professionals to demonstrate these skills.

Selecting the Most Qualified Company

The virtual-company team evaluations provide a way to see how each third-party logistics provider's professionals interact with the enterprise's professionals. The synergy that potentially develops between the involved parties should be considered as important as their ability to provide the technical expertise.

Because typical third-party logistics outsourcing contracts range from three to ten years, the third-party logistics provider must be viewed as an extension of the enterprise and a part of the company. A lot is riding on the performance of the two companies. The enterprise simply doesn't have enough time or resources to sort out personality conflicts and style differences continually and still expect to achieve world-class performance. The time to avoid such problems is before the contract is signed and the alliance solidified.

Of course, once the most qualified company has been selected, there is the need to work up a contract with that company, which should specify the services to be provided, the cost of the services, and the expected outcomes of the strategic alliance. In some cases, shared benefits and/or guaranteed cost performances are incentives for ensuring win-win relationships.

The main question to answer before signing a contract with the most qualified third-party logistics provider is, "Can my company expect to be substantially better off doing business with this company than without this company?" If the answer is yes, then proceed with the strategic alliance.

Developing and Implementing the Transition Plan

A critical part of the contract is the development of a transition plan, which must cover the transition of activities and people as they relate to the blending of logistics core competencies. Such issues as salaries, benefits, pensions, and reporting relationships must be negotiated, established, and communicated to all parties before the transition date.

The actual implementation of the transition plan should go smoothly if all issues have been addressed on a timely basis and all details have been communicated. Communication is the key!

We must not forget the customer in our communications. In fact, it is advisable to have one or two key customer representatives participate in the virtual-company team evaluations. This would not only assist the transition process but also allow for ownership and support of the strategic alliance by the key customers.

Examples of Successful Third-Party Logistics Operations

In this subsection, I'll highlight just two of the many examples of successful third-party logistics operations: the GATX Logistics operation in Bloomington, Illinois, for the Diamond-Star (Mitsubishi/Chrysler) assembly plant and the Customized Transportation, Inc., operation in Memphis, Tennessee, for General Motors Corporation. The main reasons why I selected these two examples are observations from key involved professionals.

Jim McHugh, operations and scheduling manager for GATX Logistics, commented to me in November 1992 that when GATX Logistics Distribution interfaces with Diamond-Star suppliers, it is perceived as part of Diamond-Star. He also observed that his group in fact operates as if it were part of Diamond-Star, focusing on total customer satisfaction.

Michael MacDonald, formerly the director of transportation economics and planning for General Motors, presented the Customized Transportation, Inc., example at the 1992 Council of Logistics Management (CLM) Conference in San Antonio, Texas. He commented that the GM professionals regard the Customized Transportation professionals as an extension of their company.

These two sets of comments focus on the power of two companies' joining forces with complementary core competencies and organizationally behaving as one entity. The following examples illustrate how virtual companies can become a reality in successful third-party logistics operations and further the customer's view of a supply chain as one extended company.

GATX Logistics/Diamond-Star Motors

Mitsubishi Motors and Chrysler Corporation formed Diamond-Star Motors with the opening of their Bloomington, Illinois, plant in 1988. Several companies that had been suppliers to Mitsubishi and Chrysler were established as suppliers to Diamond-Star Motors. For the lower-value-added parts and services, either the suppliers relocated their facilities to Bloomington or the products and services were outsourced.

GATX Logistics successfully bid on the outsourcing proposal for just-in-time delivery of parts and subsystems to the Bloomington assembly plant.[7] GATX operates a closed-loop transportation system to pick up at supplier locations. *Closed-loop* essentially means dedicated contract carriage that picks up parts and subsystems from suppliers, delivers them to the assembly plant, and returns to suppliers to deliver returnable containers and make more pickups.

The Diamond-Star assembly plant notifies suppliers of its assembly schedule ten weeks out. The schedule is solidified one week out, with supplier pickups routed and sequenced by Mitsubishi and GATX to match up with the assembly schedule. The sequencing is so tight that GATX must plan for deliveries every two hours, which translates into multiple pickups per day at most supplier locations.

---

7. "Facility Profile: GATX Contract Carriers and Diamond-Star," GATX Logistics, December 14, 1992.

The focus is on eliminating inventories at the assembly line *and* in the pipeline. The purpose of the ten-week advance assembly schedule is to allow suppliers to balance their own production scheduling and meet the scheduling demands of Diamond-Star.

Diamond-Star compensates GATX Logistics on a per-mile basis. Perfect order-fill rates by suppliers supersede all other productivity measures, including full truckloads. The keys to GATX's operations are twofold: (1) securing information through the use of scanners that capture supplier shipments as they are loaded on GATX's trailers and (2) locking in the assembly schedule one week out to solidify the just-in-time process.

Customized Transportation, Inc./General Motors

General Motors has multiple assembly plants across North America, with a high concentration in the upper Midwest. Its supplier base is more dispersed than Diamond-Star's, with many suppliers located in the Southwest. The net result is a longer length of haul and greater complexity than the one-plant Diamond-Star operation. Customized Transportation, Inc., uses its single-focused approach to dedicate resources to a solution for General Motors. It uses its flow-through warehousing scenario to simplify complexity, minimize costs, and ensure just-in-time service.

It is important with most automotive assemblers to minimize the inventory levels at the plants and in the pipeline. The sequencing of parts and subsystems to the assembly line is critical. However, due to the length of haul from the Southwest to the upper Midwest, it is important to ensure full truckloads.

Customized Transportation established a regional distribution center (RDC) in Memphis, Tennessee. Utilizing a systems link to General Motors and its suppliers, the multiple assembly-line requirements from the multiple suppliers are secured, batched, and sorted for pickup. These supplier parts and subsystems are brought to the Memphis RDC, cross-docked, sequenced in assembly-line order, and re-shipped to the appropriate General Motors assembly plant.[8] The sequencing timetable for the cross-dock operation is very tight. The average time for the cross-docking of the suppliers' parts and subsystems is estimated to be two to three hours. The net result is full truckloads from suppliers to the Memphis RDC and just-in-time deliveries to the GM assembly plants.

Customized Transportation also operates a closed-loop transpor-

8. "Supporting Synchronous Manufacturing for General Motors Corporation," Customized Transportation, Inc., and General Motors Corporation, October 1992.

tation system that includes scheduled pickup times at suppliers and daily container returns. Approximately 90 percent of supplier pickup locations are included in the closed-loop system. For the remaining 10 percent, alternate carriers make the pickups, with scheduled delivery times at the Memphis RDC, and container returns are infrequent. These pickups tend to involve a much longer length of haul than the closed-loop supplier locations and a lower density in their supplier base.

General Motors compensates Customized Transportation on a cost-per-hundredweight basis, which provides GM with just-in-time service at a guaranteed price. It also gives Customized Transportation an incentive to search for cost-saving methods in its operations.

The keys to Customized Transportation's operations are also twofold: (1) the use of bar-code scanners at the suppliers' locations to capture supplier shipments and feed its routing system at the Memphis RDC and (2) the fast execution at the cross-docking operation in Memphis.

The journey to world-class quality in supply chain management relies on core competencies. Logistics executives must provide leadership within their organizations to promote, not inhibit, this journey.

Assessing supply chain alternatives involves two processes: determining whether to use third-party logistics providers (the outsourcing strategic decision process) and—if the company decides to proceed with outsourcing—selecting the most qualified third party. By utilizing the right approach, the executive can achieve core competencies in logistics regardless of whether the activities in question are performed in-house or outsourced. This will enable the company to obtain the mix of infrastructure, resources, and talent needed for effective supply chain management.

The following process methodology provides the executive with a step-by-step process to identify the enterprise's true core competencies, pinpoint its *needed* core competencies, determine the advisability of outsourcing (through the outsourcing strategic decision process), and if appropriate, select the most qualified third-party partner.

Process Methodology
Core Competencies—Supply
Chain Alternatives

There comes a time when the transformation team and the enterprise's executives must answer the question, "Can the enterprise change as extensively and quickly as needed to achieve the goals and objectives of the transformation effort?" Almost all the information needed to answer this question has already been developed and should be obtained from the work that was performed during previous process methodologies. This process methodology has been designed to provide to the transformation team the missing information required to answer this question. The approach used in this process methodology is to help the transformation team determine the enterprise's core competencies, then review its strategic options and select a third-party provider if appropriate.

This process, which is illustrated in the accompanying flowchart, has three major components: performing a core competency assessment, determining the advisability of outsourcing (the outsourcing strategic decision process), and selecting a third-party logistics provider.

I.1: Perform a Core Competency Assessment

I.1.a: Internally Identify the Enterprise's Core Competencies

The transformation team needs to obtain the outputs from the previous process methodologies and the work papers from foundation process methodology step B.4 (Chapter 2), which concentrated on core

THE SUPPLY CHAIN MANAGEMENT CHANGE PROCESS
Process Methodology
Core Competencies—Phase 1

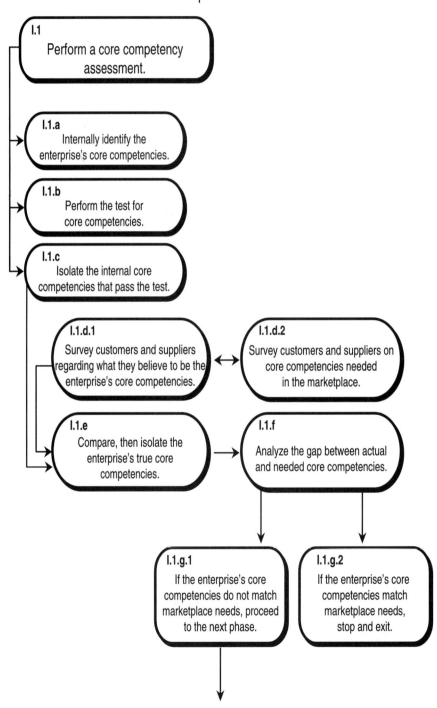

THE SUPPLY CHAIN MANAGEMENT CHANGE PROCESS
Process Methodology
Core Competencies—Phase 2

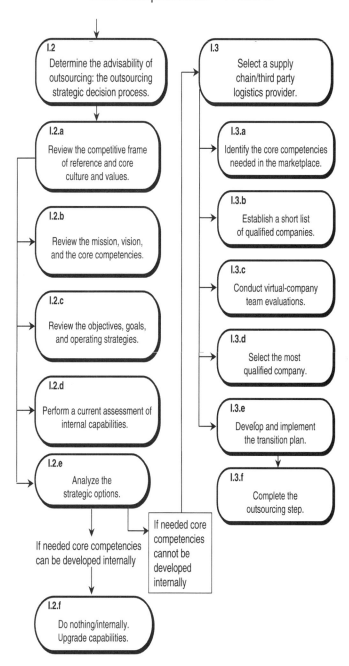

competencies at a high level. They will provide a good foundation for proceeding with the present process step.

The team should prepare a list of the key influencers within the enterprise, including no more than twenty-four names. The list should be broken into two groups of twelve or, if time permits, four groups of six.

Each group should meet for one to two hours to address the task of identifying the enterprise's core competencies. Each group should be given only the standard definition of a *core competency* (presented in the first half of this chapter) and a review of the basic rules of professional meeting behavior (everyone is equal, only one person speaks at a time, and so forth).

The output of each group's meeting should be documented for use in step I.1.b. Care should be taken to ensure that the groups do *not* have access to each other's output.

I.1.b: Perform the Test for Core Competencies

The output from the group meetings in step I.1.a should be screened by the combined transformation team and the groups involved using the test for core competencies presented in the first half of this chapter. To repeat, in order to qualify as a core competency, a perceived core competency must satisfy three criteria. It must:

1. Provide access to a wide variety of markets
2. Make a significant contribution to the perceived customer benefits of the end product
3. Be difficult for competitors to imitate

The transformation team must take each perceived core competency identified in step I.1.a and collectively decide whether it satisfies all three criteria for being a core competency. The result should be a "pass" or "fail" rating for each perceived core competency.

I.1.c: Isolate the Internal Core Competencies That Pass the Test

The results from step I.1.b must be separated into two groups:

1. The core competencies that passed the test in step I.1.b, each of which should be identified, along with a description of the rationale for determining that it was a core competency

2. The perceived core competencies identified in step I.1.a that did not pass the test in step I.1.b, each of which should be identified, along with a description of the rationale for determining that it was not a core competency

These two groups should be documented, and a presentation should be prepared for each group. These presentations should not be published at this point, however. Instead, they should be held for use in step I.1.e.

Executives can learn a lot by analyzing the group of perceived core competencies identified by the enterprise's top twenty-four influencers and the transformation team that did not pass the core competency test. Alignment, or the lack thereof, among the enterprise's key influencers can have a dramatic impact on the enterprise's employees. One can imagine what employees think the enterprise's core competencies are if there is a lack of alignment among the key influencers! Future executive effort should focus on achieving alignment and only examine root causes if time permits.

I.1.d.1: Survey Customers and Suppliers Regarding What They Believe to Be the Enterprise's Core Competencies

The transformation team should assemble a team of two to four people to survey customers and suppliers to determine their beliefs regarding the enterprise's core competencies. These two to four people should act *independently* of the influencers in step I.1.a and the reviewers in steps I.1.b and I.1.c. These people should also have the credibility to conduct objective interviews with customers and suppliers. *Above all, do not select either sales representatives or employees who have driving, directive personalities! This task must be performed by people who are "askers," not "tellers"!*

The executive sponsor should consider hiring an outside company to support the transformation team in conducting these interviews if a suitable team of two to four employees cannot be assembled. Remember, it is the objectivity of the enterprise's key supply chain partners that is important.

The list of the enterprise's core competencies as perceived by each customer and supplier should be documented and consolidated. For this step, the customers and suppliers must remain anonymous. If their confidentiality is protected, they will be willing to provide more objective feedback to the interview team. Also, there must be protection against reprisals if anyone within the enterprise regards the information as negative.

I.1.d.2: Survey Customers and Suppliers on Core Competencies Needed in the Marketplace

The team that conducts the interviews in step I.1.d.1 should concurrently ask the customers and suppliers a second set of questions, focusing on the core competencies *needed* in the marketplace.

The results of these interviews should be documented and combined, just as in the previous step, but they should be kept separate from the other results. For this step, however, the names of customers and suppliers should be included unless they object. It is critical for the enterprise's executives and employees to know what core competencies are in demand among their key supply chain partners!

I.1.e: Compare, Then Isolate the Enterprise's True Core Competencies

For this step, the transformation team must first assemble the output from steps I.1.c, I.1.d.1, and I.1.d.2. The team should now have the list of the enterprise's core competencies that was developed internally; the list of the enterprise's core competencies that was developed externally, based on information from supply chain partners; and a list of the core competencies needed in the marketplace.

The team must then merge the internally and externally developed lists of core competencies. The core competencies that match, or appear on both lists, should be placed in a group titled "True Core Competencies." The core competencies that do not match should be placed in a second group.

The team should take the second group, the nonmatching core competencies, and perform a second but abbreviated test for core competencies, the results of which will reveal the following: The enterprise may have true core competencies that are recognized internally but are not recognized by its supply chain partners, and the supply chain partners may recognize core competencies in the enterprise that were not recognized internally.

If the enterprise has true core competencies that are not readily recognized by its supply chain partners, they must be added to the "matched" list. The transformation team may also recommend that a communication or advertising campaign be developed to increase the supply chain partners' awareness of these core competencies. I say "may" because there could be a competitive advantage to allowing these core competencies to remain unrecognized.

The true core competencies recognized by the supply chain partners but overlooked internally must also be added to the matched list. The list of internally identified perceived core competencies that turned out not to be true core competencies should be set aside, together with the description of the rationale for having determined that each one was not a core competency.

The presentations that were first developed in step I.1.c must now be updated to tell the story of the entire core competency assessment process and be presented to the enterprise's employees.

I.1.f: Analyze the Gap Between Actual and Needed Core Competencies

The process of identifying the enterprise's true core competencies is very important for the whole customer-centered supply chain management change process. However, it is only the first step of an analysis that has even greater importance. The transformation team must take the enterprise's true core competencies, summarized in step I.1.e, and compare them to the core competencies *needed* in the marketplace, identified by customers and suppliers in step I.1.d.2. *The resulting gap between actual and needed core competencies represents the gap between the enterprise's current state and marketplace leadership—and perhaps marketplace dominance.*

For each supply chain work group in the enterprise, the transformation team must evaluate the group's progress, its potential for reaching the transformation goals, and the time frame the group needs to achieve these goals. The team must then analyze each work group in terms of the probability of its reaching the transformation goals within the time frame set by the executive team. This analysis must include work groups directly involved in areas of needed core competencies. (This analysis should also include areas that are not core competencies. However, the core competencies produce marketplace competitive advantages, whereas the other areas usually represent cost-control or tactical efficiency activities.)

I.1.g.1: If the Enterprise's Core Competencies Do Not Match Marketplace Needs, Proceed to the Next Phase

If the core competencies of the enterprise do *not* match the core competencies needed in the marketplace, then the transformation team should proceed to step I.2.

I.1.g.2: If the Enterprise's Core Competencies Match Marketplace Needs, Stop and Exit

If the core competencies of the enterprise *do* match the core competencies needed in the marketplace, then the transformation team should exit this process methodology. Very few companies are in this category, and almost without exception, they are the current marketplace leaders. If your enterprise is in this category, congratulations (for today).

I.2: Determine the Advisability of Outsourcing: The Outsourcing Strategic Decision Process

The outsourcing strategic decision process is designed to help the transformation team and the executive sponsor decide how to close the gap between the enterprise's *real* core competencies and the core competencies *needed* in the marketplace. There are two basic ways to close the gap: by developing the needed core competencies internally or by outsourcing the activities surrounding the core competency gap to a third party. When performed properly, this process step will enable the transformation team and the enterprise to determine which approach to use.

I.2.a: Review the Competitive Frame of Reference and Core Culture and Values

Because varying amounts of time will have elapsed between the earlier process methodologies and the present one, this step and the next two steps involve reviews by the transformation team. The team must obtain the output from steps B.1.e (a statement of the competitive frame of reference) and B.2.e (a statement of the core culture and values) of the foundation process methodology (Chapter 2) and review and summarize this output for use in upcoming steps.

I.2.b: Review the Mission and Vision and the Core Competencies

The transformation team must continue its review by obtaining the output from foundation process methodology steps B.3 (the mission statement) and B.5 (the vision statement) and the core competencies that were identified in the first phase of the present process methodology. In this review, special emphasis should be placed on the vision statement, which provides the basis for the quality process and the expectations regarding the transformation process. It will also provide the basis for defining the performance and behavior that will be expected from potential third-party providers.

I.2.c: Review the Objectives, Goals, and Operating Strategies

The transformation team's review process deepens with a review of the objectives, goals, and operating strategies determined during the design process methodology (Chapter 4). This will help the team translate the vision statement into definable expectations for the potential third parties. If the objectives, goals, or operating strategies have been modified or updated as a result of the prototype or pilot test of the to-be process, then this review should include these updates as well.

Steps I.2.a, I.2.b, and I.2.c provide the transformation team with a "refresher" that will enable it to perform step I.2.d from a strategic alignment standpoint. All too often, transformation teams get caught up in the tactical details of implementation and fail to recognize the importance of thinking strategically when considering outsourcing. The success of outsourcing will be determined by the alignment of the third-party outsourcing firm with the overall vision, objectives, goals, and operating strategies of the enterprise. Without this alignment, the outsourcing firm and the enterprise will probably have what amounts to nothing more than a vendor relationship.

I.2.d: Perform a Current Assessment of Internal Capabilities

Using the preceding reviews, the transformation team must objectively assess the internal capabilities of each work group in the enterprise. The work to date, especially the work performed during the as-is process-mapping effort, will provide valuable insights into the capabilities of each work group. These internal capabilities must be measured against the needed core competencies demanded in the marketplace and the ability to achieve the results expected from the transformation process.

An effective way to assess the internal capabilities of a work group is to ask the work groups within the supply chain that interface with the work group in question. Another way is to ask the customers. The as-is process-mapping work, together with the feedback from the interfacing work groups and the customers, will provide the team with adequate information to perform the assessment.

The assessment should enable the team to determine two things: (1) the internal work groups' *ability* to develop the required core competencies internally and (2) the estimated *time frame* that they will need in order to do so.

The work groups' performance to date will also provide a clear indicator of their ability to develop the needed core competencies. The internal work groups either do or do not have the ability to achieve a quantum leap in performance in supply chain management.

With help from its executive sponsor, the transformation team must separate capabilities from leadership during this assessment. Often, work groups have untapped capabilities that are suppressed by a lack of leadership or bad leadership. The executive sponsor's guidance is critical for this part of the assessment because evaluating the leadership of the enterprise's work groups could be politically dangerous for team members, the team employees, and the whole customer-centered supply chain management change process.

I.2.e: Analyze the Strategic Options

If the specific work groups assessed lack the ability to develop the core competencies needed in the marketplace, the transformation team should proceed to step I.3. If the work groups have the ability to develop the needed core competencies, then the transformation team should assess the time frame that the work groups will require to accomplish this task. If the time frame is acceptable, then the transformation team should proceed to step I.2.f. If the time frame is not acceptable, then the transformation team should proceed to step I.3.

It is important for the transformation team's executive sponsor to lead team members to think with their heads and not with their hearts. This has always been tough for the true "people" executives. However, the enterprise's future success may depend on the rapid development of specific core competencies. If internal work groups cannot develop these competencies in the needed time frame, the transformation team must make a decision to consider third-party providers of these services as an alternative. Remember, the performance of the supply chain as a whole reflects the combined performance of all the individual supply chain components. The supply chain can only perform as well as its poorest-performing partner. Excellent performance throughout the redesigned supply chain is a must for tomorrow's world-class enterprise!

I.2.f: Do Nothing/Internally Upgrade Capabilities

If the enterprise has the capabilities to develop the needed core competencies internally within an acceptable time frame, then the transformation team should do nothing regarding outsourcing. If the enterprise has *latent* capabilities, then the team must proceed with the task of internally upgrading those capabilities. Training, benchmarking, and leadership changes may all play a part in the upgrading process.

I.3: Select a Supply Chain/Third-Party Logistics Provider

Seeking out a third party to supplement and/or replace an internal work group to develop the needed core competencies is a major decision. This third party must be selected as a supply chain *partner*, not a vendor. This series of steps is designed to help the transformation team select the right third-party partner. Several supply chain activities and work groups are interrelated with logistics. I will use the terms *supply chain logistics* and *third-party logistics* interchangeably since "third-party logistics" has become an industry subsegment of its own in the past few years.

I.3.a: Identify the Core Competencies Needed in the Marketplace

The third-party selection criteria must be based on the core competencies that are needed in the marketplace but not present within the enterprise. Thus, the output from step I.1.d.2 should be used to guide the transformation team in the direction needed to scope out the third-party selection criteria. Since third-party logistics contracts are multiyear, the selection decision has to be right.

I.3.b: Establish a Short List of Qualified Companies

There are many third-party logistics providers in the marketplace. (Exhibit 9-2 shows some examples.) Most of these companies advertise that they offer clients a complete menu of logistics services. The transformation team must do its homework to understand the real value each third-party provider can offer to the enterprise. For example, I know of one third-party logistics provider that advertises one of its business relationships as a showcase success story. However, in private conversations with this client's senior executive, the third-party logistics provider has been "under review" two or three times and will not have its current contract renewed when it expires. It seems that the third-party provider has not delivered the quality of services to which it committed during negotiations. A few telephone calls to key executives of the third-party providers' customers will reveal the true customer satisfaction in dealing with the suppliers.

The needed core competencies identified in step I.1.d.2 will dictate what type of third-party services the enterprise will seek. For example, the enterprise may need an overnight order-to-delivery capability from a regional warehouse to its customers. This enterprise may also need a bonded warehouse to handle under-bond import shipments. To acquire these two capabilities, the transformation team should consider an asset-based third-party logistics company that has a bonded warehouse infrastructure, preferably with a private delivery fleet.

To cite another example, the enterprise may need to outsource the distribution process entirely, from the manufacturing plant to the store shelf. To acquire this capability in a customized fashion, the transformation team should consider a non-asset-based third-party provider.

Asset-based third-party logistics providers are companies like GATX Logistics and Ryder Distribution Services. GATX Logistics primarily owns and leases warehouses and specializes in third-party warehousing activities. Ryder Distribution Services primarily owns and leases over-the-road tractors and trailers and is a subsidiary of Ryder Corporation. (Ryder is trying to refocus its corporate direction to third-party logistics and is attempting to redefine itself as a non–asset-based provider rather than an asset-based provider. From the standpoint of logistics revenues, Ryder is one of the largest third-party logistics providers.)

Non–asset-based third-party providers are companies that only own assets for specific customer contracts. Customized Transportation, Inc., discussed in the first half of this chapter, is an example of a non–asset-based third-party logistics provider.

The transformation team should obtain information on third-party logistics providers from a number of sources, including the Council of Logistics Management; university research centers that focus on logistics, like Penn State University and Ohio State University; consulting firms that employ known industry experts; and companies with excellent marketplace reputations, like Frito-Lay or Saturn.

The output of this step is a list of third-party providers that have the expertise to produce the core competencies that the enterprise needs in its supply chain.

I.3.c: Conduct "Virtual-Company" Team Evaluations

The transformation team must take the output from step I.3.b and evaluate every appropriate third-party logistics provider. As I mentioned in the first portion of the chapter, there are two ways to evaluate outsourcing candidates: by using the traditional request for proposal (RFP), which details the specific services required by the enterprise, or by conducting "virtual-company" team evaluations.

The traditional RFP approach is an effective way to obtain standardized proposals from outsourcing candidates, which usually enables the transformation team to analyze all candidates in an apples-to-apples manner. However, what the team and the enterprise gain from this standardization, they lose in creativity.

As I said earlier, each third-party logistics provider is different. My recommendation is to avoid the traditional RFP process and allow the creativity of each provider to surface through the uniqueness of its own proposal. It is a must, however, to establish some boundaries for these responses. To accomplish this, I recommend virtual-company team evaluations.

The transformation team should develop a real, live business case for each third-party candidate to solve. This business case should be developed with the help of the enterprise's work groups and their key "influencers." The third-party providers should have access to selected members of these work groups and the transformation team while they are developing their proposals. As they solve the live business case and collaborate with the enterprise's work groups, the third-party providers' performance will reveal not only their technical competence but also their ability to synergize with the enterprise. As I have stated a number of times, the key is to have supply chain partners join forces and behave organizationally as an extended or unified enterprise.

The third-party logistics providers should present their recommendations and approaches to the virtual-company review team, which should include selected members of the transformation team, the work groups and their key influencers, and even selected customers of the enterprise. This review team should evaluate the presentations on creativity in the value-added of solutions, teamwork and synergy with the enterprise work groups, customer focus, and technological competence in supporting business solutions. Evaluations should be completed after each presentation.

I.3.d: Select the Most Qualified Company

The transformation team should use a forced-ranking system in the team evaluations. The evaluation scorecard should include the measures identified in step I.3.c and any pertinent information from step I.3.b. With help from the executive sponsor, the transformation team must establish a weight for each criterion used. This scorecard measuring system must be established and communicated to all virtual-company team evaluators prior to any evaluations.

The transformation team now has two options. If a clear winner or top candidate has surfaced throughout the evaluations, then the team can proceed directly to the contracting stage with the selected third-party logistics provider. If two companies are very close, then each one should go through a final set of interviews, focusing on its organizational behavior skills that would support the core competencies needed by the enterprise and differentiate the company from its competitor.

Just before contracting with a third-party logistics provider, the transformation team and the executive sponsor must answer the following questions:

- Will my enterprise be better off with this third-party logistics provider than without it?
- Will the enterprise secure the needed core competencies with this third-party logistics provider?

Given the process that the transformation team has just gone through, these questions might seem redundant. However, if there is any doubt, stop the process! These outsourcing contracts range anywhere from one or two years up to ten years, so the enterprise is selecting a business partner for the long term! During the selection process, the enterprise must be confident that this provider will produce the core competencies it needs.

I.3.e: Develop and Implement the Transition Plan

As part of the third-party logistics contract, the transformation team must now develop a transition plan, which includes the activities of the outsourced work groups and their employees. The responsibility-charting exercise presented in Chapter 7 will be useful in developing this transition plan. Direct participation of the involved work groups and the work groups with which they interface is necessary to carry out the transition plan.

Responsibility for developing this plan often falls on the third-party logistics provider. In my opinion, however, this plan must be jointly developed. The more closely the enterprise works with the third-party provider in transitioning the activities and people, the more integrated the supply chain operations will become.

The employees of the outsourced work groups must be handled with extreme care. Prior to start-up, the salaries, benefits, pensions, and reporting relationships must all be defined, reviewed, and communicated, and buy-in must be secured from every employee.

There will probably be some employees who will not want to transition to the third-party logistics provider. Rather than forcing any transition, it is best to offer alternatives if possible. Options might include transfers to other internal work groups and outplacement packages. Either way, the team must be prepared to approach the employees of the outsourced group with a complete plan and treat those employees with the same empathy with which they themselves would want to be treated if the roles were reversed.

At times, work groups will be completely eliminated by outsourcing. In these cases, outplacement packages for the entire work group may be the only alternative. *Be careful and get sound legal and human resources advice!* I know of some companies that eliminated whole work groups through outsourcing, yet tried to keep a few selected employees through side deals. Every one of these companies incurred lawsuits as a result. The best policy is to handle the process with integrity and keep everything aboveboard, professional, legal, and consistent with company policies.

I.3.f: Complete the Outsourcing Step

Completion of the outsourcing step may be spread over a period of time because the actual start-up date, the transition of employees, and the effective date of the signed contract are not necessarily simultaneous. In reality, a letter of intent is usually signed prior to the official start-up date, allowing for the ramp-up of outsourced activities and the transition of employees. The signing of the formal contract is often the final event. Be careful, because a letter of intent is a legal document and is only as good as its content. All agreements and contracts should be reviewed by the appropriate enterprise counsel as identified by the transition team's executive sponsor.

Because start-up problems can be expected to occur, a start-up issue resolution team must be assigned, with funding by the executive sponsor, to solve these problems *immediately*. The tone of the relationship between the third party and the enterprise is often determined within the first ninety days of start-up.

Conclusion

Now that the transformation team has completed the supply chain alternatives process methodology, the enterprise will have developed a firm direction for the whole customer-centered supply chain management change process. The complementary core competencies of the to-be supply chain should be aligned with the core competencies needed in the marketplace. Thus, the extended enterprise should be positioned for supply chain leadership within its marketplace.

Chapter 10

The Executive Perspective

Pulling It All Together

In December 1996, I was shopping at a new Wal-Mart store in Plano, Texas. It was early morning, and the store had just opened. As luck would have it, the Frito-Lay route salesman was just finishing his delivery.

I introduced myself as a former Frito-Lay employee, and to my surprise, we knew each other. When I had first joined Frito-Lay several years earlier, the route salesman and I had worked a route together as part of my company orientation. (In fact, it used to be Frito-Lay's policy that all new hires, regardless of level, had to work a route with a route sales representative on the first or second day of employment. This policy was designed to impress on all employees that the whole Frito-Lay organization must be focused on the ultimate consumer and retail trade customer.)

This man had been with Frito-Lay for more than twenty-five years and had experienced a lot of change during his career. After the normal pleasantries, I asked him how his job had changed in the past few years. He proceeded to tell me about how the movement to reduce the supply chain cycle time from the date of manufacture to the date of delivery to the sales representative from seven to four days had increased the freshness of his product on the store shelf. He told me how his managers used point-of-sale (POS) data (he left out category management tools, but that was certainly OK) to help him adjust his store-shelf plan-o-grams. He even described how the Borden snacks decision and the Eagle Snacks/Anheuser-Busch decision to exit the snack business had trickled down to his own store-shelf plan-o-grams!

He also complained a little. He said that his handheld computer had been dropped on the shipping dock, and he could not get a spare for a few days because it was a holiday season and all the spare handhelds were in use. He had to fill out his orders on the old paper forms, which were kept just for emergencies like this. He was amazed at how long it took him and never wanted to go back to the old, manual way! Furthermore, he could not understand why other companies delivering to retailers still use the manual method of placing orders.

The Wal-Mart associate overheard our conversation and began telling us about a start-up problem involving the opening of a new store. It seemed that during the few days just prior to the opening, there were upload difficulties with the handheld terminals. As it turned out, it was a hardware problem, and it only lasted less than a day.

However, this associate was able to describe in detail how many phone calls and forms were used to keep track of the merchandise and the orders. She knew exactly what the distribution center had to do to fill her shelves and was somewhat aware that the process went beyond the distribution center to the suppliers. She was also able to describe in detail the impact that all of this had on her store shelves and how critical it would be for such hardware failures not to occur now that the store was open. (What was amazing was that she knew the supply chain process one or two steps upstream from her store. Even more amazing was that she kept referring to the store shelves as "my shelves.")

These two individuals are examples of employees who, despite being at the lowest levels in their organizations, are the backbone of their respective companies. They are on the front lines and are the last step in the supply chain before the ultimate consumer buys the merchandise. They are the workers who must benefit from transforming the supply chain and instituting supporting technology. In my opinion, the executive knows that the process is working when employees at the lowest levels of the organization understand how their job duties and responsibilities affect others throughout the customer supply chain.

At this point in the customer-centered supply chain management change process, we have completed all of the process methodologies: getting started, foundation, quality, transformation design, innovation, as-is, bridge, performance results, and supply chain alternatives.

The prototype or pilot should be complete, and the rollout plan described in Chapter 8 should be in full swing. It is now time to review the progress to date and proceed with a continuous improvement or renewal process (Exhibit 10-1).

The Renewal Process

The renewal process is critical to maintain the momentum of the customer-centered supply chain management change process. Remember, this is a journey, not a one-time event! The renewal process involves the following steps:

1. Reviewing what's working according to the migration plan
2. Identifying what's not working
3. Assessing the root causes behind what's not working
4. Renewing operations and/or strategy, whichever is applicable

Reviewing What's Working According to the Migration Plan

The transformation team needs to work with each work group within the enterprise and with the enterprise's customer supply chain partners to assess what's working according to the migration plan. This assessment should be framed using the key areas that are embedded in the migration plan. As you'll recall, these areas are:

- Performance against process and metric goals
- Performance-based rewards
- Technology
- The people process
- The organizational structure
- Outcome-driven task/process definition
- Process mapping

The transformation team should review each area in the order listed. This is the reverse of the order in which we developed the migration plan. It first focuses on the performance against goals, then works back through to the process mapping. This way, all work will initially be anchored by performance measurements and goals to which the transformation team and the executive sponsor have committed the enterprise.

Exhibit 10-1. The customer-centered supply chain management change process.

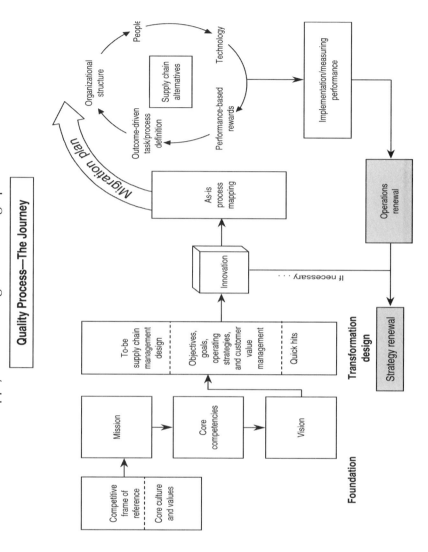

To help maintain momentum and enthusiasm for the overall process, the team should focus on what's working. These items should be documented and circulated among the executives of each work group. In addition, selected items should be communicated to all employees through in-house publications, meetings, and so forth.

Identifying What's Not Working

The transformation team should then review and identify what's not working according to the migration plan. These items should be categorized in two groups:

1. Minor variances to goals
2. Major variances to goals

The team must prepare this list with caution. Performance to goals has two variables—performance and goal setting. At this stage in the change process, a variance to a goal could be attributable to either (or both) of these factors. Thus, in preparing this list, the team must use the right documentation in order to categorize the variances properly.

Assessing the Root Causes Behind What's Not Working

For the minor variances, there are two courses of action. The first is to assess the root causes and make minor adjustments in the supply chain operations. Perhaps the responsibility charting for a particular activity needs to be redone due to employee turnover or a change in the enterprise's product portfolio. Whatever the reason(s), it (they) must be identified for each minor variance. The second course of action for the minor variances is to adjust the goals.

For the major variances, the transformation team should focus on either significant disconnects between execution and the migration plan or major events that have had an impact on the enterprise since the migration plan was developed. It is important to separate the two. Frequently, I have led transformation teams that have categorized variances as "controllable" or "noncontrollable." Performance itself can be controlled to a large extent. When the original goals are rendered meaningless by structural changes to the enterprise (mergers, divestitures, and so forth), then employees should not be held accountable for achieving these goals. However, it is critical for the team to identify the root causes for the senior executives, or the whole process could be judged according to irrelevant performance measurements.

Renewing Operations and/or Strategy, Whichever Is Applicable

Minor variances can be corrected with minimal effort if they are identified and communicated properly. Remember the Whirlpool example presented in Chapter 3? After the implementation of its change process, the on-time delivery rate increased to 99.8 percent, from what the company guesstimated had been a rate in the low 80s before the change process. But what if Whirlpool's on-time delivery rate after the change process had increased from 80.0 percent to 95.0 percent and its goal had been 99.8 percent? Such a performance improvement could hardly have been considered a failure. Perhaps there was something wrong with a measurement metric that fed the overall measurement, such as expecting overnight delivery from Dallas, Texas, to Buenos Aires, Argentina.

The team must perform this review with this type of calibration in mind, document the root causes, communicate the changes to all involved, and implement the changes. Communication is the key. Senior executives usually accept changes in goal setting if there is sufficient documentation to justify them. They will usually resist if these changes are made without the proper documentation and communication.

Major variances to goals require closer scrutiny by the transformation team. The team should assess the performance side of the equation and identify changes to the enterprise's business since the migration plan was developed. If the assessment identifies changes to the business, then an operations review of the customer-centered supply chain management change process should be performed. This review should start with the innovation process methodology and proceed through the performance results process methodology. Since this is only a review, the analysis need not be done in the same depth as the first time through these process methodologies. Any performance improvement opportunities that are identified should be implemented immediately. All documentation should be updated to reflect any changes.

Major variances that result from major changes to the enterprise's business (merger, acquisition, divestiture) will force a review of the enterprise's strategy. The transformation team should review the quality, foundation, and design process methodologies to realign the customer-centered supply chain management change process to the newly structured enterprise. Once this review and realignment are completed, the team should proceed through the operations renewal to build on the strategy renewal work.

This whole renewal effort should be an ongoing process. At a minimum, monthly progress reports should be obtained from the work groups and quarterly updates from the key executives. The enterprise should not have to wait until something is "broken." The best customer supply chain companies, like Wal-Mart, continually upgrade their capabilities in order to be proactive in the marketplace.

The Future of Customer-Centered Supply Chain Management

This section presents a collection of my thoughts and opinions (and remember, they are only opinions) on the future of customer-centered supply chain management.

An associate of mine who was the chief executive officer of a *Fortune* 500 company observed to me recently that he was glad he was not starting his career in the late 1990s. He said point-blank that he would not have become a CEO as fast or by following the same career path. This was a very objective observation from a man who, in the opinion of many, had earned the privilege of running the company by working hard and producing results. In fact, this executive said that, if he were currently on his way up the career path with his former company, he would have to expand his skill sets continually, open himself to the ideas of others, and empower his people more. He also said that, in private conversations with other current and former CEOs, he has learned that many of his peers share his opinion.

These observations are directly related to the rate of change in the global economy and the forces of change that are driving the rate and pace of change. We saw in Chapter 2 that, between 1971 and 1993, more than 40 percent of the companies on the *Fortune* top 50 list turned over and that the churn continued well into 1997. Many think that the late 1990s and the 2000s will bring an even greater turnover in leading companies.

The next seven to ten years will serve as the cornerstone for global companies to establish their positions of marketplace leadership in the twenty-first century. The design, implementation, and preservation of supply chain management will be a key factor for global companies that compete on cycle time, cost, and quality as they relate to customer satisfaction. Recognizing the forces of change in the global economy and adapting customer supply chain management to take advantage of change are two critical success factors that will differentiate winners from losers in the coming decade.

Outlook for the Forces of Change

In my opinion, globalism will continue to escalate in the businesses of manufacturing and logistics. In the past, the placement of manufacturing facilities was dictated by proximity to sources of raw materials and labor. Currently and in the future, it will be dictated by proximity to markets for products and sources of technology. The labor content of manufacturing costs will continue to shrink. In making plant location decisions, these lower wage costs as a percentage of total costs will be offset by increased logistics, telecommunications, and finance costs. As a result, certain manufacturing jobs that had been shifted offshore to achieve labor savings will increasingly be returning to the United States. (The wild swings in the dollar's value from 1994 to 1997 dictate that the value of the dollar will also affect this movement.)

The movement of manufacturing facilities closer to their markets and sources of technology is driving the need for small and medium-size companies to form alliances and partnerships to access global markets. These alliances and partnerships, which must be focused on the blending of core competencies to provide the best-of-the-best menu of product and service offerings to the marketplace, are further complicating supply chain management. Leading companies must define the alliances and partnerships in terms of a common vision, mission, objectives, goals, and strategies. Successful companies will also define how alliances and partnerships will terminate when the usefulness of the relationship has ended.

In addition, companies will have to invest in emerging countries. Many of these countries have neither the management expertise, the training on how to adapt to change, nor the capital needed to reposition their companies for an open, global economy. North American enterprises will have to invest in joint ventures and alliances with the needed expertise and capital, with the understanding that their return will come from future streams of revenues and profits. For the "live by immediate returns" North American CEO, investing in emerging countries will be a very disappointing experience. For the future-oriented, vision-minded CEO, the eventual returns can be significant. (Just look at Coca-Cola's global investment strategy through the years versus PepsiCo's. Over the last twenty years, Coca-Cola invested much more heavily in global markets than PepsiCo and is now reaping significantly greater profits from international operations.)

Customer-Led Supply Chain

The movement toward the customer's dictating how the supply chain will respond to marketplace demands will continue to accelerate. The customer-led supply chain will continue to reduce many vertical supply chain functions—like transportation, manufacturing assembly, and warehousing—to commodity status. Traditional manufacturing industries, like the high-tech industry, have been and are looking to "unbundle" their companies and outsource the assembly operations for their products. This unbundling of a company's operations will accelerate within certain industries, with the unbundled activities being performed by third-party providers or supply chain partners.

Value-added activities will be dictated by the customer. In fact, I believe that there will be momentum toward these activities' being truly customized for each customer (one-to-one marketing). Currently, many companies are attempting to design and implement value-added activities to meet customer needs. However, most companies I visit are trying to identify the overlapping needs across multiple customers and focus on developing a standard set of value-added activities that will fit horizontally across a group of customers. Short-term, this "pushing" of services to multiple customers to leverage internal resources may work. Customers will appreciate some progress toward meeting their needs versus no progress. Ultimately, however, the customers' total needs must be met, and those companies that succeed in meeting them will emerge as marketplace leaders. The key is to listen to the voice of the customers and translate what is heard into successful products and services.

Purchasing: An Early Experience

Several years ago, as a terminal manager for a large less-than-truck-load (LTL) carrier, I had the responsibility for making sales calls on the terminal's biggest customers. Two of these customers were a manufacturer of marine engines and a manufacturer of hoses for automotive and home use. Because of the competitiveness of our region, it was critical for me to integrate my company's operations with the terminal's customer operations. This meant that I had to integrate the terminal's operations into the purchasing strategies of these two companies and effectively bridge the gap between their suppliers and their assembly operations. The contrast between these two companies was like night and day.

The hose company was a traditional manufacturer, receiving raw materials, forming and packaging the end product, inventorying standard items, and shipping the products when orders were received. Nonstandard items, which represented 80 percent of the line items but 20 percent of the volume, were produced once a week.

The purchasing department of the hose company was an ordering and expediting group. All purchasing specifications were provided by the corporate office's engineering function, which deliberately established specifications generic enough to cover a wide range of customers. The product tolerances were loose by design. The intent was to simplify manufacturing and reduce the line-item complexity for the warehouse.

The purchasing department was responsible not only for ordering from suppliers but also for processing defective and returned products. Both returns and customer dissatisfaction were high. The purchasing professionals could not influence the engineering department to translate the customers' needs into higher-quality products that fit those needs. The engineering function's inward, efficiency focus precluded any external, customer focus.

The purchasing professionals' frustrations came to a head when the hose company's largest customers started to increase their orders for nonstandard items. After a trip to the hose company's largest customer, I realized that the customer was customizing products for *its* customers. The hose company's manufacturing operations became disrupted when the rate of growth in the orders for nonstandard, customized items resulted in a fifty-fifty mix of standard versus nonstandard items.

This hose company fought to keep the purchasing/manufacturing model that had served it well over the years and actually asked its customers to change! Six months after being promoted and leaving the freight terminal, I learned that the hose company lost its largest customer and, with it, 20 percent of its business.

The marine engine manufacturer was a different story. Its purchasing professionals were accountable for customer satisfaction as it related to the parts and subsystems that they purchased, and they were authorized to order changes in engineering specifications if returns, warranty claims, or customer complaints dictated the need to do so.

These purchasing professionals were required to attend their customer meetings and get to know their customers' business. This approach successfully bridged the gap between the customers' needs and the enterprise's suppliers and vendors. As a transportation provider on both the inbound and outbound side of this company's manufacturing assembly operations, my company was required to support the purchasing professionals and help them bridge this gap between their suppliers and vendors.

The contrasting directions taken by these two companies illustrate what I believe will be accelerating trends within the global businesses of manufacturing and logistics. One trend is for purchasing to play a growing role as a leader in logistics and supply chain management, bridging the gap between customer needs and supplier expectations. The other trend is for companies to hold fast to a manufacturing model that may make sense internally but misses the mark in meeting the customers' needs. This second trend will spell the end of many companies as we know them today.

Purchasing: The Dawn of a New Era

The stereotype of the purchasing professional as a junior back-room product expediter is quickly evaporating. For many reasons, I believe the purchasing executive will play a leadership role within companies that rely on supply chain management as a means to achieve customer satisfaction.

As the example of the hose manufacturer and the marine engine manufacturer implied, quality of a product and process must begin with the end, or customer, in mind. Quality must start at the beginning of the supply chain to minimize the cost of reworking defective material, minimize the cycle time from order to customer delivery, and most important, minimize the possibility of producing defective products and delivering them to the customer.

To accomplish this, vendors and suppliers must be involved in defining the supply chain's ultimate customer satisfaction criteria. They must also be involved in designing the products and services that are developed to meet the customers' satisfaction criteria. The enterprise's link between the vendor/supplier and the supply chain customer is the purchasing professional. This is a dramatic departure from the old procurement role within a manufacturing plant to which many purchasing professionals were relegated.

The alliances and partnerships within a supply chain involve the linkages of the supply chain: the movement of goods, financial transactions, and information between supply chain partners. How supply chain partners interact is highly dependent on the terms of agreement in purchasing contracts; how purchasing contracts are executed, implemented, and administered; and the actions of the executives within each company. The purchasing professional is quickly becoming the focal point for defining and driving these supply chain partner relationships.

The behavior of vendors and suppliers within the supply chain has an impact on transportation, order processing, warehousing, production scheduling, and inventory management. In fact, the purchasing professional may play *the* lead logistics role within many enterprises, especially as these enterprises are "unbundled." Although this may give many of my logistics and manufacturing executive associates heartburn, I believe that we are entering a new era that has logistics activities reporting to and controlled by purchasing and perhaps purchasing reporting to and controlled by an expanded customer service organization that includes sales and marketing.

Another factor behind the rise in purchasing's influence within the enterprise is the obvious one: For a broad range of manufacturing industries, the purchase price of raw materials and components represents either the major part or a significant percentage of the total manufacturing cost for their respective finished products. The overall financial impact of purchasing cannot be overlooked, either by the rest of the enterprise or by the enterprise's downstream customers (retailers, for example).

The marine engine manufacturer may have been ahead of its time, but it had the right approach. Its purchasing professionals treated the LTL company for which I worked as an extension of their company, and we had to respond as the needs of their customers and suppliers dictated.

People: Skill Sets

The future of supply chain management depends heavily on people. The need for competent, flexible, and results-producing employees will be overshadowed only by the need to listen to the customer. In fact, it is highly unlikely that employees will be able to produce results in the future without listening to the customer.

Supply chain management will require people whose skill sets are significantly different from those of traditional employees. In the future, employees will need the people skills necessary to "connect" with employees of other companies within the supply chain. This requires an understanding of your customers' personality and style and how your personality and style "fit" those of the customers.

For example, command-and-control directive personalities want options, with the answers presented first. People issues frequently do not matter to them. Expressive people want "a show." They are open, telling people who like to present a positive image above all else. Amiable people focus on teamwork and harmony, whereas analytical people focus on "the process."

The ability to adapt one's style to fit the style of the employee of a supply chain partner increases the probability of connecting with that employee, which, in turn, increases the opportunity to influence his or her behavior. Adapting one's style can be done through oral and written communications, such as meetings, reports, and presentations.

In order to be effective, it will be a must for professionals to have a working knowledge of most supply chain functions. This includes an understanding of the interdependencies among functions and among companies. The focus will be on how these interdependencies can be leveraged to maximize the use of supply chain resources, minimize the cost of the final product and service, and maximize customer satisfaction. The value of an employee's being a "transportation" expert or a "warehousing" expert will diminish as a qualification for playing a leadership role within the enterprise, while the value of an employee's having multifunctional, multicompany knowledge will increase dramatically.

The supply chain management professional must be flexible enough to adapt quickly to the ever-changing customer demands. In fact, the truly successful people will anticipate customer needs and help customers define their demands in order to satisfy them. This translates into the need for people to be self-directed. It also translates into the need for the leaders in supply chain management to share their knowledge openly and transfer it freely to other supply chain participants. In addition, these leaders must be willing to let others share in the supply chain management successes as well as failures.

The work of many professionals within the vertical supply chain functions will be relegated to "commodity" status. These functions, like basic transportation point-to-point service and warehousing receive/store/ship service, are essential to the performance of the supply chain as a whole but will not necessarily produce a competitive advantage in the marketplace for their companies. Performing these functions requires limited skills and education. The leaders of supply chain management will be challenged to increase the productivity of these workers in the service functions that must be low-cost, high-service. Achieving the necessary productivity increases will depend on the motivation and organizational behavior and design skill sets of the supply chain management leaders.

There will be an increasing demand for professionals (and executives) who speak more than one language. The globalization of economies is accelerating with NAFTA, MERCOSUR, the Andean Pact, the European Common Market, and so forth. For many one-language executives, it will no longer be acceptable to recruit others who speak more than one language and consider themselves totally safe from this trend.

Executive positions will quickly become working positions and not just command-and-control positions. Micromanagement will only be successful in selected situations; in more typical situations, it will quickly lead to low morale and declining productivity.

The toughest task for executives will be to recognize that *they* must change first if they are to lead their organization though a successful change process.

The University Connection

It is obvious that universities and business alike must combine their efforts to prepare people with the required skill sets. The shift from the command-and-control directive style to the people-oriented influence style of management needed for successful supply chain management won't just happen by itself. A combination of training and development in the areas of organizational behavior, organizational design, and human performance must complement the traditional business training in functional activities like manufacturing, computer science, and engineering.

Career Management

The successful leaders of supply chain management will also take charge in shaping and directing their careers. The traditional logistics and purchasing departments will slowly diminish, giving rise to horizontal business units and "umbrella" organizations. (For example, units like customer service will include purchasing, transportation, distribution, and sales and marketing.) The clear, distinct career path within one vertical function will give way to an unclear career path that may involve multiple functions. Knowledge, people skills, flexibility, and continuous learning skills are what will determine whether an employee becomes a leader or a follower. Followers run the risk of "peaking" in their careers much earlier than their parents, due to a growing oversupply of people and a steady decline in middle and upper management positions. It is my opinion, though, that leaders will be in increasingly high demand throughout the supply chain.

The "Deans" of Supply Chain Management

The three individuals profiled in this section have, in my estimation, had a significant impact on customer-centered supply chain management. Although I know there have been many more who have made noteworthy contributions, and some may argue that others are as deserving of mention, I have chosen these three for their overall accomplishments in their respective enterprises, their industries, and supply chain management.

Charlie Cotton

Charlie Cotton, an industrial engineer thrust into the ever-changing world of manufacturing and logistics, was the consummate supply chain management professional. Charlie had a sense of how the world would change and was fearless in challenging conventional wisdom with his forward-thinking ideas.

Charlie started with Frito-Lay as director of industrial engineering and held several positions at the company, including vice president of manufacturing and vice president of logistics. Bill Elston, then Frito-Lay's area manufacturing vice president and Charlie's main internal customer, says:

> Charlie brought a fresh approach to the industrial engineering function with a *heavy* emphasis on *internal customer service.* Charlie worked very hard at bringing innovative approaches to new manufacturing processes/systems to the manufacturing group. He helped lead the manufacturing group in its strategic-planning process and was very active in identifying resources and investigating best practices (benchmarking) before it became a favorite fad of the consulting companies.

In the early to mid-1980s, Charlie began a journey to pull together multiple vertical supply chain functions to organizationally create a horizontal supply chain focused on the end consumer.

One of Charlie's first moves was to recruit strategic-thinking managers. He then sought out key integrating functions within the supply chain. The first function to move to logistics was order entry, which connected logistics on the front end of the supply chain process. Charlie's goal of dramatically improving the timing and quality of the order-entry process was achieved in a matter of a few months. He proceeded to utilize the order-entry process to improve production scheduling, transport scheduling, and warehouse planning and allocation.

Charlie sought to integrate the manufacturing and logistics functions through this process, further automating the distribution routing system (initiated in the early 1970s by Steve Johnson and Ernest Harris) and plant service area economic models. These models would determine the least landed cost options for Frito-Lay as a whole, after service to sales commitments were ensured. This effort permitted objective discussions to take place among manufacturing, logistics, and sales executives concerning balancing service to sales and cost.

As legislation allowed, Charlie was one of the first in the marketplace to integrate the procurement of raw materials and packaging materials into the supply chain process. He was also one of the first to utilize the empty returns of the private-fleet deliveries to Frito-Lay sales representatives to transport raw materials and outside, for-hire loads. Eventually, the management of the route sales representatives' facilities and equipment was combined with the logistics group to extend the customer supply chain management design.

The complexity of the management of the supply chain grew with Charlie, yet the costs per unit declined virtually every year. Although he had a little help with larger trailers and favorable fuel prices, the operating efficiencies that resulted from pulling vertical functions together and focusing them collectively on the customer were significant as well. The year after Charlie left Frito-Lay, 1991, is still a topic of conversation among many Frito-Lay supply chain managers, a few of whom privately praise it as the "year of the star fleet."

The Frito-Lay supply chain is a significant one. There were many participants up and down the organization who helped make a lot of those accomplishments a reality. Charlie would be the first to recognize the contributions of all concerned and downplay his own role in Frito-Lay's supply chain successes. However, if it weren't for his strategic visioning capability and his zeal to push the envelope of what's possible, many of those successes would have been delayed for several years. As Bill Elston says:

> Charlie was not afraid to take an unpopular stand when it was backed by data/facts which were often challenged by the status quo group. I always invited Charlie to my customer forums when I was running GATX Logistics because he could always be counted on to inject thought-provoking subject matter into our strategic and tactical topics.

Charlie Cotton left this world in March 1994 at the relatively young age of forty-nine after a two-year battle with cancer. Despite his untimely death, his accomplishments were many. He has truly earned the recognition as a dean of customer supply chain management.

H. Lee Scott

H. Lee Scott is currently president of Wal-Mart's Stores Division. I first met Lee in the mid- to late 1970s, when we were both with Yellow Freight System. Lee joined Wal-Mart in 1979 as the assistant director of transportation. In that year, Wal-Mart's sales topped $1 billion for the first time.

Lee would proceed to rise through the ranks of Wal-Mart, earning the positions of director of transportation, vice president of transportation, vice president of distribution, senior vice president of logistics, executive vice president of logistics, and executive vice president of merchandise and sales. As I stayed in periodic contact with Lee, it became very evident that he had one special gift that was similar to Charlie Cotton's: Lee was always able to focus on the tactical execution necessary to service sales while utilizing his strategic visioning skills to drive Wal-Mart's supply chain process forward.

In the early 1980s, I visited Lee in Bentonville, Arkansas. Wal-Mart was growing rapidly (at a rate of more than 30 percent per year), and Lee's organization was doing everything it could just to keep up with the growth. Yet Lee told me that he *had* to take the time to develop the vision for how the supply chain was evolving and take immediate action to align some of the supply chain components and activities to avoid inhibiting Wal-Mart's future growth. The topics on which he commented ranged from standardizing/converting private-fleet tractor leases to Wal-Mart equipment to standardizing delivery options for Wal-Mart stores. The rate at which Wal-Mart was opening up stores and distribution centers was astounding, yet Lee had the vision to balance the tactical execution and the strategic positioning of the supply chain.

In the mid- to late 1980s, I again visited Lee in Bentonville. This meeting occurred just after the historic top-to-top meeting between Wal-Mart and Proctor & Gamble, which initiated the "buying on a fifty-two-week everyday low price basis" agreement. Prior to my meeting with Lee, he was working with a few associates on the need to ensure that three bids were obtained for all purchase agreements. His comment to me was that Sam Walton personally inspected files of buyers at random and that everyone had to be prepared! Lee spent just a few minutes reflecting on the historic agreement, then proceeded to discuss the need to stick to the Wal-Mart way of purchasing items, no matter how busy people were in keeping up with the growth. Lee had once again impressed me by demonstrating the balance between tactical execution and strategic process mapping.

In addition, virtually every meeting I have had with Lee included either discussions on merchandising or a walk-through of the Wal-Mart store in Rogers, Arkansas. Lee always sent the message to everyone that the placement of the right merchandise on the store shelves was his top priority.

In my opinion, Wal-Mart could not have achieved its customer supply chain excellence as fast as it did without Lee's significant contributions. For those contributions, I have included him as a dean of customer-centered supply chain management.

Dr. John J. Coyle

Dr. John J. Coyle is a professor of business administration at Pennsylvania State University (Penn State) and executive director of Penn State's Center for Logistics Research. He earned his doctorate at Indiana University in Bloomington, where he was a U.S. Steel Fellow.

In his thirty-six years at Penn State, Dr. Coyle has written more than a hundred publications in the areas of transportation, logistics, and supply chain management. He has coauthored two best-selling textbooks—*The Management of Business Logistics* and *Transportation*—and edited the *Journal of Business Logistics* from 1990 to 1996.

Dr. Coyle has been active in bringing his vast academic gifts into the corporate world. He has consulted and provided in-house educational programs to more than two hundred companies. At Penn State, he has participated regularly, as both a lecturer and faculty director, in executive education programs, including the Executive Management Program, the National Industrial Distributors Program, the Materials Management–Physical Distribution Program, and the Emerging Executives Program. In addition, his instructional television taped modules, for which he has received several teaching awards, are being used by a number of *Fortune* 500 companies.

Currently, Dr. Coyle is focusing his research on the interfaces between manufacturing, marketing, and logistics, with particular emphasis on customer service, channels of distribution, and supply chain issues. He has also continued his research on the use of educational technology in the delivery of credit and noncredit programs.

In 1991, Dr. Coyle received the top honor of the Council of Logistics Management—the Distinguished Service Award, which recognizes "an individual who has made a significant contribution to the art and science of logistics."

However, above and beyond all these awards, Dr. Coyle's greatest achievements have perhaps been in adding value to the many lives he has touched during his years at Penn State. Dr. Coyle has encouraged and enhanced the professional aspirations of thousands of students, professors, and businesspeople throughout the world. He has tirelessly promoted logistics and supply chain management, yet has somehow found the time to work with people (including me) at all levels in companies and at Penn State. His gifts as an educator have enhanced his contributions to the overall evolution of supply chain management. For all the above reasons and many more, Dr. Coyle has truly earned the title of dean of customer supply chain management.

There are many others who arguably should be recognized as deans of customer supply chain management. In the academic field, it is hard to overlook the significant contributions of Dr. Donald J. Bowersox of Michigan State University, Dr. Bernard J. LaLonde of Ohio State University, and Dr. Les Waters, professor emeritus of Indiana University. (In fact, if I were assembling a "deans of transportation" list, Dr. Waters would be *the* dean.) In the business world, it is hard to overlook the impact that Eiji Toyoda and Taiichi Ohno of Toyota had on supply chain management through their development efforts with the Toyota Production and just-in-time systems. However, the three I picked are individuals who I knew from firsthand experience had the impact and the peer recognition in the marketplace to deserve being singled out in this way.

The key here is that these three represent professionals who made an impact on customer-centered supply chain management. The world is changing at a rapid pace, and the need to evolve customer supply chain management is changing equally rapidly. Who will be the deans of customer-centered supply chain management in the coming decade? Tomorrow's deans are actively pursuing excellence in this area and earning their reputations for success as this book is going to press.

Conclusion

Congratulations! You've reached the end of this book but are still only in the middle of the journey toward excellence in customer supply chain management. The customer-centered supply chain management change process is a journey and should be approached as such. In fact, an associate of mine once told me that if we perform change processes right, we are perpetually in a "transition state." Although I think he might have been influenced by the fine work of Richard Beckhard and John Kenneth Galbraith, I remember his remark and support his philosophy.

The business professional need not be a "dean" to achieve success in customer-centered supply chain management. This book was written to provide an integrated methodology that all business professionals can follow to help them manage the supply chain successfully. As you embark on the customer-centered supply chain management change process, I wish you luck in your journey. Maybe your name will appear on the next "deans" list!

Index

virtual-company team evaluations, 228, 244–245
vision
  in establishing foundation, 34
  failure of, 44–46
  framework for, 42–46
  in outsourcing strategic decision, 224, 240–241
  process of, 46–49
  quality and, 61–62
vision statement, 48–49, 58–59

Wal-Mart
  in Brazil, 131
  core competency of, 48
  customer focus of, 193
  ECR practice of, 103
  H. Lee Scott in, 263–264
  insourcing in, 225
  logistics in, 173–174, 175
  power of, 5
  principles of, 57
  quick response in, 174–176
  start-up problems of, 249

supply chain in, 173–176
technology in, 173–176
waste, elimination of, 171
Waters, Dr. Les, 265
Welch, Jack, on quality and price, 71
Westinghouse Electric Corporation, 66
what-if scenarios, 128
Whirlpool, Quality Express, 73–74
world economy, 36–37, 260
world-class performance standards, 55, 115
Wright, Tom, on Whirlpool, 73–74

Xerox
  customer satisfaction in, 77–79
  integrated global supply chain of, 105

Yellow Freight System, 187
zero defects concept, 72–73, 81
zero waste, 92